# CHALLENGING CITIZENSHIP

# Challenging Citizenship

Group Membership and Cultural Identity in a Global Age

*Edited by*
SOR-HOON TAN

ASHGATE

Published by
Ashgate Publishing Limited
Gower House
Croft Road
Aldershot
Hampshire GU11 3HR
England

Ashgate Publishing Company
Suite 420
101 Cherry Street
Burlington, VT 05401-4405
USA

Ashgate website: http://www.ashgate.com

**British Library Cataloguing in Publication Data**
Challenging citizenship : group membership and cultural
  identity in a global age
  1.World citizenship 2.Globalization - Social aspects
  3.Globalization - Political aspects 4.Group identity -
  Political aspects 5.Identity (Psychology) - Political
  aspects
  I.Tan, Sor-hoon, 1965-
  303.4'82

**Library of Congress Cataloging-in-Publication Data**
Challenging citizenship : group membership and cultural identity in a global age /
[edited] by Sor-hoon Tan.
     p. cm.
  Includes bibliographical references and index.
  ISBN 0-7546-4367-0
 1. World citizenship. 2. Globalization--Social aspects. 3. Globalization--Political
aspects. 4. Group identity--Political aspects. 5. Identity (Psychology)--Political
aspects. I. Tan, Sor-hoon, 1965-

 JZ1320.4.C43 2004
 303.48'2--dc22

                                                                    2004021067

ISBN 0 7546 4367 0

Printed and bound in Great Britain by MPG Books Ltd, Bodmin, Cornwall

# Contents

List of Contributors                                                vii
Foreword                                                             ix
Acknowledgements                                                     xi

1   Introduction: Globalization and Citizenship                      1
    Sor-hoon Tan

2   Migration and Cultural Diversity:
    Implications for National and Global Citizenship
    April Carter                                                    15

3   A Refugee and a Citizen of the World
    C.L. Ten                                                        31

4   Justice for Migrant Workers?
    Foreign Domestic Workers in Hong Kong and Singapore
    Daniel A. Bell                                                  41

5   The Globalization of Citizenship
    Barry Hindess                                                   63

6   Active Citizens or an Inert People?
    James E. Tiles                                                  75

7   Socratic Citizenship: The Limits of Deliberative Democracy
    Catherine Audard                                                89

8   Liberalism, Identity, Minority Rights
    Alan Montefiore                                                 98

9   Models of Multicultural Citizenship: Comparing Asia and the West
    Will Kymlicka                                                  110

10  Montaigne's Cannibals and Multiculturalism
    Cecilia Wee                                                    137

11  Citizenship and Cultural Equality
    Baogang He                                                     151

12   On the Confucian Idea of Citizenship
     *A.T. Nuyen*                                                              169

13   Exemplary World Citizens as Civilized Local Communicators:
     Politics and Culture in the Global Aspirations of Confucianism
     *Sor-hoon Tan*                                                           183

14   Conclusion: Meeting Challenges                                           197
     *Sor-hoon Tan*

*Index*                                                                       *199*

# List of Contributors

**Catherine Audard**, Lecturer in Philosophy at the London School of Economics, is author of *Anthologie Historique et Critique d'Utilisme, Citoyenneté et Individualité Morale* and *Individu et Justice Sociale*. She has also translated John Rawls's *A Theory of Justice* and J.S. Mill's *Utilitarianism* into French.

**Daniel A. Bell**, Associate Professor at the City University of Hong Kong, has published several works, including *Communitarianism and Its Critics*, *East Meets West: Human Rights* and *Democracy in East Asia*, *Toward Illiberal Democracy in Pacific Asia*, and *The East Asian Challenge to Human Rights*.

**April Carter**, formerly of Oxford and Queensland universities, is author of *The Political Theory of Global Citizenship*, *Authority and Democracy*, and *Direct Action and Liberal Democracy*. She also edited *The Politics of Women's Rights*, *Democratic Theory Today: Challenges for the 21st century*, and *Liberal Democracy and its Critics*.

**Baogang He**, Associate Professor at Tasmania University in Australia, has authored *The Democratization of China*, *The Democratic Implications of Civil Society in China*, and several journal articles and book chapters on democracy, national identity, and civil society.

**Barry Hindess**, Professor at the Research Center for Social Sciences, Australia National University, is author of *Choice, Rationality and Social Theory*, *Politics and Class Analysis*, *Freedom Equality and the Market*, *Philosophy and Methodology in the Social Sciences*, *Sociological Theories of the Economy Reactions to the Right*, and chapters in several volumes on citizenship and politics.

**Will Kymlicka**, Professor at Queens University, Kingston, Canada, is author and editor of several works, including *Multicultural Citizenship*, *Liberalism, Community and Culture*, *Contemporary Political Philosophy*, *The Rights of Minority Culture*, and *Ethnicity and Group Rights*.

**Alan Montefiore**, President of the Forum for European Philosophy and Emeritus Fellow of Balliol College, Oxford, taught Philosophy for many years. His works include *A Modern Introduction to Moral Philosophy*, *Integrity in Public and Private Domains*, *Neutrality and Impartiality: The University and Political Commitment*, and *The Public Responsibility of Intellectuals*.

**A.T. Nuyen**, formerly Reader at Queens University, Australia and now Associate Professor at the National University of Singapore, has published many articles and book chapters on Continental Philosophy and Confucianism, among a wide range of interests. He is working on a volume on Self and Others in Eastern and Western Philosophy.

**Sor-hoon Tan**, Associate Professor at the National University of Singapore, is author of *Confucian Democracy: A Deweyan Reconstruction* and several articles and book chapters on Comparative Philosophy, Pragmatism, and Confucianism. She also co-edited *The Moral Circle and the Self: Chinese and Western Approaches* and *Filial Piety in Chinese Thought and History*.

**C.L. Ten**, Professor at the National University of Singapore, is author of *Mill on Liberty*, *Mill's Moral, Political and Legal Philosophy*, and *Crime, Guilt and Punishment*. He edited the *Utilitas* special issue on *Punishment* and the volume on *The Nineteen Century* in the *Routledge History of Philosophy*. He is also one of the editors of *The Moral Circle and the Self: Chinese and Western Approaches*.

**James E. Tiles**, Professor at the University of Hawai'i at Manoa, is author of *John Dewey* ("Arguments of the Philosophers" Series), *Moral Measures*, *An Introduction to Historical Epistemology*, and several articles and book chapters on Pragmatism. He also edited *John Dewey: Critical Assessments*.

**Cecilia Wee**, Associate Professor at the National University of Singapore, has published articles and book chapters on Aristotle, Descartes, and Environmental Philosophy. She has a forthcoming monograph on Descartes.

# Foreword

The contributors to this volume were invited to reflect on the concepts of globalization and citizenship and on the connections between them. The results, revised in the light of the lively and intense discussion the first drafts evoked, are embodied in this volume. Unsurprisingly, they display a diversity of understandings of both these concepts, of the problems they raise and of perspectives of political theorists and philosophers coming from the Anglo-Saxon West (including the United States, Britain, and Australia) and what Westerners call the 'Far East' (but excluding points between, and the South).

The chapters in this volume amply confirm that 'globalization' captures some genuinely novel developments in our world, some of them extensions of earlier trends, whose novelty consists in their very intensification. Chief among these, and central to our discussions, are the ever-more salient facts of cultural diversity and cultural conflict and of transnational migration. These raise acute issues of policy – of different models of 'multiculturalism', of how to accommodate national minorities, of what to do with refugees, of how to treat migrant labour, and so on. They also raise difficult issues of principle – of whether 'cultures' can be ranked, or even meaningfully compared, of whether moral and other judgments can be made across cultural boundaries, of whether cosmopolitan concepts and ideals make sense in our time and, if so, what sense they make.

They also raise the interesting question of what thinking about such issues in terms of 'citizenship' entails. What are the positive and what the negative implications of framing them in terms of this increasingly prevalent notion? The positive implications are amply exhibited in the essays here collected. 'Citizenship' focuses our attention on a range of urgent and basic matters. What should be the criteria of membership as citizens of states? What are members' obligations to other members and to non-members who reside within their territories or are trying to enter them? What are the appropriate units of membership? Are nation-states still viable and effective, and in what respects? What rights and obligations does the status of citizen confer and how far do they extend? What do citizens owe non-citizens? Which non-citizens have the greater claims (if any)? To what extent and in what respects is the nation-state still an appropriate source for the identification of citizens and focus for their self-identification? And what constitutes being a *good* citizen? What demands should citizens meet in order for states and other political entities below and above the level of the state to function well? How are such citizens to be formed? What institutional and cultural preconditions must exist for citizens to function as good citizens? How do systems of so-called 'Asian values', notably Confucianism, address and answer these last questions and how do these answers relate to the 'liberal' and 'republican' answers of the West?

It is noticeable that these questions all reflect a range of contemporary preoccupations (are they perhaps more central to the concerns of political theorists and philosophers than to those of their fellow citizens?) that are marked by the buzz-words of our times: 'identity,' 'values,' 'governance,' and indeed, 'multiculturalism.' The 'citizenship' frame focuses our attention on these issues. They concern how best to respond to a social environment characterized by exponentially increasing mobility and insecurity, in which the inherited political structures and institutions appear increasingly ineffective to control unintended consequences and increasingly unresponsive to people's demands and aspirations. But it may be worth asking what this way of framing questions neglects to address.

'Citizenship' talk is un-, even anti-ideological. It operates, in large part, above the fray, in abstraction from politically partisan positions. The questions of citizenship, such as those listed above, concern, or should concern, people from all, or most, contemporary political standpoints. But there are also fundamental and urgent questions that divide us politically. If you frame these in terms of 'injustice' and 'inequality,' and, more polemically still, 'exploitation,' 'colonialism' and 'imperialism,' you will focus on other aspects of the questions above indicated, and indeed on other questions. We live in a period in which the market-driven politics of neo-liberalism has swept across the globe. In part this was the result of the impersonal pressures of the global economy and in part the outcome of political policy-making inspired by neo-liberal ideology, and one result is that non-market areas of social life are virtually everywhere being transformed into markets. Such alternative vocabularies, expressing a range of different theories and policy standpoints, focus our attention upon the increasingly unequal distribution of resources and opportunities within nation-states and across the globe, and upon the enduring institutional structures which impose vastly unequal access to them. Perhaps, in short, the concept of citizenship offers an interpretation of globalization that directs our attention to some central and urgent questions and away from others.

Steven M. Lukes<br>
Professor of Sociology<br>
New York University

# Acknowledgements

The idea for a volume of essays on citizenship in the current context of globalization, exploring the intersections between group memberships and overlapping or conflicting identities, was first suggested by Alan Montefiore and Catherine Audard during their visit to Singapore in year 2000. I am indebted to them for the idea, and especially to Alan for his continued advice and support throughout the process of bringing this book to the press.

C.L. Ten, as Head of Philosophy Department at the National University of Singapore, has been unstinting in his encouragement and assistance. I am grateful for a research grant from the Faculty of Arts and Social Sciences at the National University of Singapore that facilitated the project. A sixth-month attachment in 2004 at the Asia Research Institute provided the much needed time and a very conducive environment to complete the editing of the work, in the midst of other research.

Taylor and Francis has kindly given permission to use, in Chapter 12, materials from A.T. Nuyen's 'Confucianism and the Idea of Citizenship' in *Asian Philosophy*, vol. 12, no.2, pp.127-39 (available at http://www.tandf.co.uk/journals). The figures on page 84 are reproduced from Thomas Janoski's *Citizenship and Civil Society* (Cambridge University Press, 1998), with the author's and publisher's kind permission.

Last but not least, my heartfelt gratitude goes to all the contributors, for their cooperation and patience in the editing process; to Kim-Chong Chong and Alan K.L. Chan, with whom I collaborated on previous projects, for teaching me the finer points of editing a volume of collected essays; and to the editors at Ashgate, especially Kirstin Howgate and Sarah Horsley, for their guidance in preparing the work for publication. I am solely responsible for any errors or omissions.

# Chapter 1

# Introduction:
# Globalization and Citizenship

Sor-hoon Tan

Though the idea of citizenship may be implicit in the city-states politics of Ancient Greece, making it as old as Western political philosophy, its significance as a key to understanding political problems of group membership and individual identity is characteristic of the modern era. The rise of humanism during the renaissance brings with it a radically changed view of human agency and identity; people came to view their destinies as subject to their own individual and collective efforts rather than given by God. The French Revolution pushed the *citoyen* to the forefront of the political stage, replacing the subject under autocracy, signalling the freedom and equality that go with membership in a democratic polity wherein its members do not only obey but have a role in making laws and deciding other matters of the state. Membership in a new form of nation-state, a political identity demarcated by rights and obligations defined by the law, vies with previous primordial and parochial ties as a primary locus of loyalty.

Citizenship used to be the privilege of the few and has been used to exclude entire groups on the basis of gender, race, religion, class, property, ethnicity, place of origin, age, or years of residence in a country. While such exclusion continues, the wave of independence movements after World War II leads to an overwhelming majority of people acquiring citizenship of some sovereign country. Sovereignty or secession movements by various national minorities in existing countries, and migration, mean that many are striving to change their citizenship and some have succeeded. Regional conflicts, political persecution, and even economic deprivation have created large numbers of refugees and migrants both legal and illegal residing where they are without citizenship.

From its very inception, citizenship has been a subject of constant contestation. Periodically, the question of whether the concept can be or needs to be retained is raised. In practice, where the boundaries are drawn between citizens and non-citizens, what rights and obligations belong to citizens, have all been disputed from time to time. Conceptually, its contested nature bears witness to the ever changing relationship between state and individual, to the complex interaction between political and other collective identities, and the impact of these changes on political organization and action. According to Robert Nisbet (1974, p.612), 'Citizenship in the West is more than simply a condition or a status; it is a process, with identifiable phases in time and with contexts in history which unite it in some degree with other processes such as individualism and secularism'. If so, then even as the concept becomes more widespread, its meaning and relevance become more problematic.

While the workings of the modern nation-state focus attention on citizenship as a legal status, political affiliation has never been totally separate from other affinities. Until the twentieth century, it is often taken for granted that a sovereign state is also a nation, with one language, one culture, and one religion. Diversity is seen as a transient imperfection or dealt with by subordinating primordial ties and obligations of special relationship to a singular political loyalty and civic duties. Immigrants and indigenous population in empires created by colonization have been excluded from citizenship or subjected to harsh assimilation programs even in states that profess respect for freedom and equality. Such approaches have come under attack as resistance to imperialism and ethnocentrism mounts; increasingly cultural diversity and pluralism come to be valued. Citizenship has been associated with the struggle first for political rights, then extended to economic and social rights. It has become a battle ground for cultural equality, a troubled expression of identity caught between political affiliation and cultural affinities.

## Globalization as Context

According to Martin Albrow, we now live in the Global Age, which is not just a stage of modernity or its culmination. The Global Age signifies a rupture with the past; it marks the end to modernity, but not the end of history. Nor is it a postmodern age; to Albrow (1996, p.78), 'the postmodern imagination is indeed the hypertrophy of modern innovation rather than the expression of the new age'. He advocates holding on to 'the transhistorical and cross-cultural potential of theory' in order to grasp the nature of novelty by developing concepts more suited to this new age (Albrow, 1996, p.79). The concept of citizenship is certainly among those that need to be reinvented, given its historical association with a concept of the modern nation-state central to the project of modernity. Albrow argues that the Global Age is witnessing the emergence of a new kind of citizenship, which he calls 'performative citizenship', opposed to both the ancient and the modern citizenship. Ancient citizenship is participatory as Aristotle defines a citizen not as one 'who has legal rights' (1275a9) but as one who 'shares in the administration of justice and in offices' (1275a20-21). Modern citizenship, in contrast, focuses on rights and duties in the relationship between the state and the individual citizen. Performative citizenship leaves behind both ancient and modern conceptions of the state and is premised on the activities of individuals 'acting as world citizens' in 'collective organization for global ends'. Albrow believes that 'the encroachments of the modern state on everyday life have actually assisted in the empowerment of people, through education of course, but also in requiring participation in everyday bureaucracy'. So much so that, in the Global Age, 'world citizens are turning to the task of building the global state and it is being made in and through their activities' (Albrow, 1996, p.177).

None of the contributors in this volume assumes a total break with modernity. The global age that contextualizes their discussion implies no more than recognition of the importance of globalization and reactions to or against it in contemporary life. A few imply that, whether or not globalization is important, the most important philosophical problem with citizenship lies elsewhere. Since it was coined in the 1960s, 'globalization' has become the new fad in and out of academia. According to Albrow (1996, p.88), the general informed usage of the term includes making or being made global in individual instances,

1.  by the active dissemination of practices, values, technology and other human products throughout the globe;
2.  when global practices and so on exercise an increasing influence over people's lives;
3.  when the globe serves as a focus for, or a premise in shaping, human activities;
4.  in the incremental change occasioned by the interaction of any such instances.

It also includes the generalization and abstraction of such individual instances of making or being made global. Globalization can also mean a process of making or being made global or the historical transformation constituted by the sum of particular forms and instances of making global or being made global.

A recent 'critical introduction' to the topic identifies five conceptions of globalization (Scholte, 2000, pp.44-6). Most uses define globalization as internationalization, an increase in interaction and interdependence between people in different countries. This definition favours the sceptics as internationalization is arguably not new since the nineteenth century witnessed comparable levels of cross-border migration, direct investment, finance, and trade. Others define globalization as liberalization, the removal of regulatory barriers to transfers of resources between countries. Thus defined, it is difficult to see how the concept is distinctive or uniquely useful in understanding contemporary economy and society against the background of an already well-developed discourse about free trade. A third common conception of globalization is universalization, the spread of people, cultural phenomena, ideas, and practices to every part of the globe; but then, past ages already saw worldwide spread of religions and distribution of certain goods in global markets. Definition of globalization as Westernization is popular in arguments over postcolonial imperialism. This definition implies that the West (or more specifically the United States) is the winner in globalization, which is making the world more Western or American. If so, what does globalization as Westernization add to the discourses of postcolonialism and imperialism?

Jan Scholte (2000, pp.46-50) dismisses the above four definitions in favour of a definition of globalization that he believes will provide a new vocabulary to remake an old analysis. This fifth definition of globalization is deterritorialization, the growth of 'supraterritorial' relations between people that fundamentally changes the nature of social space. This approximates Anthony Giddens' (2000a, p.92) definition of globalization as 'the intensification of worldwide social relations which link distant localities in such a way that local happenings are shaped by events occurring many miles away and vice versa'. Theoretically, the only consensus about globalization seems to be the contested nature of the concept, even as we see a veritable deluge of publications on globalization.[1] As globalization forms the context rather than the subject of their discussion, the authors in this volume mostly assume rather than argue for any specific definition of globalization and their implicit preferences differ.

Not only do those who study and write about globalization disagree about its definition, they disagree about the extent and impact of globalization. Globalists believe globalization is the most important single fact of contemporary history and insist that contemporary social relations have become thoroughly globalized. Opposing them, sceptics dismiss globalization as myth and maintain that, appearances notwithstanding, the world is fundamentally not much different from what it has been for many years or even returning to what it had been in an earlier era.[2] Like many others, the contributors to this volume occupy positions between these two extremes, treating globalization as a significant trend, but coexisting with various other historical changes as well as continuities.

Technological advances from the invention of the steam locomotive to the internet have revolutionized communication and worldwide travel, making them faster, cheaper, more reliable, and capable of meeting more varied goals. While one should not exaggerate their availability to one and all, significantly more people now travel greater distances and more frequently, come into contact with or are affected by people, things, and events from places far away from their residential locality, and enjoy a wider range of choices of where to live, study, work or play than could be envisaged a century ago. Most understandings of globalization are based on a sense of expanding interdependence stretching across the globe, some going so far as to entertain a vision of a world community, but others see the global age as economically and politically 'a highly fragmented order for what has disintegrated is the stable force of a civic realm and its replacement by disembodied space'.[3] Globalization is far from complete, affecting different countries, classes, cultures, and genders unevenly. It also has no absolute logic, inherent direction, or necessary end-point (Albrow, 1996, p.95).

Even as we struggle to find out how much globalization has and will change the world and our lives, whether and how we could control or at least influence the process, disagreement is rife about the value of globalization. Globalists include both promoters and strong critics of globalization. Kenichi Omae (1990 and 1995) and John Naisbitt (1994) praise the 'borderless world'. They see globalization in terms of an economic logic and celebrate the emergence of a single global market and the principle of global competition as the harbingers of human progress. Others warn of global corporations ruling the world, usurping the power of states and local governments without undertaking their social responsibilities (Barnet and Cavanagh, 1994). Street protests against WTO meetings and other world economic summits – Seattle in 1999, Genoa in 2001, Cancún in 2003 – have drawn cross border participants and have been given worldwide media coverage. This 'citizen backlash to economic globalization' or 'global' backlash includes those who wish to roll-back globalization as well as those who are agitating to change the nature of globalization.[4] Richard Falk (1999) and others advocate resisting 'globalization from above' with 'globalization from below'. Politically, Francis Fukuyama (1992) looks forward to the 'end of history' and the triumph of liberal democracy on a global scale, provoking a spate of Asian exceptionalism drawing a line between 'the West and the rest' (Mahbubani, 1992).[5] Nor do sceptics of globalization necessarily believe its opposite would be good for the world's future. Samuel Huntington (1996) predicts a 'clash of civilizations' instead of a new world order of global peace and prosperity.[6]

Religious revivalists and reactionary nationalists attack globalization for destroying traditional cultures. Some view this 'destruction' positively as making room for new identities of hybridity. Postmodernists perceive globalization as contributing to the de-centring of the subject, further fragmenting modern identities. In particular, globalization dislocates that aspect of modern cultural identity formed through one's membership of a *national* culture.[7] Debate continues about whether the phenomenal growth in the global circulation of cultural goods that is one dimension of globalization will lead to cultural homogenization, which some see as a form of Western imperialism, or greater diversity of cultural participation in global activities and improved quality of life with expanded individual choices.[8] Some evidence exists of erosion of national identities. Successful packaging of ethnicity for global consumer markets leads to protests against 'MacDonaldization'. However, such US-centric views perhaps ignore evidence that culture flows are not always one-way. Cultural imports need not destroy local cultures; instead they could work to produce a 'complex interpenetration of the global and the local' wherein the local becomes more globally integrated without losing its distinctiveness (Miller, 1995). Or 'local' particularistic identities could be strengthened by resistance to globalization and the weakening of the nation-state identity.[9]

The weakening of nation-state identity could also strengthen universalistic identities which might oppose globalization at least rhetorically. Resistance to globalization in one form could involve globalization in some other form. Some perceive the terrorist attack on the World Trade Centre in New York as targeting the symbol of the global economy. The means employed in planning and carrying out the attack are available only in this global age. As Craig Calhoun (2002, p.87) comments, 'in a sense, the non-cosmopolitan side of globalization struck back on 11 September'. For Teresa Brennan (2003, p.2), 'the new anxieties over terrorist attacks are only the latest in a series of fears generated by globalization in the West'. While many, including some of its promoters, recognize that there are losers and winners in globalization, Brennan argues that even people living in those countries which purport to benefit from it in fact suffer because globalization not only generates cutbacks in welfare, education, and health benefits, but also 'abets terrorism, which is a self-conscious response to global economic policy'.

The results of globalizations are a mixture of good and bad; no conclusive judgment on its normative aspect is likely given the wide range of approaches and perspectives, and the open-endedness of globalization itself. The significance of globalization for this book must be set out in terms of the actual challenges that globalization, variously understood, poses to the concept and practice of citizenship in the new millennium.

**Challenges Old and New**

The fortunes of citizenship as a major political concept have been bounded up with the rise of liberal democracy in the West. In practice citizenship today is still mostly understood in liberal terms of rights and obligations that accompany politically and legally defined membership in a nation-state. The articles collected in this volume approach citizenship from a variety of perspectives. Some adopt a largely liberal position; others challenge liberal conception of citizenship. Some discuss perennial problems that remain relevant in this global age; others address new challenges and new possibilities generated by globalization. Questions about the adequacy of liberal approaches that dominate theories of modern citizenship, the tensions that confront citizenship when political affiliation and cultural affinity do not coincide, whether citizenship is a 'universal' concept or an ethnocentric Western notion with limited usefulness, are problems that pre-date today's globalization; in a global age, they are posed with greater urgency and intensity. There are also new challenges generated by the varied phenomena identified as globalization. In this global age, could we still think in terms of being citizens of nation-states or do we need to re-conceptualize citizenship and what it entails?

Some see 'the most potent of the meanings of globalization' in terms of 'the transcendence of nation-state boundaries' (Albrow, 1996, p.91). Others worry about the 'auto-destruction' of the global system (James, 2001). Ulrich Beck (2000, p.20) identifies 'one constant feature' in the various dimensions of globalization and the associated disputes, 'the overturning of the central premise of the first modernity: namely, the idea that *we live and act in the self-enclosed space of national states and their respective national societies*'. Beck (2000, p.11) himself defines globalization as 'the processes through which sovereign nation-states are criss-crossed and undermined by transnational actors with varying prospects of power, orientation, identities, and networks'. Richard Langhorne's (2001) study of globalization shows how it produces the many different overlapping plates of activity and organization, global markets and other forms of e-trading, entertainment and leisure interest of every kind, news and information so varied that no complete list could be made, which are creating 'short-circuits' within and challenging existing institutions of nation-states and pre-existing structures of commerce. Global flows of information, goods, capital, and people are changing the way nation-states and individuals perceive themselves and their place in the world, their rights and obligations vis-à-vis groups and individuals. This does not mean that the nation-state is going to 'wither away' anytime soon. And paradoxically, greater mobility across national boundaries has also prompted efforts by nation-states to control if not stamp the flows altogether, and as Michael Smith (1999, p.11) observes, sometimes 'transnational migration has resulted in outbursts of entrenched, essentialist nationalism in both sending and receiving locales' (also Westwood and Phizacklea, 2000). Nevertheless, there is a need to re-imagine political community; nation-states of the global age need to change their self-definition, the way they operate and relate to one another, to their own respective members, and to other groups and individuals.[10] The 'transnational' and 'supraterritorial' aspects of globalization put tremendous pressures on the prevalent concept of citizenship that was in the words of T. H. Marshall (1964, p.72) 'by definition national'.

In the wake of globalization and the challenges it posed to the traditional nation-state, there has been a revival of interest in cosmopolitanism and its accompanying concept of the citizen of the world, and the closely related concept of global citizenship.[11] In Chapter 2, April Carter poses the question of how 'global citizenship' could deal with the cultural diversity resulting from new forms of migration today. She examines how far both republican and liberal approaches could be adapted to the global arena to deal with the contentious and theoretically complex problems about national identity, multiculturalism, and citizenship raised by a significant level of immigration from diverse cultures. Comparing today's migrant with the Enlightenment 'citizen of the world', she notes that the demanding republican conception of citizenship is in tension with the ideal of global citizenship. Carter presents as alternatives three liberal approaches, the first emphasizing freedom of trade and travel, the second offering a critique of economic globalization in the name of social justice, the third a Kantian cosmopolitanism; she argues that the last two provide the starting point for an understanding of global citizenship. In her view, terrorism on a world wide scale are among the problems that obstruct the realization but do not render obsolete the idea of global citizenship, which requires 'a committed defence of cosmopolitan ideals, rather than belief in an emerging world order more conducive to peace, freedom of migration, and respect for both individual and cultural rights'.

The UNDP (1999) reported that economic globalization is increasing the gap between rich and poor states as well as between peoples in the global economy. The problem of justice has worsened in this global age. The media publicizes to a worldwide audience the prosperity gaps between North and South, West and East. Some of the very worst off have responded to their plight by leaving their homeland and seeking a better life elsewhere. Not only has this increased migration, but the number of refugees has increased manifold in recent decades, and their numbers include those seeking entry into a foreign land for economic reasons. C.L. Ten believes the category of refugee should include not only those who suffer persecution for their politics or religion but also those who live in such appalling social and economic conditions that their lives are at serious risk. In Chapter 3, he argues that a country's obligation to accept refugees is a matter of justice rather than charity, because the basic interests of the refugees are at stake, by comparison with which the sacrifices made by members of the host country are relatively small. These obligations to refugees, however, do not extend to other immigrants seeking better economic opportunities. Ten is therefore sceptical of global citizenship if it suggests that nation-state boundaries are *always* morally irrelevant. Existence of standards of global justice is compatible with non-universal special relationship and local identification that does not extend to the entire humanity. Membership in a common humanity takes priority only when human lives are at stake. Less universal affiliations have their place and could be more important in certain contexts.

In contrast to Carter and Ten's liberal approach, Daniel Bell's dialogue in Chapter 4 comparing the lots of foreign domestic workers in Hong Kong and

Singapore offers a different perspective on the increased movement of people across nation-states that characterizes the global age; it questions liberal emphases. The entire system of migrant labour is arguably based on global injustice. Unfortunately, the day when such inequalities will be eliminated is nowhere in sight. In the meantime, export contract labour is one way to deal with Third World poverty, and the liberal-democratic prioritization of equal citizenship for foreign workers might have negative implications for people in poor countries. Arguments of global citizenship seem far removed from the realities of these foreign domestic workers' lives. From their perspective and that of the NGOs representing them, the most pressing issues are not the fight for equal citizenship or legal protection of rights. Bell is sceptical whether the common cure of 'good governance', implementing basic human rights and democracy within states will alleviate global injustices. It is debatable if agitating for equal rights, including those of citizenship, is the only or best way of improving their work and living conditions.

With the greater interdependence brought about by prevailing globalization processes, demands of justice at the global level have become more pressing, but appear to be more difficult to achieve than ever. Existing national and global institutional systems are not designed to meet these demands; worst, they might be inherently unjust. Barry Hindess argues in Chapter 5 that there are important structural or systemic limitations on the role of citizens in the government of contemporary states, however internally democratic they may be, and what should concern us is the grossly unequal character of the international order from which these limitations derive. Historically the globalization of citizenship, not a move to global citizenship but the extension of citizenship status to more people as more nation-states gain independence in the postcolonial era, has merely changed not removed constraints and inequality. Nor will cosmopolitanism eliminate these inequalities. Hindess finds the *status quo* so unsatisfactory that he considers it a positive development for commitments that cut across national boundaries to threaten not only the role of citizenship within the larger system of states but possibly the design of the system more generally.

Chapter 6 offers a possible alternative to the existing system wherein citizenship is very much based on the liberal understanding of how individuals are related to the state. Even without globalization, liberal citizenship is inadequate as it is compatible with an inert people, which some consider 'the greatest menace to freedom'. James Tiles points out that the tradition of civic republicanism, beginning with Aristotle, recognizes that active citizens are required for a democracy wherein citizens take turns to rule. Can an ordinary citizen meet the demands of active participation? Is the republican view of participation too narrow and elitist, focusing on government at the level of the sovereign state? Tiles suggests that a more flexible and inclusive view of participation is available in John Dewey's vision of democracy as the problem of organizing inchoate publics. In a global age, such publics comprehend far more than is or can be catered to by any individual state. To face the challenges of globalization, transnational publics must find themselves and seek better instruments for furthering the interests that constitute them. Moreover, these publics must be coordinated so that they mutually support rather than obstruct one another. Citizenship is not well understood as membership in one comprehensive organization, be it local or global; it is better understood as membership in multiple organizations that brings with it a comprehensive responsibility. Citizenship in a Deweyan democracy of the global age is not easily achieved. Building transnational institutions will not be enough; the more important task is to facilitate truly democratic and effective processes of communication and deliberation within and among local and global organizations.

Contemporary political theorists who advocate deliberative democracy, which implies active citizenship, share Dewey's emphasis on communication and deliberation. Among them is Jürgen Habermas (1994), who has acknowledged a certain debt to Dewey even though their views about democracy are significantly different in some respects. Habermas (2001) has explored the extension of his model of deliberative democracy, which finds in public deliberation the source of legitimization for principles and norms governing democratic life, beyond the nation-state. In Chapter 7, Catherine Audard criticizes the Habermasian model and insists that the citizen's decision to enter public deliberation needs justifying. She argues that abstention may not be apathy but may instead create a space for moral individuality and integrity. Audard favours a conception of Socratic citizenship. Socrates was *par excellence* a practitioner of deliberative democracy. Paradoxically, the resulting vision of citizenship he held, richer and more demanding than most conceptions, sets him apart from the rest of his citizens. For Socrates, the welfare of Athens depended not on the result of public deliberation, but on his individual moral and intellectual integrity in this process. Democratic processes will not necessarily produce the *right* results. Moral individuality must set limits to the deliberative process. Socratic citizens set these limits by claiming the right to dissent and retreat. Audard's arguments are made mostly in the context of national rather than global citizenship. Can the model of Socratic citizenship be extended on a global scale? From the perspective of individual integrity, being a citizen of a global order or disorder is probably not very different from being a citizen of a nation-state. However, global links could provide resources or strengthen personal capacity for dissent or retreat from national or local political participation.

Implicit in Audard's views is a tension between being a member of a group with a collective identity, and being an autonomous individual capable of critical reflection, a theme taken up in Chapter 8. Alan Montefiore acknowledges that the power of self-determination based on individual identity do eventually have to acknowledge certain internal limitations, in particular the limitations stemming from the fact that all individual identities are at least in part necessarily functions of communities to which the individual may properly be held to belong to and of the roles which they may be thought to occupy in virtue of their community membership. However, acknowledging one's membership in a community does not necessarily mean always 'identifying' oneself with that community. Liberal toleration of diversity and the rights of minorities cannot extend to recognition of any right, which a minority might claim, to determine who should be identified as belonging among its members in cases where the individuals concerned explicitly identify themselves otherwise. A coherent and nuanced approach to reconcile liberalism's commitment to individuals' freedom to live their own lives in whatever way may seem best to them and its commitment to maximum toleration of religious, cultural, and other social sub-group diversity is needed in view of the greater likelihood of conflict between these commitments with the increased mobility of population and more frequent encounters among different cultures and other forms of diversity in a global world.

In Chapter 9, Will Kymlicka takes up the question of whether Western models of multicultural citizenship are relevant for Asia. Many Asian countries have multiethnic and multicultural populations. How do Asian States deal with such diversity which has increased with globalization? Though the phenomenon of minority nationalism appears to be universal, Kymlicka notes that territorial autonomy for minorities have been strongly resisted almost everywhere outside Western liberal democracies. In Asia, only India has many hallmarks of a genuinely multination federalism; the rest of Asia remains pessimistic that minorities would exercise any autonomy given to them in a way that benefits both their own members and the larger community. Instead, many Asians expect minority nationalism to fade away, something which most Westerners have come to accept will never happen. Kymlicka highlights the importance of security concerns in any attempt to accommodate diversity. In many parts of Asia, majorities fear that minorities will ally themselves with neighbouring 'kin-states' to the detriment of the larger state – such alliances would be facilitated by new global networks that escape the monitoring and control of individual nation-states. In view of this perception of security threat, Asian countries are unlikely to adopt Western models of multicultural citizenship.

While multicultural citizenship is a twentieth-century innovation and may or may not be useful in meeting the challenges of globalization, the problem of how to deal with different cultures has a longer history. One criticism of multiculturalism is that it involves moral relativism and precludes criticism or elimination of certain cultural practices that might seem outright inhuman. Chapter 10 shows how the sixteenth-century French philosopher Montaigne's views about other cultures are relevant to contemporary concerns about accommodating divergent traditions without succumbing to moral relativism, even though the multicultural state was not an issue in sixteenth-century France. Many consider Montaigne a moral relativist who believes that reason cannot transcend custom; Cecila Wee argues on the contrary that Montaigne's acceptance of foreign cultural practices is compatible with conscious moral evaluation of these practices according to some universal standards. She applies Montaigne's restricted universalism to contemporary problems of group-differentiated rights in multicultural states and considers justifiability of disapproval of, or even intervention in, the practices of another culture.

Baogang He resists relativism differently by defending a concept of cultural equality that assumes interaction between cultures understood as open and dynamic. From a universal cross-cultural perspective, he sees equality as the basis for the communication, production, and distribution of culture both internally and externally. In Chapter 11, he offers a critical response to Brian Barry's attack on cultural equality by re-examining the various meanings of cultural equality and the arguments for and against it, and by exploring the strategies for dealing with some of its problems. Despite its problems, and controversy is only to be expected of such a new idea, he defends cultural equality as the idea provides transnational activism with a normative basis to deal with the issue of structural inequalities. It meets the need of global citizenship to negotiate cultural differences in order to develop some minimal overlapping consensus.

Chapter 12 demonstrates the benefits of mutual learning and mutual transformation that have become possible with the more frequent and intense cultural encounters facilitated by globalization. A.T. Nuyen argues that it is not necessary to choose between rejecting citizenship as an ethnocentric Western idea irrelevant to other cultures and imposing a procrustean universal concept on all. Other cultures could accommodate the idea of citizenship, and in the process modify it and raise questions for certain traditional Western conceptions. Nuyen portrays Confucianism as sympathetic to criticisms of liberalism's metaphysics of the individualistic self. Confucianism offers an alternative that sees the essence of being a citizen in participating in the making of one's own world, one's own community. With its understanding of the individual person as a social being whose rights and responsibilities are governed by the moral concept of *li* (rites or ritual propriety), Confucianism would be compatible with a practice of 'deep' or 'thick' citizenship that would be able to deal better with the problems minorities face, which have increased and intensified in the midst of globalization.

In Chapter 13, Sor-hoon Tan considers how the negotiation of cultural differences might be achieved by examining the interaction between politics and culture in contemporary Confucianism's global aspirations. She argues that such global aspirations are not realizable except through local efforts at civilized communication. What Confucianism could contribute to discussions of global citizenship is not another proposal of macro institutional framework. Instead, it should draw attention to the importance of fostering certain local processes that would reduce the likelihood of conflict, promote understanding between cultures, and provide resources for bringing about such processes. Aspiration to be a citizen of the world is needed in this age of globalization where demands on us and impact of our actions are no longer strictly local. However, we cannot realize that aspiration without learning to act and communicate in civilized ways with cultural others in local encounters.

## Notes

1  For various debates over the different dimensions of globalization, see Held and McGrew, 2000; Giddens, 2000b, chapter 1. Recent studies of globalization have become too numerous to enumerate, most of them focus on some specific aspect or adopt a specific perspective. Multifaceted works on globalization include Germain, 2000; Held, 2000; Robertson and White, 2003.

2  For a mapping of the globalization debate into hyperglobalists, sceptics, and transformationalists, see McGrew, 1998. For detailed globalist arguments, see Albrow, 1996; Omae, 1990; Naisbitt, 1994; Greider, 1997. Works by globalization sceptics include Hirst and Thompson, 1996; Boyer and Drache, 1996.

3    Delanty, 2000, p.3. In response, various arguments have been for the need for global
     governance, an example of which may be found in Cable, 1999; also Väyrynen, 1999.
4    See Broad, 2002 for the various perspectives against current globalization.
5    For debate about Fukuyama's thesis, see *National Interest*, vol.17.
6    For a collection of essays on globalization from an international relations perspective,
     see O'Meara *et al.*, 2000.
7    For how globalization affects cultural identity and the different possible outcomes, see
     Hall, 1992; also Jameson and Miyoshi, 1998. Further discussion of the relationship
     between globalization and postmodernism may be found in Featherstone, 1995.
8    One account of this debate is found in MacKay, 2000; also Holton, 1998, chapter 7.
9    Resistance to globalization is not confined to the cultural arena but also has generated
     tensions in economic arena, prompting some to ask if globalization has gone too far.
     For a defence of globalization as liberalization in the context of tensions produced by
     globalization, see Rodrik, 1997.
10   For a study of the complex impact of globalization on the nation-state that criticizes
     those who announce the demise of the nation-state under the onslaught of the global
     economy, see Holton, 1998; Archibugi *et al.*, 1998.
11   Recent works on global citizenship include Carter, 2001; Dower and Williams, 2002.

## References

Albrow, Martin (1996), *The Global Age*, Polity, Cambridge.
Archibugi, Daniele, David Held and Martin Köhler (eds.) (1998), *Re-imagining Political
     Community: Studies in Cosmopolitan Democracy*, Polity, Cambridge.
Aristotle (1984), *The Complete Works of Aristotle*, Jonathan Barnes (ed.). Princeton
     University, Princeton.
Barnet, R.J. and J. Cavanagh (1994), *Global Dreams: Imperial Corporations and the New
     World Order*, Simon and Schuster, New York.
Beck, Ulrich (2000), *What is Globalization?* Patrick Camiller (trans.), Polity, Cambridge.
Boyer, Robert and Daniel Drache (eds.) (1996), *States against Markets: the Limits of
     Globalization*, Routledge, London.
Brennan, Teresa (2003), *Globalization and its Terrors: Daily life in the West*, Routledge,
     London.
Broad, Robin (2002), *Global Backlash: Citizen Initiatives for a Just World Economy*,
     Rowman & Littlefield, Lanham.
Cable, Vincent (1999), *Globalization and Global Governance*, Royal Institute of
     International Affairs, London.
Calhoun, Craig (2002), 'The Class Consciousness of Frequent Travellers: Towards a
     Critique of Actually Existing Cosmopolitanism', in Steven Vertovec and Robin Cohen
     (eds.), *Conceiving Cosmopolitanism*, Oxford University, Oxford, pp.86-109.
Carter, April (2001), *The Political Theory of Global Citizenship*, Routledge, London.
Delanty, Gerald (2000), *Citizenship in a Global Age*, Open University, Buckingham.
Dower, Nigel and John Williams (eds.) (2002), *Global Citizenship: a critical reader*,
     Edinburgh University, Edinburgh.
Falk, Richard (1999), *Predatory Globalization*, Polity, Malden.
Featherstone, Mike (ed.) (1995), *Undoing Culture: Globalization, Postmodernism, and
     Identity*, Sage, London.
Fukuyama, Francis (1992), *The End of History and the Last Man*, Macmillan, New York.

Germain, Randall (ed.) (2000), *Globalization and its critics: perspectives from political economy*, Macmillan, Basingstoke.

Giddens, Anthony (2000a), 'The Globalizing of Modernity', in Held and McGrew, 2000, pp.92-8.

Giddens, Anthony (2000b), *Runaway World – How Globalization is reshaping our lives*, Routledge, New York.

Greider, William (1997), *One World, ready or not: the manic logic of global capitalism*, Simon ad Schuster, New York.

Habermas, Jürgen (1994), 'Citizenship and National Identity', in Bart von Steenbergen,*The Condition of Citizenship*, Sage, London, pp.20-35.

Habermas, Jürgen (2001), 'The Postnational Constellation and the Future of Democracy', in Max Pensky (ed. and trans.), *The Postnational Constellation: Political Essays*, MIT, Cambridge, pp.58-112.

Hall, Stuart (1992), 'The Question of Cultural Identity', in Stuart Hall, David Held and Anthony McGrew (eds.), *Modernity and its Futures*, Polity, Cambridge, pp.274-325.

Held, David (ed.) (2000), *A Globalizing World? Culture, Economics, Politics*, Routledge, London.

Held, David and Anthony McGrew (eds.) (2000), *The Global Transformations Reader*, Polity, Malden.

Hirst, Paul and Graham Thompson (1996), *Globalization in Question*, Polity, Cambridge.

Holton, Robert J. (1998), *Globalization and the Nation-State*, St. Martin's, New York.

Huntington, Samuel (1996), *The Clash of Civilization and the Remaking of the World Order*, Simon and Schuster, New York.

James, Harold (2001), *The End of Globalization: Lessons from the Great Depression*, Harvard University, Cambridge.

Jameson, Fredric and Masao Miyoshi (eds.) (1998), *The Cultures of Globalization*, Duke University, Durham.

Langhorne, Richard (2001), *The Coming of Globalization*, Palgrave, Basingstoke.

Mahbubani, Kishore (1992), 'The West and the Rest', *The National Interest*, vol.28, pp.3-12.

Marshall, T.H. (1964), *Class, Citizenship and Social Development*, Double Day, New York.

McGrew, Anthony (1998), 'Globalization: Conceptualizing a Moving Target', in John Eatwell *et al.*, *Understanding Globalization*, Swedish Ministry of Foreign Affairs, Stockholm, pp.7-27.

MacKay, Hugh (2000), 'The Globalization of Culture', in Held, 2000, pp.48-84.

Miller, Daniel (ed.) (1995), *Worlds Apart: modernity through the prism of the local*, Routledge, New York.

Naisbitt, John (1994) *Global Paradox: the Bigger the World Economy, the more Powerful its Smallest Players*, Brealey, London.

Nisbet, Robert (1974), 'Citizenship: Two Traditions', *Social Research*, vol.41, pp.612-37.

Omae, Kenichi (1990), *The Borderless World: Power and Strategy in the Interlinked Economy*, Fontana, London.

Omae, Kenichi (1995), *The End of the Nation-state: the Rise of Regional Economies*, Free Press, New York.

O'Meara, Patrick, Howard Mehlinger, and Matthew Krain (eds.) (2000), *Globalization and the Challenges of a New Century*, Indiana University, Bloomington.

Robertson, Roland and Kathleen E. White (eds.) (2003), *Globalization: Critical Concepts in Sociology*, Rouledge, London.

Rodrik, Dani (1997), *Has Globalization gone too far?* Institute for International Economics, Washington, DC.

Scholte, Jan Aart (2000), *Globalization: a critical introduction*, St. Martin's, New York.

Smith, Michael (1999), 'New Approaches to Migration and Transnationalism: Locating transnational practices', keynote address given at the Conference *New Approaches to Migration: Transnational Communities and Transformation of Home*, University of Sussex, 21-22 September.

UNDP (1999), *Globalization with a Human Face: Human Development Report 1999*, Oxford University, New York.

Väyrynen, Raimo (ed.) (1999), *Globalization and Global Governance*, Rowman & Littlefield, Lanham.

Westwood, Sallie and Annie Phizacklea (2000), *Transnationalism and the Politics of Belonging*, Routledge, London.

Chapter 2

# Migration and Cultural Diversity Implications for National and Global Citizenship

April Carter

A great deal has been written in the last two decades about national citizenship since the topic became fashionable again (Kymlicka and Norman, 1994). Global citizenship and the closely linked concept of cosmopolitanism have also received increasing attention since the 1990s (Dower and Williams, 2002; Falk, 1994; Hutchings and Dannreuther, 1999; Linklater, 1998, pp.179-212; Nussbaum, 1997; Carter, 2001). This chapter approaches national and global citizenship somewhat obliquely, through the important political issue of migration, which is now one facet of globalization.

In a national context a significant level of immigration from diverse cultures raises questions about national identity, multiculturalism, and citizenship which are politically contentious and theoretically complex. I outline briefly evolving civic republican views of citizenship and the role of migrants, and then consider two versions of liberalism, the first giving priority to universal individual rights and the second recognizing that groups have cultural rights.[1]

Liberalism, even when adapted to recognize group rights, tends to set limits to the cultural rights of migrants. For a stronger version of multiculturalism, linked to cosmopolitanism, I turn to the work of Bhiku Parekh (2000a; 2000b), who questions liberal universalism and whether, in a context of global migration and reduction in the power of the nation-state, citizenship can be resolved in a purely national context.

In a global context migration raises questions about rights of migrants under international law and how far migrants can claim to be global citizens. I note differing interpretations of the Englightenment concept of the travelling philosopher as world citizen (Waldron, 1995 and 2000), before considering the view put forward by Yasemin Nohoglu Soysal (1994) that migrants are 'postnational' citizens with rights protected by international law.

The plight of many migrants excluded from such rights raises however wider questions about global obligations and the role of global citizenship. I explore how far republican or liberal approaches can be adapted to the global arena.

**National Citizenship and Migrants: Republicanism**

Although liberal beliefs and attitudes are predominant in Western political theory, there has been a revival of civic republican ideas.[2] This revival is sufficiently strong for an alternative interpretation of republicanism, focusing on freedom from domination and on the rule of law, to have emerged (Sunstein, 1993; Pettit, 1997). This kind of constitutional republicanism is – despite important differences of interpretation – closer to liberalism. I focus here on civic republicanism, which promotes the ideals of political community and active citizenship.

Classical republicanism, which evolved in the city state, suggests the private realm be subordinate to the public realm and individual virtue is essential for good citizenship. Citizens have rights but also duties, such as implies both active participation in a direct democracy and taking up arms when required for the republic. Classical civic republicanism also implies strong communal purpose, linked to a deep patriotism. Although strangers may be allowed to live in the land, contribute to the economy and enjoy certain civil rights, they are excluded from the political rights of citizenship. (Switzerland, which at some levels is the country closest to classical republicanism, adopts just such an exclusionary policy towards migrants.)

The modern republicanism which was fostered by the French Revolution, and declared 'the rights of man and citizen', was more egalitarian and democratic than some earlier versions which excluded from citizenship those without property.[3] The activity of the Paris communes and the rhetoric of the Jacobins emphasized the ideal of expressing and legislating for the popular will. The Revolution adapted to the modern age by taking the nation-state for granted and associating republicanism with nationalism.

The French Revolution also, however, had a strongly internationalist slant and therefore citizenship was in principle open to strangers who came to live in France. But the price of that citizenship has been acceptance of the political and social beliefs of the new republic. To this day the tendency of French policies is assimilationist – hence the major and continuing public debate sparked since the 1990s by Muslim girls choosing to wear headscarves (*hijab*) to school.

Theorists of civic republicanism today have modified it to fit the spirit of the times and have abandoned the older emphasis on subordinating the private to the public and the requirement of military service. Benjamin Barber envisages a period of compulsory service for citizens, but sees it primarily as social. David Miller (1999, p.83) argues that public service is more likely to take the form of voluntary work in civil society. He suggests that the republican citizen should be active in safeguarding the rights of other members of the society and should participate fully in all aspects of politics. So a republican would expect immigrants who become citizens to move beyond protecting the rights of their immigrant group – as many do – to participate fully in public life. There is clearly a tension between this expectation and the reality of the life of many migrants – particularly of women living in cultural groups where they are expected to stay out of the public realm, who may not even learn the language of their new country. There is also the problem that active engagement by migrants from very different backgrounds may mean pressure for national policies alien to the dominant values of the host country. Conflict between religious beliefs and secular values is particularly likely. Republicanism finds these questions especially difficult because it believes citizens should be bound by agreed beliefs and values.

## National Citizenship and Migrants: Liberalism

Liberalism seems prima facie a doctrine more suited to accepting the presence of immigrant groups with diverse languages, religions, social attitudes, and modes of behaviour – although avowedly liberal states have often pursued racist policies at home and used racial criteria to exclude migrants.

Liberal theorists since John Locke have generally urged religious toleration.[4] Liberals have also argued eloquently for toleration of social differences and the rights of minorities to dissent from the majority. They have argued too for a maximum sphere of individual freedom not controlled by the state. Awareness of different beliefs about 'the good' and different life styles is one of the reasons for Isaiah Berlin's commitment to 'negative liberty' (Berlin, 1969). So cultural pluralism appears to be embedded in a liberal view of the world but the universalist model of liberal citizenship also suggests giving priority to the rights of individuals and their potential for autonomy and self-development. This is the mainstream tradition of humanist liberalism represented by Immanuel Kant, John Stuart Mill, and John Rawls.

There are, therefore, several problems for a liberal state in responding to significant social diversity and claims for group rights. One is primarily theoretical, but has been highlighted in court cases: the potential for conflict between the rights of individuals and respect for group cultural or religious beliefs. The second problem is primarily political, but has been reflected in theoretical debates: the growth of a militant identity politics has required states to move beyond tolerance of difference in the private sphere to making changes in the law and offering state support to maintain cultural differences.

The first problem is not restricted to new immigrant groups – it has been posed by long established religious sects such as the Jehovah's Witnesses refusing forms of medical treatment for their children, or the Amish in the United States refusing to send their children to high school (Galston, 1995). However, the increasing number of migrant communities whose culture is far removed from Western liberal ideas of individual freedom does present this problem in a more acute form.

Even liberals prepared to rethink the role of group rights in liberal theory, like Will Kymlicka, have argued that group rights must be limited by some inalienable individual rights. Kymlicka (1999, p.31) suggests that liberals should support minority groups claiming rights against the dominant society – these are 'external protections' such as guaranteeing political representation and the survival of a language, or compensation for past oppression and injustice; but liberals should not support groups imposing 'internal restrictions' on their own members. He also makes a distinction between territorially based national minorities and indigenous peoples asserting their rights and cultures on the one hand, and migrants on the other. He argues that migrants have chosen to seek a new life in their adoptive country. Therefore, whilst they should of course be protected against discrimination and should have the right to maintain their own language and ethnic heritage in the private sphere, they should be educated to fluency in the mainstream language and accept the principles of a liberal host country. He is, however, prepared to recognize that immigrant groups may seek some minor changes in public laws or institutions, for example to exempt Jews and Muslims from Sunday closing legislation (Kymlicka, 1995, pp.78-9).

Kymlicka's liberal interpretation of group rights is, in varying degrees, challenged by the new politics of multiculturalism. Third generation migrants are now more likely to demand education in their original native language as Turks in Germany have done, or to assert their own identity as the Muslim girls in the *hijab* dispute in France did, or to press for separate religious schools. Some second or third generation migrants in Germany have also demonstrated a revived nationalism and strict adherence to Islam (Joppke, 1999, pp.221-2).

**Cosmopolitan Multiculturalism**

This new politics is the context within which Bhiku Parekh argues, in *Rethinking Multiculturalism*, for strong multicultural rights for migrant groups. Parekh agrees with the importance of recognizing the claims of indigenous peoples and ethnic minorities: in a later essay, 'Reconstituting the modern state', he discusses these issues focusing on Canada and India (Parekh, 2002). He refuses to accept Kymlicka's distinction between national minorities and immigrants, since even recent migrants are 'citizens in waiting'. His central theoretical claim is that Kymlicka's position is inconsistent, since Kymlicka has argued that culture is a primary good. Therefore, it could not be right for a country accepting migrants to demand that they should abandon such a good.

Parekh is also unwilling to accept unconditionally a specifically Western liberal framework for framing policy. He argues that liberalism 'represents a particular cultural perspective and cannot provide a broad and impartial enough framework to conceptualize other cultures or their relations with it' (Parekh, 2000b, p.14). Multiculturalism requires that the values which determine relations between cultural groups must emerge from dialogue between them.

The other strand in Parekh's argument is that it is no longer possible to think purely in terms of the nation-state: in an era of mass migration culture cannot be confined to a particular country. His goal is 'cosmopolitan multiculturalism'. In the *Parekh Report* – an enquiry by a Commission chaired by Parekh into the nature of British citizenship and identity today – the aim is to safeguard the rights of all cultural communities, indigenous and migrant. The report envisages 'a community of communities...proud of and learning from its own internal diversity' (Parekh, 2000a, pp.3-4). It also argues that the ground rules for negotiating issues such as the content of education are provided by international human rights conventions, thus moving the argument away from liberalism within the nation-state to the international setting, where international law is playing an increasing role (Parekh, 2000a, p.90). Parekh therefore raises two central theoretical and political issues:

1. Whether the tension between universalism and respect for cultural pluralism within liberalism can be resolved satisfactorily within a liberal framework, or whether it is necessary accept a new version of cosmopolitan multiculturalism.
2. Whether we need to move beyond national citizenship to think in terms of transnational or global citizenship both for migrants and for everyone.

**Cosmopolitanism: Universalism versus Multiculturalism?**

The tension between the universal right of a group to respect for its culture and the universal rights of individuals are reflected not only within liberal cosmopolitanism, but also within international law. On the one hand immigrants can appeal to international recognition of their rights to maintain their religious and cultural beliefs and practices; on the other hand, national governments may recognize that some cultures discriminate against certain individuals. British immigration rules issued in 1999, for example, provided for asylum for homosexuals escaping from severe discrimination in their home culture. Brian Barry (2001, p.61), who cites this ruling, notes that it appears to assume a universal right to a private sexual life. Moreover, if respect for individual human rights leads Western liberal countries to give asylum to those discriminated against elsewhere, then it is incoherent simultaneously to permit immigrants to practise such discrimination within their own groups.

Barry, one of the most incisive critics of multiculturalism, has specifically attacked *The Parekh Report*. He argues that it is liable to be 'harmful to women and children in minority communities and to those within them who deviate from their prevailing norms' (Barry, 2001, p.58). He fears, for example, that in the British context multicultural policies may mean official endorsement of culturally-based restrictions on women in marriage, and that the report will tend to reinforce sensitivity to cultural rights rather than uphold individual rights.

Barry's main concern is with the wider implications of Parekh's position and its international application. If it is accepted that there are some universal standards, but that other practices should be defined by cultural values, then the crucial issue is where to draw the line. Barry (2001, p.63) suggests that Parekh, after starting with the 1948 Universal Declaration of Rights, then denudes it of most of its force by upholding the legitimacy of South Asian political systems and cultural values which negate much of the Declaration.

Barry's central argument is that appeal to 'an alleged consensus' based on religious and cultural traditions, is bound to support 'unequal treatment based on ethnicity and sex'. He adds that 'this is true of every society's traditions, including those of Britain' (Barry, 2001, p.62). Much the same point is made by Susan Moller Okin in her essay 'Is multiculturalism bad for women?' (1999, p.17): 'Most cultures are patriarchal...and many (though not all) of the cultural minorities that claim group rights are more patriarchal than the surrounding cultures'. Okin's argument here assumes a Western context, and she specifically notes that feminist agitation has helped to reduce previous entrenched discrimination against women in the West. But her argument also ranges over oppression of women in other parts of the world and the dangers of endorsing the suppression of women's voices in the name of respect for culture.

The case made against Okin by some of her respondents is that liberal cosmopolitanism, stressing individual rights, reflects a Western liberal tendency to impose their own liberal standards on the world, and also a liberal assumption of superior morality. This is also the case made by Parekh. Has it any validity?

Certainly it can be argued that claims to colonial rule in the nineteenth and early twentieth centuries were often linked to the assumed superiority of Western civilization, which in turn implied (selective) commitment to liberal beliefs. Even the progressive John Stuart Mill justified British rule over India (1962, pp.336-65). We also appear now to be seeing an emerging justification for American and British neo-imperial domination based on appeals to liberal democracy, for example, to replace dictatorship in Iraq (Frum and Perle, 2004), and even – in the case of the war on Afghanistan – appeals to the rights of women.[5] However, some liberals have always opposed colonialism, and liberal cosmopolitanism should not be equated with imperialist and militaristic attempts to co-opt liberal values to justify *realpolitik*.

Second, Western liberals have often been ignorant of the complexities of other cultures and have held oversimplified views, for example, about the position of women under Islam. These attitudes towards Islam and their evolution in academic disciplines during the colonial period have been discussed in the literature on 'orientalism' (Said, 1978). Such attitudes are not intrinsic to liberalism, but may be encouraged by belief in the superiority of liberal values. It is in addition important to note that, in the past, countries where Islam or Hinduism were dominant have often been very tolerant of a variety of religious beliefs and cultural practices in their midst. So tolerance is by no means exclusive to Western liberalism. Many immigrants in Britain might justifiably resent Home Office proposals in October 2002 that they should 'take lessons in tolerance'.[6]

If we did not live in a globalized world, and if different cultures were more or less limited to specific geographical areas, it might be politically prudent and morally right to give priority to the need for mutual tolerance and respect. But we are moving towards a Kantian position where 'The people's of the earth have thus entered in varying degrees into a universal community...where a violation of rights in *one* part of the world is felt *everywhere*' (Reiss, 1991, pp.107-8). Moreover, widespread immigration – the starting point of this paper – ensures cultural mingling, so potentially conflicting demands for the rights of different cultures and the rights of individuals cannot be ignored.

Recognition of social diversity is the basis for both liberal pluralism and Parekh's emphasis on 'pluralist universalism'. Whereas liberalism assumes individual choice, Parekh tends to imply that the 'cultural embeddedness' of the individual defines many personal choices. Second, liberalism assumes that we should seek universally valid principles, whereas Parekh's multiculturalism appears ultimately to undermine claims to universalism. Even though he appeals to cosmopolitanism and a core of international human rights, he also argues that 'different societies may legitimately define, trade-off, prioritize and realize the universal values differently, and even occasionally override some of them' (Parekh, 2000b, p.136). But stressing the cultural autonomy of particular societies tends to undermine *both* a commitment to individual rights *and* a universal requirement of tolerance to other cultures – since not all existing societies are tolerant. So although Parekh argues eloquently for a cosmopolitan multiculturalism and has made a strong case for states treating migrants in the same way as other cultural groups, he has not yet produced a convincing alternative to liberal cosmopolitanism.

The basis of living together has ultimately to be provided by law and politics. But given the erosion of the nation-state by global trends it is arguable that the role of national citizen should be transcended by a normative concept of global citizenship. Parekh (2002, p.53) notes 'the growing spirit of global citizenship' in response to global problems of poverty and interdependence, but does not elaborate on its implications.

I examine below the embryonic sense of global citizenship emerging out of migration, before considering whether the transfer of republican and liberal views to the global sphere is adequate.

### Migrants as Global or Transnational Citizens?

The right of individuals to travel the world they share as members of a common humanity, and the right to settle in other lands, can be traced back to the early theorists of international law, but found its most vigorous exposition in the writings of the Enlightenment *philosophes*. Montesquieu and Voltaire claimed that individuals had a fundamental right to travel wherever they wished and to live where they felt at home. Kant claimed both a right to travel and to leave one's native country permanently (Carter, 2001, p.43).

Many *philosophes* also saw themselves as 'citizens of the world' who could be at home anywhere. Today, scientists, academics, and other professionals who work abroad – who are often multilingual, with transferable skills such as computer literacy, and transnational organizational links – can be seen as contemporary versions of the Enlightenment citizens of the world. Experience of varied cultures may also promote a cosmopolitan outlook. This kind of cosmopolitanism may be in part a life style preference, although it clearly implies a rejection of a narrow nationalism. The Chinese astrophysicist Fang Lizhi (1990), for example, draws on his own observations when travelling, the experience of scientific cooperation across borders during World War I, the astronomical perspective on a small world within the universe, and his belief that human rights transcend national borders, to condemn exclusive patriotism.

Jeremy Waldron, himself a travelling philosopher, moves from this first understanding of cosmopolitanism as rejection of national or communal loyalties towards a more specifically Kantian political position. Waldron (1995) defines cosmopolitanism as a lack of identification with any single place or culture. In a later article 'What is cosmopolitanism?' (2000) he accepts that serious engagement with a particular culture is compatible with wider cosmopolitan sympathies and obligations. His new understanding gives weight to Kant's concept of cosmopolitan right, which creates 'certain universal laws' relating to the world which nations share in common (Reiss, 1991, pp.106-8, pp.172-3). Waldron notes that 'cosmopolitan right' imposes moral constraints on how travellers behave towards the people in the country where they are visiting or settling. It also suggests acceptance of cultural diversity and respect for other cultures.

The Enlightenment world citizens and today's cosmopolitan intellectuals reflect the attitudes of an elite. The main issues raised by immigration now arise out of the movements of large numbers of people, many from a peasant or worker background. There is a second important difference. The Enlightenment *philosophes* and their counterparts today value their experience of diverse cultures. In contrast, many migrants seeking work and economic betterment in this age of globalization cling to their inherited culture as a source of identity and continuity.

Today's discussion of migration tends to focus primarily on migrants' rights: civil rights to freedom of speech, association and movement, rights to social welfare, and economic rights such as a minimum wage or trade union membership. Political rights have usually been reserved for citizens of the state; but, as Tomas Hammar (1990, p.115) and others have argued, there is a democratic case for granting long term migrants, or 'denizens', a voice in the policies of the state in which they are living.

The evolution of European Union (EU) citizenship as a semi-supranational status has resulted in the transfer of not only civil, social, and economic rights but also limited political rights across frontiers. EU citizens can in principle vote and stand in both local and EU elections anywhere in the Union – though not in national elections. How far EU citizenship really transcends national citizenship is still hotly debated (Meehan, 1993; Rosas and Antola, 1995; Lehning and Weale, 1997). Even if it does, it is debatable whether it provides a model for global citizenship – EU citizenship, symbolized by the EU passport, is in many ways exclusive.

Nevertheless, the example of transferable rights between territories within the EU has global implications. First, many of the rights granted to migrant EU citizens are also granted in some European countries to migrants from other parts of the world. This is true even of rights to vote in local elections, and is one of the grounds for contesting the existence of a true European citizenship (d'Oliveira, 1995, pp.77-81). Even in Germany, which initially resisted extending rights of EU citizens to other migrants, there are both legal and moral pressures to do so. Christian Joppke (1999, p.191) notes that the 'European Court of Justice increasingly applies the prohibition of nationality-based discrimination to the 1.5 million Turks living in Germany' and that 'every new privilege for EU immigrants raises the question why non-European immigrants should not have it'. Therefore, the principles of transferring rights across frontiers have been established on a significant scale. This principle is also underpinned by the development of global conventions making individuals bearers of rights.

The increased significance of international law in shaping the policies of national governments is one trend changing the nature of both politics and citizenship. Although international law does not require states to accept migrants – as opposed to general obligations to grant asylum – the 1965 Convention on the Elimination of Racial Discrimination does in principle prevent discriminating against migrants on the basis of race. Since the United States abandoned its national-origins quota in 1965 other Western governments have phased out racial and ethnic requirements (Joppke, 1999, pp.256-66). The Convention also requires governments to prevent discrimination against all racial minorities (Parekh, 2000a, p.92). The European Human Rights Convention has also been used to extend immigrant rights – for example, its incorporation into British law has enabled immigrants to argue that it is illegal to *require* immigrants to learn and use English.[7]

Because of the increased salience of international law in the justification of national policy, Soysal has argued that migrants in European countries are able to base their claims to cultural identity on international law and therefore these migrants can be seen as moving towards a form of 'postnational citizenship'. Soysal (1994, p.166) does not argue that migrants are full global citizens, but that they demonstrate the possibility of multiple membership in diverse societies and the acceptance of multiple identities with 'intersecting complexes of rights, duties and loyalties'. David Jacobson (1997, p.v) also suggests that human rights allow migrants to make claims on government without having to become naturalized or to assimilate into the society they have entered. If migrants throughout the world were able to claim civil, political, socio-economic, and cultural rights under international law, this would be an expression of global citizenship – but at present such an outcome appears wholly utopian.

Indeed the thesis of 'postnational citizenship' has been disputed by some other experts on migration, such as Joppke, who emphasize that acceptance of international obligations depends upon a prior national political commitment to respect rights. Certainly the existence of international agreements does not mean that all countries accede to them, or honour them. Even if they do take international obligations seriously, they may opt out of certain provisions. Still, Soysal's analysis does suggest that Parekh's concept of cosmopolitan multiculturalism has some basis in political and legal reality.

It is, however, a very partial reality for migrants. The rights granted to those legally admitted to the EU constitute an argument for restricting external migration in the first place. This logic became manifest in the 1990s, when the EU stressed the need to strengthen external border controls as internal controls were relaxed, and when there were fears of very large numbers seeking entry from the former Soviet bloc and Africa. But restrictive measures have not prevented large numbers of people fleeing both poverty and oppression entering the European Union illegally. Illegal immigrants enjoy virtually no rights, are always subject to deportation and may often be subject to exploitation by criminal groups – even though their labour is practically indispensable in cities like London.

The moral problem posed by plight of illegal migrants, and the economic and political pressures which create mass migration and refugees, suggest the need for a new global politics. Therefore, the next question is whether it is possible to elaborate republican or liberal concepts of global citizenship, and the policy implications – including policies on migration – of identifying as a global citizen.

**Republican and Liberal Theories of Global Citizenship**

There are conflicting tendencies within the civic republican tradition in assessing the scope for a form of global citizenship. A republican view of citizenship within the nation-state tends either towards exclusiveness (as in Switzerland) or towards a strong emphasis on cultural assimilation (as in France). It seems therefore to be clearly opposed to a concept of postnational citizenship in which migrants can claim under international law the right to retain a separate language and culture which may be at odds with the country's social and political values.

Yet there is a cosmopolitan strand in republicanism dating from the Enlightenment. Tom Paine and others saw no contradiction between their republican patriotism and their claim to be citizens of the world. The French Revolution in its declaration of the 'rights of man' had a universal application. The new French Republic in the 1790s also adopted a radical position on how easily foreigners could gain citizenship rights after a brief period of residence – a precedent appealed to by Jürgen Habermas (1992) in his rejection of the German ethnic view of citizenship. As noted above, however, this generous policy towards accepting strangers also implies that the new citizens should adopt republican beliefs.

It can be argued that the subsequent rise of nationalism (partially promoted by the French Revolution and its aftermath) made republicanism and cosmopolitanism incompatible; but now that the nation-state is being undermined by regional and global trends, some argue that republicanism should become cosmopolitan. Alastair Davidson has adopted this position. In his study of Australian citizenship he argues that newcomers should be able to take part in politics and 'reshape the public space' (Davidson, 1997, pp.257-8). He looks back to the French Revolution to argue that migrants should rapidly be allowed to acquire citizen rights and looks forward to an ideal of freedom of movement between many countries and the acquisition of many citizenships. He recognizes, however, problems posed for Australia by the fact that many migrants will come from countries in the region with more authoritarian traditions (Davidson, 1997, pp.280-86). Davidson therefore espouses a republican cosmopolitanism but suggests that it may be difficult to maintain the republican element in a multicultural world. He does, however, evaluate positively the role of regional bodies in underpinning multicultural rights and promoting a supranational form of citizenship in a book co-authored with Stephen Castles (Castles and Davidson, 2000). The postscript to the book is however more pessimistic about the results of globalization such as the arms trade, the drugs trade, and the spread of HIV/Aids.

The activist republican ideal of citizenship might suggest that at a global level there is a duty to defend the rights of the poor and exploited and to hold national governments, international organizations, and other centres of power such as multinational corporations to account. But some republicans argue that the criteria for real political citizenship cannot be met globally. Michael Walzer (1996, p.125) for example – though he is sympathetic to the idea of a cosmopolitan education – denies that he can be a citizen of the world because there are no institutional structures, decision procedures, clear rights and duties, or common celebrations of citizenship. Miller does not accept that the nation-state is being seriously undermined and provides a defence of some forms of nationalism; but nationalism does not, from this perspective, exclude a belief in wider human obligations towards those suffering political persecution or economic need (Miller, 1999).

One republican theorist who *does* accept the reality of globalization, Benjamin Barber, stresses its negative side. 'We have globalized crime, globalized the rogue weapons trade, globalized terror and hate propaganda – sometimes using the Internet itself...globalized drugs, pornography and the trade in women and children made possible by "porn tourism"' (Barber, 2001, p.302) Barber fears the future is represented by a 'mafiacracy-cum-anarchy' and that transnational government or civil society bodies cannot exert meaningful power. So there is no global democratic framework for effective citizenship – though Barber believes responsible individual action is the only hope.

Civic republicanism's demanding view of citizenship and of the kind of society that can nurture true citizens is in tension with an ideal of global citizenship. Liberalism is inherently cosmopolitan in its emphasis on universal individual rights and embodies the values of the Enlightenment. In practice since the nineteenth-century liberals within nation-states have relied on nationalism as a background to liberal politics, but with a few exceptions (such as Mill) liberal theory has until very recently ignored the role of nationalism (Mill, 1962, chapter 6; Canovan, 1996). Given the growth of international law and international institutions (generally approved by liberals) and the pressures of economic globalization (enthusiastically endorsed by some liberals and viewed with alarm by others) liberals are now coming to grips with the partial decline of the Western nation-state.

There are several possible liberal approaches to globalization and global citizenship, some of them primarily internationalist with a continuing emphasis on the central role of the state (Rawls, 1999). I focus here on three cosmopolitan approaches: a neo-liberal emphasis on freedom of trade and travel; a social liberal critique of economic globalization in the name of social justice, and a Kantian cosmopolitanism.

Neo-liberalism in the abstract appears to be the approach most inclined to transcend national borders, with its emphasis on free trade and movement of capital. Moreover the merchant was in the Enlightenment one embodiment of world citizenship, and a contemporary theorist of citizenship, Herman van Gunsteren (1988, p.741), has suggested that the emergence of a global business class 'multilingual, multicultural and migrant' is 'a real development of world citizenship'. Neo-liberalism could suggest that individuals see themselves as bearers of rights in a global context and provide a 'thin' model of global citizenship. In theory, free movement might also imply unrestricted movement for economic migrants in search of work; but neo-liberalism can also plausibly be seen as an ideological justification of policies which allow multinational corporations to exercise control over the resources of the poorer sections of the globe and find the cheapest labour. Neo-liberalism in practice distinguishes sharply between freedom for capital and freedom for workers. The advocates of free movement for migrant labour usually come from the political left (Hayter, 2000).

Strongly opposed to global neo-liberalism are those liberals who believe in the need to constrain the market in the interests of social justice. At the end of the nineteenth century social liberals argued for welfare and trade union rights within the nation-state. Today social liberals are likely to advocate policies which promote the interests of developing countries, support restraints on multinationals including protection of worker rights, and are concerned to preserve the environment. They probably support voluntary bodies such as Oxfam and *Medecins Sans Frontieres* and Greenpeace which they see as contributing to the creation of a global civil society. They emphasize the importance of alleviating poverty and oppression round the world – policies which would if effectively implemented greatly reduce the pressure to migrate to the developed countries. But their stance also suggests a generous attitude to migrants (and refugees) seeking entry now to the West. Richard Falk, who appears to fall into this broad category, has strongly criticized neo-liberalism. He argues that such criticism does not denote a desire to 'annihilate capital-driven forces' but 'to work toward their containment and partial transformation' (Falk, 1999, p.3). He has also addressed the danger that attempts to protect citizens' welfare against economic globalization can mean distinguishing more sharply between citizens and resident aliens. He suggests that a partial answer may be regional agreements to promote social welfare – along the lines of the EU Social Charter – thus promoting 'a more meaningful conception of transnational or regional citizenship than has existed in the past' (Falk, 1999, p.165).

There are two ways of reading Kant's interpretation of cosmopolitanism and global citizenship (Franceschet, 2001). The first is to focus on Kant's actual arguments, which reflect the role of nation-states within an international society, but point to moral rights and duties transcending frontiers. The second – often adopted by international relations theorists – is to use Kant as a model for a more radical 'cosmopolitan' view of the world in which the rights and duties of individuals to each other are paramount. Recent developments towards 'cosmopolitan' law – such as conventions on refugees and human rights – give this second Kantian model some basis in an emerging reality. An approach based on Kant gives weight to the moral duties of a global citizen. Indeed Kant's concept of citizenship has republican elements, although his legacy is usually seen as central to liberalism. In his own time he argued that despite the benefits of trade, Western traders and settlers must respect the rights and cultures of other lands. There is a clearly anti-colonial emphasis in his writings. Today this suggests that a Kantian model would be severely critical of many of the claims made by multinational companies to the resources of other peoples and to a Western attack on other modes of life. Kantianism also suggests obligations to individuals whose rights or means of life are under threat, and so implies offering asylum to refugees and opportunities to economic migrants – although since this is a universal obligation it might also suggest some agreed sharing of these obligations between all the more secure and affluent countries.

Kant seemed in the 1990s to offer a particularly promising theoretical framework for thinking about global citizenship. His thought combines a strong sense of moral duty with a political grasp of the real-world obstacles to his ideal goals. Despite numerous grounds for pessimism about the impact of global neo-liberalism and the extent of warfare and brutality in many part of the world, there were grounds for believing that many developed states were becoming more committed to both international institutions and cosmopolitan law. Indeed the severity of shared problems, such as environmental deterioration, seemed to provide a possible spur to greater commitment to the global commons.

One contemporary theorist of cosmopolitanism who has drawn heavily on Kant is Andrew Linklater, who believes globalization has eroded the capacity of individuals to control their lives in their capacity as national citizens. Kant clearly provides for an ethical universalism – an aspect explored by Martha Nussbaum (1997). Linklater (1999, p.41) asks whether 'ethical universalism can be linked with a thicker conception of citizenship which draws upon classical conceptions of participation in the public sphere'. Linklater argues that a Kantian conception suggests personal responsibility for individual actions which impinge on the environment, and a need for action across frontiers based on compassion for 'peoples everywhere'; but he thinks Kant's framework is still too limited to the role of nation-states within an international society. It can, however, act as a bridge to a 'dialogic conception of world citizenship which assumes that sovereignty ultimately resides in the whole human race' (Linklater, 1999, p.41) and support 'efforts to create new communities of discourse which bring citizens and aliens together as co-legislators' (*ibid.*, p.49). Emphasis on dialogue also allows for recognition that people adhere to different cultures and sets of beliefs.

## Conclusion

The precise implications of a principle of global citizenship depend of course on ideological perspectives; but social liberal and Kantian perspectives can provide a starting point for developing a cosmopolitan understanding. They can also promote coherent ideals of global citizenship, which could be applied to urge policies on key global issues such as social injustice between the affluent and poor areas of the world, the erosion of the environment, and the claims of migrants and refugees (Dower and Williams, 2002).

However, the September 11 attack on New York and Washington and the response by the United States (and Britain) have made a concept of global citizenship within a framework of international law and institutions much less realistic.

The position of immigrants has also worsened. Respect for the rights of strangers is under severe attack in the West, not only in response to right-wing populism or nationalism, but even more crucially as a result of the wide ranging disregard for civil liberties arising out of the 'War on Terror'.

The rise in fundamentalism in many parts of the world, including within the West, clearly puts greater strains on liberal multicultural policies, and indeed undermines defence of civil liberties when immigrant communities express support for or take part in fundamentalist violence.[8]

There is still a role for global citizenship; but it implies a committed defence of cosmopolitan ideals, rather than belief in an emerging world order more conducive to peace, freedom of migration, and respect for both individual and cultural rights.

## Notes

1    For a classification of citizenship in relation to migration policy related more directly to actual practice, see Castles and Miller, 1993.
2    Hannah Arendt (1973) inspires today's civic republicanism. See also Barber, 1984; Sandel, 1996; Miller, 2000.
3    The Italian city republics limited citizenship to an elite, and James Harrington in *Oceania* excluded those without property.
4    Tolerance has not of course always been unlimited: Locke argued against tolerance for Catholics, partly on political grounds.
5    On Afghanistan and women's rights, see *Guardian*, 8 October 2001, pp.10-11. Both Mrs Bush and Mrs Blair made public statements about the rights of women in Afghanistan in support of the war on the Taliban and Al Quaeda.
6    'Immigrants who seek British citizenship will have to take lessons in tolerance', *Independent*, 29 October 2002, p.1.
7    BBC, Radio Four, 'Today Programme', 18 August 2001.
8    The issue of whether British Muslims fighting for the Taliban in Afghanistan should be charged with treason was discussed in an editorial, *Independent*, 31 October 2001, p.3.

## References

Arendt, Hannah (1973), *On Revolution*, revised edition, Penguin, Harmondsworth.
Barber, Benjamin (1984), *Strong Democracy: Participatory Politics for a New Age*, University of California Press, Berkeley.
Barber, Benjamin (2001), 'Challenges to Democracy in an Age of Globalization', in Roland Axtmann (ed.), *Balancing Democracy*, Contiuum, London, pp.295-311.
Barry, Brian (2001), 'Muddles of Multiculturalism', *New Left Review*, no.8, pp.49-71.
Berlin, Isaiah (1969), 'Two Concepts of Liberty', in *Four Essays on Liberty*, Oxford University Press, Oxford, 1969, pp.118-72.
Canovan, Margaret (1996), *Nationhood and Political Theory*, Edward Elgar, Cheltenham.
Carter, April (2001), *The Political Theory of Global Citizenship*, Routledge, London.
Castles, Stephen and Alastair Davidson (2000), *Citizenship and Migration: Globalization and the Politics of Belonging*, Macmillan, Basingstoke.
Castles, Stephen and Mark Miller (1993), *The Age of Migration: International Population*

*Movements in the Modern World*, Macmillan, London.

Davidson, Alastair (1997), *From Subject to Citizen*, Cambridge University Press, Melbourne.

Dower, Nigel and John Williams (eds.) (2002), *Global Citizenship: A Critical Reader*, Edinburgh University Press, Edinburgh.

Falk, Richard (1994), 'The Making of Global Citizenship', in Bart Van Steenbergen (ed.), *The Condition of Citizenship*, Sage, London, pp.127-40.

Falk, Richard (1999), *Predatory Globalization*, Polity, Cambridge.

Fang Lizhi (1990), 'Patriotism and Cosmopolitanism', in Fang Lizhi, *Bringing Down the Great Wall: Writings on Science, Culture and Democracy in China*, J.H. Williams (ed.), Alfred A. Knopf, New York, pp.244-9.

Franceschet, Antonio (2001), 'Sovereigny and Freedom: Immanuel Kant's Liberal Internationalist "Legacy,"' *Review of International Studies*, vol.27, pp.209-28.

Frum, David and Richard Perle (2004), *An End to Evil*, Random House, New York.

Galston, William A. (1995), 'Two Concepts of Liberalism', *Ethics*, vol.105, pp.516-34.

Habermas, Jürgen (1992), 'Citizenship and National Identity: Some Reflections on the Future of Europe', *Praxis International*, vol.12, pp.1-19.

Hammar, Tomas (1990), *Democracy and the Nation-state*, Avebury, Aldershot.

Hayter, Teresa (2000), *Open Borders*, Pluto, London.

Hutchings, Kimberly and Roland Dannreuther (eds.) (1999), *Cosmopolitan Citizenship*, Macmillan, Basingstoke.

Jacobson, David (1997), *Rights Across Borders: Immigration and the Decline of Citizenship*, John Hopkins University Press, Baltimore.

Joppke, Christian (1999), *Immigration and the Nation-State: The United States, Germany and Great Britain*, Oxford University Press, Oxford.

Kymlicka, Will (1995), *Multicultural Citizenship: A Liberal Theory of Minority Rights*, Clarendon, Oxford.

Kymlicka, Will (1999), 'Liberal Complacencies', in Okin *et al.*, 1999, pp.31-4.

Kymlicka, Will and Wayne Norman (1994), 'Return of the citizen: A survey of recent work on citizenship theory', *Ethics*, vol.104, pp.352-81.

Lehning, Percy B. and Albert Weale (eds.) (1997), *Citizenship, Democracy and Justice in the New Europe*, Routledge, London.

Linklater, Andrew (1998), *The Transformation of Political Community*, Polity, Cambridge.

Linklater, Andrew (1999), 'Cosmopolitan citizenship', in Hutchings and Dannrether, 1999, pp.35-59.

Meehan, Elizabeth (1993), *Citizenship and the European Community*, Sage, London.

Mill, John Stuart (1962), *Considerations on Representative Government*, Henry Regnery, Chicago.

Miller, David (1999), 'Bounded citizenship', in Hutchings and Dannreuther, 1999, pp.60-80.

Miller, David (2000), *Citizenship and National Identity*, Polity, Cambridge.

Nussbaum, Martha (1997), 'Kant and, Stoic cosmopolitanism', *Journal of Political Philosophy*, vol.5, pp.1-25.

Okin, Susan Moller *et al.* (1999), *Is Multiculturalism Bad for Women?* Joshua Cohen *et. al.* (eds.), Princeton Universirty Press, Princeton.

d'Oliveira, Hans Ulrich Jessurun (1995), 'Union Citizenship: Pie in the Sky', in Rosas and Antola, 1995, pp.58-84.

Parekh, Bhiku (2000a), *The Future of Multi-Ethnic Britain: The Parekh Report*, Profile Books, London.

Parekh, Bhiku (2000b), *Rethinking Multiculturalism: Cultural Diversity and Political Theory*,

Macmillan, Basingstoke.

Parekh, Bhiku (2002), 'Reconstituting the Modern State', in James Anderson (ed.), *Transnational Democracy: Political Spaces and Border Crossings*, Routledge, London, pp.39-55.

Pettit, Philip (1997), *Republicanism: A Theory of Freedom and Government*, Oxford University Press, Oxford.

Rawls, John (1999), *The Law of Peoples*, Harvard University Press, Cambridge.

Reiss, Hans (ed.) (1991), *Kant's Political Writings*, 2nd edition, Cambridge University Press, Cambridge.

Rosas, Anton and Esko Antola (eds.) (1995), *A Citizens' Europe: In Search of a New Social Order*, Sage, London.

Said, Edward (1978), *Orientalism*, Routledge, London.

Sandel, Michael (1996), *Democracy's Discontent: America in Search of a Public Philosophy*, Belknap, Cambridge.

Soysal, Yasemin Nuhoglu (1994), *The Limits of Citizenship: Migrants and Postnational Membership in Europe*, University of Chicago Press, Chicago.

Sunstein, Cass R. (1993), *The Partial Constitution*, Harvard University Press, Cambridge.

van Gunsteren, Herman (1988), 'Admission to Citizenship', *Ethics*, vol.98, pp.731-41.

Waldron, Jeremy (1995), 'Minority Cultures and the Cosmopolitan Alternatives', in Will Kymlicka (ed.), *The Rights of Minority Cultures*, Oxford University Press, New York, pp.93-119.

Waldron, Jeremy (2000), 'What is Cosmopolitanism?' *Journal of Political Philosophy*, vol.8, pp.227-43.

Walzer, Michael (1996), 'Spheres of affection', in Martha Nussbaum *et al.*, *For Love of Country*, Joshua Cohen (ed.), Beacon, Boston, pp.125-7.

# Chapter 3

# A Refugee and a Citizen of the World

C.L. Ten

During the last federal elections in Australia, prominent members of the government, including the Prime Minister, claimed that some asylum-seekers, seeking to enter the country in overcrowded boats, deliberately threw their children into the sea, and photographs were shown to back up the claim. The electorate was prepared to believe that these asylum-seekers had unworthy moral characters and should be denied admission to the country. The Howard government was returned to power partly because of the tough stand it took against asylum-seekers, reflecting the popular mood; but as it turned out after the elections, the specific claims about children being thrown overboard in order to attract attention were false. Apparently the Prime Minister was not told, even though senior bureaucrats knew.

It is often said that each state has the exclusive right to determine for itself who gets admitted or excluded from its territory; but from the moral perspective no such right can be absolute if we are to recognize the urgent claims of those whose lives or liberties are threatened by various forms of persecution. The Geneva Convention of 1951 defined a refugee as a person who, 'owing to a well-founded fear of being persecuted for reasons of race, religion, nationality, membership of a particular social group or political opinion, is outside the country of his nationality and is unable or, owing to such a fear, is unwilling to avail himself of the protection of that country' (Shacknove, 1985, p.275). However, it is quite clear that on simple humanitarian grounds there are also others who have as strong claims to protection, and it is therefore desirable to extend the category of refugees to include those who, although not victims of political, racial, or religious persecution, live in such appalling social and economic conditions that their lives are at serious risk. Loescher (2001, p.235) points out that most refugees are 'fleeing from generalized political violence' rather than from individual persecution. Shacknove (1985, p.282) has argued further that refugee status should be extended to those whose governments fail to protect their basic needs, who have 'no remaining recourse than to seek international restitution of these needs', and who are 'so situated that international assistance is possible'. Of course part of the obligations of various states to this broader group of refugees can be met by the provision of more generous foreign aid directed to alleviating the conditions that produce refugees.[1] However, there are many constraints on the effectiveness of such aid, including the difficulty or impossibility, at least in the short run, of restoring severely devastated societies to some degree of stability, and the dangers of aid being diverted into the hands of those who do not need it. There can therefore be no substitute for a substantial intake of refugees.

I said that the moral claims of refugees to our help rest on simple humanitarian grounds; but there are those who think that moral obligations can only arise out of reciprocity or from voluntary undertakings. Since those who live in relatively wealthy societies have not voluntarily agreed to look after the refugees who languish in refugee camps or head for safer shores in boats, the refugees cannot make any claims on them. Nor can refugees appeal to a relation of reciprocity because while the residents of a rich country are in a position to help them, they are not in a position to return any help given, at least in the short run. Of course in the long run it is likely that many refugees would make positive contributions to their host country. Often they have qualities that enable them to take advantage of opportunities given, but it is their current plight, and not any good they might perform in future, which should be the basis of their moral claims.

There should not be a problem here because moral relations include many which are asymmetrical or not based on voluntary agreements. For example, we acknowledge certain obligations to future generations not to damage the environment to such an extent as to cause them serious harm, even if by so doing we can maximize benefits to ourselves; yet these obligations are not based on reciprocity. If we avoid harming them, we do not expect them to reciprocate by not harming us in turn because they are incapable of harming us. Again, some of the most elementary moral obligations not to inflict unnecessary suffering on animals rest simply on their capacity to suffer pain. Nor are these obligations dependent on whether we have voluntarily undertaken them. They are quite unlike the specific contractual obligations from which we can escape by simply showing that we were not willing parties to the contract.

It might be thought that the general obligations which we have to others not to harm them are merely negative, and can be discharged by our simply refraining from attacking them. On this view, we are never required to give them positive aid. Now consider a case in which you come across someone dying of thirst and there is a life-saving bucket of water just outside his reach. He feebly begs you to give him a drink from the bucket. You would not bend so low as to take some water from the bucket to him. He pleads with you, 'Just kick it to me!' He is a stranger. So you refuse to kick the bucket to him, and as a result he kicks the bucket. Have you not violated a fundamental obligation to help him? In cases where a small sacrifice on our part can prevent a serious harm, we have a positive duty to perform the beneficial act.[2]

Once it is acknowledged that we have such positive duties to help others, which are not based on reciprocity or on our voluntary commitments to them, then it is hard to see how we can avoid the conclusion that we have obligations to admit refugees. These obligations are part of the requirements of justice, and should not be relegated to discretionary acts of supererogatory charity. The social sacrifices made in admitting refugees are relatively small when their numbers are not so large as to threaten the stability of society or put an intolerable strain on normal social services. Thus there does not appear to be any convincing reason as to why

Australia, for example, cannot comfortably absorb many more refugees than it currently accepts.

Sometimes a false analogy is used to suggest that the burden of admitting refugees, even in small numbers, is unacceptably high. Suppose you have a couple of spare bedrooms in your house and there are two homeless tramps seeking shelter. Do you have an obligation to take them in and care for them indefinitely? Many would regard your extension of hospitality to the tramps as saintly acts of supererogation not required by the demands of justice. So how could it be otherwise with a country's admission of refugees? But in fact the analogy is false. Sharing your home with strangers is for most people, who value their privacy, a major sacrifice. Living in close proximity with others requires a degree of intimacy or tolerance, which can be strained or undermined by clashes of personal preferences, habits, and personalities; in contrast, living in a society with total strangers does not involve the same kind of unavoidable intimate and stressful contacts. We already live in the same society with many who are strangers in some sense.

However, what makes a country's obligation to accept refugees a matter of justice rather than charity is the fact that the basic interests of refugees are at stake, by comparison with which the sacrifices made by members of the host country are relatively small. Of course admitting refugees to our country does not end our obligations to them. There is also the need to provide them with resources and opportunities to achieve at least a certain minimal level of well-being that will enable them to function properly in their new home; but again, meeting these further obligations through the payment of additional taxes does not require unreasonably heavy sacrifices on our part.

These obligations to refugees do not extend to other would-be immigrants. Typically, these other immigrants are looking for better economic opportunities for themselves or their children, or they are seeking a more congenial lifestyle. Because their claims for admission are so much weaker than those of genuine refugees, those opposed to the intake of refugees have sometimes tried to undermine the refugee status of certain people by claiming that they are not victims of persecution. The narrowness of the Geneva Convention definition of a refugee facilitates the exclusion even of those whose very lives are threatened by the breakdown of social and economic structures. The denigration of refugees goes well beyond claims that they are simply attracted by the allegedly generous provision of welfare payments by the host country. When a specific case is exposed of an immigrant who is indeed such a blatant free-rider on members of the host country, the case is given great publicity by the media, and the claims of very different people seeking admission are irretrievably weakened.

Nothing that I have said so far invokes the idea of citizenship. The rights and duties of citizens are confined to people who share political institutions and who are therefore related to one another in a more specific manner than they are related to refugees or others who are trying to get into a country. However, this notion of citizenship might be disputed by those who appeal to the idea of global citizenship. Thus Martha Nussbaum (1996, p.6) quotes with approval a remark of Diogenes, 'I am a citizen of the world'. She contrasts this with the view of those who have identified themselves with a citizenship that is more restrictive and not universal, such as, 'I am an Indian citizen', or a Greek citizen. Similarly, the idea of global citizenship arises in discussions of globalization and its implications. It is not clear what point is being made by the various appeals to global citizenship. If the idea is that there are common interests which transcend state or national boundaries, and which call for greater international co-operation, then no one can deny this. For example, such common interests exist in the protection of the environment and in the combat of terrorism. Again, complaints are sometimes made against the narrowness and parochialism of national educational programs for citizenship, which breed blissful ignorance about the conditions of life and problems of other countries. But the idea of global citizenship is misguided if it is invoked to deny that our cultural and political identities, which are narrower than our membership of the human species, can give rise to distinctive moral claims and commitments.

It has been suggested that the boundaries of countries are morally arbitrary, and that only a common humanity can be the basis of moral obligations. If we take this notion of global citizenship seriously, then it looks as if we are committed to a policy of 'open borders' for immigrants of all kinds. For on this view, the boundaries of a state are indeed morally arbitrary, and cannot be the basis for differential treatment between those who happen to be on one side and those who are on the other side. I have already acknowledged in my account of refugees that, where the demands of minimal justice are concerned, the boundaries between countries are morally irrelevant. However, there are many other sources of morality, including our personal projects and non-global identities.

Consider the principle of mutual love, propounded by David Richards, that 'people should not show personal affection and love to others on the basis of arbitrary physical characteristics alone, but rather on the basis of personality and character related to acting on moral principles' (Williams, 1981, p.43). Bernard Williams (1981, p.43) has called it a 'righteous absurdity', and so indeed it is, if the reference here is to personal love rather than the basis of general benevolence. Such love, and the associated moral claims, is based on features distinctive of the loved ones, rather than on features shared by all. Similarly, the accusation of moral arbitrariness in the case of moral claims based on non-global citizenship is also absurd.

Our relationships with our fellow citizens, and perhaps even with those who reside in the same country, can also generate special moral commitments which do not extend to others not similarly related to us. The exact nature of these commitments and their detailed justification will no doubt be disputed. However, if we already acknowledge special commitments elsewhere in our personal relationships, then I doubt that we can simply rule them out here. If our society is basically just to its members, then we share with them a political identity based on important values like mutual toleration. We participate together in a common political enterprise of developing sound institutions, rules and principles for regulating our lives and shaping our futures. We recognize that our present circumstances are the products of a partly common history that we ourselves might not have significantly influenced, but which nonetheless we acknowledge as ours. We see ourselves as embarking on the same journey, even though some of us join at an earlier stage than others. If we connect in these and in other ways, then we have special relationships which are the sources of some mutual obligations. We owe one another an obligation to protect and strengthen the conditions which enable us to flourish together. Human beings are not, and could not be, attracted to one another simply and solely by properties shared by all. Specific histories and experiences, differences in character and personality, and other features not shared by all, can give rise to relationships of intrinsic value. Again, for people to live in a society to which they can feel a sense of belonging and commitment, it is often the case that they should be able to participate in decisions that shape the society. A society which covers the whole world is unlikely to be one that can provide any meaningful common participation. Its government will be too remote from the lives of its own members.

I have stressed the normative force of non-universal special relationships and commitments, that is, the justifications they provide for rights and duties different from those grounded in a common humanity; but there is also the issue of motivational force. For most people the idea of a common humanity cannot provide the motivational basis for extensive moral obligations beyond those of the requirements of minimal justice, whereas special relationships can do so. In 'A Free Man's Worship', Bertrand Russell tried to rally his atheistic troops by claiming that human beings in a godless world are united by 'the strongest of all ties, the tie of a common doom' (Greenspan and Anderson, 1999, p.38). However, this common doom has not been sufficient to generate solidarity in the way that the members of a nation, surrounded by a specific common enemy, have rallied together. Nor have believers fared better than Russell in extracting motivation from the claim that we are all the children of God. The children of God have been prepared to slaughter one another in the name of the revered Father. Sometimes, as in the case of ordinary people in Europe rising to acts of great courage in rescuing and protecting Jews from Nazi persecution, we find a sense of common humanity having great motivational force. But we have no reason to believe that such force can be sustained for long periods across very different groups of people afflicted with all kinds of problems.

It has also been thought that that the necessary motivation can come from the natural development and strengthening of features which are already present in the personalities and character of most people. Thus many have pointed out that human beings are not motivated solely by self-interest but also by a natural sentiment of sympathy for others. The natural alternative, once we move away from self-interested motivation, is not the extensive adoption of the perspective of an impartial and wholly benevolent agent. Rather, it is the perspective of someone embedded in rich personal relationships, characterized by deep partial concerns. It is from this perspective that most of the great selfless conduct emerge. It is interesting to note Rawls's view that when people are required to make sacrifices for the benefit of others, they are more willing to do so when such sacrifices are grounded in reciprocity, rather than in the weaker disposition of sympathy (Rawls, 2001, p.127).[3] This may well be true, although Rawls is mistaken in thinking that all the demands of justice rest on reciprocity. However, the more general misconception, of which Rawls is certainly not guilty, is the belief that there is a single common centre of moral concern from which all moral demands and claims are generated. Rawls himself focuses on the claims of justice, which is not the whole of morality, but others have overlooked the variety of normative and motivational factors (Ten, 2003).

There is a problem of another kind: if the motivations generated by personal relationships and the like are so powerful and attractive, would they not crowd out the requirements of universal justice? This would indeed be the case if the different types of moral claims are in perpetual conflict; but they are not, and we have ample evidence to show that people understand that the pursuit of personal projects is constrained by the requirements of justice. For example, public officials acknowledge that they are not entitled to use public funds for the special benefit of their loved ones, but instead have to operate in accordance with strict impartiality. Indeed, it might even be the case that people, who are secure in their own identity arising out of partial commitments, are better able to meet the demands of universal justice than others not similarly placed. Thus Isaiah Berlin (2000, pp.202-3) quoted a remark of Herder's, 'The savage who loves himself, his wife and his child...and works for the good of his tribe as for his own...is in my view more genuine than that cultivated ghost, the...citizen of the world, who, burning with love for all his fellow ghosts, loves a chimera. The savage in his hut has room for any stranger...the saturated heart of the superfluous cosmopolitan is a home for no one'.

Another worry is the fear that once we base moral claims on considerations other than a common humanity, there will be a slide down the slippery slope to the justification of, for example, vicious forms of racism. As Nussbaum (1996, p.5) has argued against those who resist the idea of world citizenship: if I am first an Indian, and then only a citizen of the world, then why not, 'I am a Hindu first, and an Indian second, or I am an upper-caste landlord first, and a Hindu second'. This is now no longer a motivational issue but an issue about the normative force or justification of certain kinds of partialities, which have clear motivational force. There are two responses one could make.

The first is that, although, for example, racist identity can have powerful motivational force, motivation is not justification. The motivational force of various identities has to be justified ultimately by defending the activities, the relationships, and the forms of life associated with them or generated by them. Some identities will not pass the test and have to be unravelled as best we can.

The second response is that people often have multiple identities which are the bases of different, but not necessarily incompatible, moral rights and obligations. It is not a question of a person being first and foremost an Indian, and then something else, although in some contexts this form of expression might be quite useful in underlining certain responsibilities. Fundamentally, it is a matter of recognizing separate spheres and different levels of social interaction. It is a matter of locating the right identity at the appropriate level. Thus, in a multicultural and multireligious society, the cultural or religious identity should not operate at the level of the state, the political level. The political identity should rest on values which all can share, such as mutual toleration and a common participation in democratic politics. It does not rest on distinctive religious or cultural values that not all can fairly share. This is the important sense in which Rawls's political liberalism is correct. It is the bane of theocratic societies that they fail to observe this separation of identities, seeking instead one single, all-pervasive identity. Some secular societies are no better, leaving too little space for religious life. The aspiration to an all-pervasive political identity will lead to varying degrees of tyranny, or unjust discrimination. For example, in the days of the White Australia immigration policy, the leader of the Labour Party, Arthur Calwell, famously remarked, 'Two Wongs don't make a white', an anti-Asian sentiment that even today resonates in some white Christian hearts. Similarly, Simon Heffer (2001), the biographer of Enoch Powell, recently defended Powell's immigration views expressed in Britain in the late 1960s by arguing that Powell was concerned about culture, not race or colour: 'It was not so much the colour of people's skins that Powell was alerting us to in his speech; it was the problem of allowing their culture to supplant the indigenous ones'. But cultural identity in Powell's sense is an identity not shared by blacks or Asians in multicultural Britain, and he should not make it the basis of a common political identity. It is worth spending some time on Powell's view because it is still implicitly shared by many members of majority groups in predominantly white societies, which feel threatened by non-white immigrants, be they refugees or not.

Powell argued for the voluntary repatriation of 'coloured immigrants', and tried to stop more such immigrants from entering the country. Referring to them as 'alien' elements in the country, he predicted great harmful conflicts resulting from their continued presence. In a famous speech in Birmingham in 1968, he exclaimed, 'Like the Roman, I seem to see "the River Tiber foaming with much blood"' (Smithies and Fiddick, 1969, p.43). Leading up to this remark, Powell related stories about the sense of harassment experienced by some whites because of the presence and activities of blacks. The most dramatic of these stories is that of the old-aged white pensioner who had excreta pushed through her letter-box. In his definitive biography of Powell, *Like A Roman*, Simon Heffer (1998) documents very well this and other speeches, and the contexts in which they were made.

Powell identified British culture with a homogeneous mainstream culture of white British citizens, and all cultures of black or Asian immigrants different from this mainstream culture are therefore regarded as alien and disruptive of a unified British identity. This idea, that there is a single substantive culture which is the basis of political identity, is the central source of the refusal in some quarters to admit a large number of non-white immigrants to countries such as Australia and Britain or to welcome them as equal citizens or permanent residents once they have been admitted. But the proper starting point of our discussion of the treatment and selection of immigrants must be an acknowledgement that societies like Australia are, as a matter of brute sociological fact, multicultural, multiethnic, and multifaith. Powell's suggestion of voluntary repatriation of coloured immigrants is an attempt to turn back the clock in a manner that is offensive because it treats them as undesired aliens, no matter how long they have been in the country, and no matter what the circumstances of their arrival, or the nature of their contribution may be. Many coloured immigrants were born in Britain and the only language they can speak is English. I remember reading a news item many years ago of a coloured youth being harassed in London by a group of white ruffians. 'Go home! Go home! Why don't you go back to your own country!' The youth finally responded, 'Yes, I'll go home – to Birmingham!' Neither being Christian nor being white is a requirement for citizenship in a multicultural and multifaith country, or for participating on equal terms with others in the political life of the country.

Once we understand the significance of religious toleration, we should also acknowledge that, for example, neither Britain nor Australia is a Christian society, except perhaps in a sociologically descriptive sense, or in some relatively trivial ceremonial sense. Christianity, like Islam and Buddhism, or any other specific religion, has no justificatory role in political life. Laws may have Christian origins, but this speaks to their history, or to the causal influences on their enactment, but not to the way they are to be justified.

What holds good for religion should also be extended to cultural differences more generally. No single substantive culture should be the source of political identity, in the manner envisaged by Enoch Powell. Of course there will be some level at which different cultural groups give expression to their different cultural identities, in the same way that each religious group will carry out its own practices without seeking to impose them on others. When members of different cultural groups come together to deliberate at the political level, the source of their unity and identity is not a homogenous culture which they cannot share. Rather, it is their mutual toleration of their separate cultural identities. This is what unity in diversity means: unity in the endorsement of the value of mutual toleration, and diversity partly as the result of the practice of toleration. There is more than one source or level of identity, and the separateness of identity at one level does not preclude a commonality of values and a shared identity at another level.

It might be thought that the separateness will threaten social cohesion; but in fact there is no danger to social cohesion in the mere fact that people have, at some level, different sources of identity or in the fact that each person has a variety of social identities. Rather, danger arises if social, economic, and political circumstances prevent the formation of cross-cutting identities. If religious, ethnic, cultural, or economic divisions all coincide, then conflicts in one area will spread with severe multiplier effects. Freedom of association is an important element in the emergence of cross-cutting identities, but such freedom may not in itself be sufficient. We might also need more direct and active measures to encourage different groups to find more common interests, and more occasions for mixing together.

In a recent newspaper article, the columnist Karim Raslan (2002) reported the illuminating research findings of an academic, Ashutosh Varshney, who studied ethnic conflicts and civic life among Hindus and Muslims in India. Varshney found two forms of engagement which ensured harmony and prevented or lowered the level of violence. The first consists of 'everyday forms' of engagement found in 'simple routine interactions of life, such as whether families from different communities visit each other, eat together regularly, jointly participate in festivals, and allow their children to play together in the neighbourhood'. The second form of engagement is through 'associational forms', which include 'business organizations, trade unions, professional associations, political parties and NGOs, as well as film clubs and sports clubs'. These networks of forms of engagement do not develop spontaneously. Rather, they need active cultivation.

Few today would openly adopt an immigration policy based on outright racial discrimination, but the subtler policy of cultural discrimination still has many supporters. Powell might not be a racist; but his techniques of persuasion had the effect, intended or not, of stirring up racial prejudices against coloured immigrants. It is a technique that lesser minds have followed. It relies on playing to the fears of his audience by exaggerated claims about a 'massive wave of immigration', and about the black man dominating very soon over white people in the white's very homeland. It consists in telling stories, attributed to ordinary suffering whites, of coloured people doing nasty things. It paints a picture of black immigrants as alien and unable to integrate into British life.

Non-white migrants are justified in being suspicious when influential members of the white community adopt Powell's tactics. However, it is disappointing to read about the hostile reactions of some ethnic community leaders in Britain to the suggestion of the Home Secretary, David Blunkett, that members of the ethnic community should learn English, especially when this went along with an apparent commitment on the part of the government to provide facilities for learning the language.[4] Non-English-speaking migrants in Britain should welcome opportunities for them to learn English, provided that they are encouraged, but not compelled, to do so, and provided that due respect is paid to those who, for whatever reason, have difficulty in learning the language, even in its spoken form. We have seen how everyday and associational forms of engagement can play a role in reducing ethnic and religious conflicts. There can be no significant engagement without a common medium of communication. Acquiring the common language of the society is a powerful tool for breaking out of one's narrow social confines to engage with others from different groups. Narrow-minded leaders of minority ethnic groups deprive their own members of these opportunities and condemn them to social isolation.

Returning to Nussbaum's fear that we might slide into undesirable forms of particularist identity, we can reiterate that there is a level of social life at which it would be appropriate for a person to say that he or she is a Hindu. This would not, however, be the person's political identity which, in the case of India, is shared with Muslim fellow citizens. Although motivation is not justification, I have argued that identities that cannot generate sufficient motivational force, or can only gain such force by destroying desirable normative structures, lack normative credibility. If refugees, or others on their behalf, wish to stake their claims for entry to a particular country by declaring that they are citizens of the world, then I would not stop them. For the claims of refugees are indisputable, however we choose to describe them. We should respond to them at least in the name of justice and on the basis of a common humanity. But they are not our fellow citizens, in any significant normative sense, at least not yet.

**Notes**

1   See the interesting discussion on the importance and difficulty of preventing and averting refugee movements, in Loescher, 2001.
2   Compare this with Singer's qualified, but I think still stronger, principle, 'if it is in our power to prevent something very bad from happening, without thereby sacrificing anything morally significant, we ought, morally, to do it' (Singer, 1992, p.454). Singer uses a simple illustration of getting my clothes muddy by pulling a drowning child from a shallow pond. However, he draws some radical conclusions about our obligations to the needy in distant countries.
3   That is one reason why Rawls thinks his difference principle is superior to the utility principle, which rests on the 'considerably weaker disposition, that of sympathy, or better, our capacity for identification with the interests of others'.
4   'Ethnic Groups Blast Calls to Embrace "British Way of Life,"' *The Straits Times*, 12 December 2001.

**References**

Berlin, Isaiah (2000), *Three Critics of the Enlightenment*, Princeton University Press, Princeton and Oxford.
Greenspan, Louis and Stefan Anderson (eds.) (1999), *Russell on Religion*, Routledge, London and New York.
Heffer, Simon (1998), *Like a Roman: The Life of Enoch Powell*, Weidenfeld & Nicholson, London.
Heffer, Simon (2001), 'What Enoch Was Really Saying', *The Spectator*, 24 November.
Karim Raslan (2002), 'Civic Networks Can Rein In Religious Violence', *The Business Times*, 9-10 March.
Loescher, Gil (2001), 'Refugees: A Global Human Rights And Security Crisis', in Tim Dunne and Nicholas J. Wheeler (eds.), *Human Rights in Global Politics*, Cambridge University Press, Cambridge, pp.233-58.
Nussbaum, Martha (1996), 'Patriotism and Cosmopolitanism' in Joshua Cohen (ed.), *For Love of Country*, Beacon Press, Boston, pp.3-17.
Rawls, John (2001), *Justice as Fairness: A Restatement*, Harvard University Press, Cambridge.
Shacknove, Andrew E. (1985), 'Who Is A Refugee?' *Ethics*, vol.95, pp.274-84.
Singer, Peter (1992), 'Famine, Affluence and Morality', in Steven Luper-Foy and Curtis Brown (eds.), *The Moral Life*, Harcourt Brace Jovanovich, Fort Worth, pp.454-9.
Smithies, Bill and Peter Fiddick (1969), *Enoch Powell on Immigration, An Analysis*, Sphere, London.
Ten, C.L. (2003), 'The Moral Circle', in Kim-chong Chong, Sor-hoon Tan, and C.L. Ten (eds.), *The Moral Circle and the Self*, Open Court, Chicago, pp.17-25.
Williams, Bernard (1981), *Moral Luck*, Cambridge University Press, Cambridge.

Chapter 4

# Justice for Migrant Workers?
# Foreign Domestic Workers
# in Hong Kong and Singapore[1]

Daniel A. Bell

[The two main characters of this dialogue are fictitious. However, I agree with (and mean to defend) the views expressed by Professor Villanueva. They draw on my own research as well as interviews conducted in Hong Kong, December 2002, with Cynthia CA Abdon-Tellez, Director of the Mission for Filipino Migrant Workers Society in Hong Kong; Holly Allen, Director of Helpers for Domestic Helpers as well as one volunteer workers at that organization; and four Filipina domestic workers with experience in both Singapore and Hong Kong interviewed at the Tsimtsatsui YMCA. Citations and statistics are intended to be factual. Unfootnoted statistics can be found on the websites for the Asia Pacific Mission for Migrants (www.apmm.cjb.net) and the Asian Migrants Coordinating Body (amcb@migrants.net)].

SCENE: Hong Kong, 29 December 2002. Sam Demo, the East Asia program officer for the US-based National Endowment for Human Rights and Democracy (NEHRD), is in Professor Flor Villanueva's office for a prearranged interview. Professor Villanueva is a respected political scientist who has also participated in various campaigns on behalf of foreign domestic workers in Hong Kong.

**The Political Concerns of Foreign Domestic Workers**

DEMO: Thanks so much for agreeing to see me during the holiday season.

VILLANUEVA: You mean 'a' holiday season. I was pretty surprised the first time around, but Christmas isn't such a big deal here. The serious holiday in Hong Kong starts in about one month – the whole city shuts down for a few days during the Lunar New Year...As for myself, I've just returned from my annual pilgrimage back home – the Philippines, as you know. It's a pleasure to meet you (shakes Demo's hand).

DEMO (adjusting his tie): As I mentioned in my phone call, I'm the Asian rep for

NHERD, a US-based foundation. Our mission is to promote democracy, and we try to work through local civil society organizations. Basically, we give funds to NGOs that work to bring about peaceful evolution to democratic forms of rule in their own societies. What we mean by democracy is equal rights for all citizens. I was shocked to learn that foreign domestic workers in Hong Kong are treated as permanent second class citizens and I'd like to find out about the NGOs that are trying to do something about it.

VILLANUEVA: Oh, oh. I'm afraid I may disappoint you. The issue of equal rights is not widely regarded as the most pressing issue for foreign domestic workers.

DEMO: Well, surely it's the most troubling issue! What kind of government sanctions two classes of residents with unequal rights and privileges? In extreme cases, it's a kind of apartheid, with one group of people relegated to permanent second class citizenship.

VILLANUEVA (raises left eyebrow): That's not quite how most of the foreign domestic workers see it. Yes, they do the dirty, dangerous, and difficult work – the 3 Ds, as we say – but they don't plan to stay permanently. The average stay is four years, the large majority return home after they've earned enough cash for their families.

DEMO: But some Filipina domestic workers have been working 18 years in Hong Kong, and they still can't become citizens![2] I'm not saying that foreign resident workers should be given equal rights the minute they step off the airplane, but they should at least be put on the road to citizenship. Whatever the short term arrangement, those who live and work within a territory, pay taxes, send children to school, and participate in neighborhood activities should not be treated as permanent second class citizens – or perhaps I should say 'non-citizens'. They belong, and belonging matters morally. Long-term membership in civil society creates a moral entitlement to all the legal rights of membership, including citizenship itself. After a certain time, say five or ten years, the state should give equal rights to workers in its territory, regardless of their background (Carens, 2001, pp.3-5).

VILLANUEVA: I'm not sure if the situation you describe applies here. Foreign domestic workers don't pay taxes. Nor do they send their children to local schools. Of course they're not given the opportunity to do so, since they can't bring their children to live here…(short pause)…In any case, wealthy industrialized countries in the West also import foreign labourers to do the low-status but socially necessary work that locals won't do. It's an unfortunate fact about our global world today that workers of poor countries seek the opportunity to work in rich countries, and that's not likely to change so long as there's abject poverty in the Third World.

DEMO: In Western liberal democracies, however, there's a trend towards extending to long-term residents most if not all the legal rights of citizens and improving access to citizenship for the descendants of immigrants and for immigrants themselves. Hong Kong seems to be resisting this trend. Foreign workers who are paid to do housework and childrearing are denied the rights of citizenship and have no realistic hope of ever becoming equal members of the political community. I've read that the contracts of domestic workers can be renewed indefinitely, but they can never apply for permanent residence. Such an arrangement is morally intolerable.

VILLANUEVA: Look, I don't deny there's a problem, but let's look at this from the point of view of domestic workers. I've carried out many interviews, I've worked with local NGOs, and that's not what people seem to care about. There are far more pressing issues that have nothing to do with legal arrangements, not to mention the fight for equal citizenship.

DEMO: Please elaborate.

VILLANUEVA: Well, for one thing, the informal rules of engagement within the home have great impact on the welfare of foreign resident workers. In Hong Kong, for example, contracts between employers and foreign domestic workers don't specify maximum number of work hours. There's nothing illegal about making domestic workers work 16 hour days – which isn't uncommon, by the way. So from the point of view of domestic workers, one of the most important considerations is to find a 'nice' employer. Conversely, they strive hard to avoid 'exploitative' employers.

DEMO: In the West, governments legislate the maximum number of work hours, and workers are supposed to be paid overtime if they work longer. Surely the exploitation of workers could be avoided if governments play a more active role in protecting their interests. What you call 'informal rules of engagement' should be constrained by just legal regimes, and in the Hong Kong case the problem is that the legal regime is unjust.

VILLANUEVA: Actually, in Hong Kong it's the employers who are calling for specified work hours...(reaching for her bookshelf)...Here, look at this. An urban councilor named Jennifer Chow, herself an employer of three domestic workers, told the press:

> The working hours for live-in maids in Hong Kong are not specified and I think it should be in the contract. We should look at the system in Singapore where they set the work at 16 hours a day, which seems reasonable. I have had complaints from several employers saying their domestic helpers started work around 8 a.m. and are going into their rooms at 9 p.m. and will not do any more work – if we set the working hours these situations would not happen (Williams, 1998).

DEMO (laughs): It's hard to feel sorry for those employers. I suspect the pro-worker NGOs have a different story to tell.

VILLANUEVA: Well, perhaps not what you'd expect. Cynthia Tellez, Director of the Mission for Filipino Migrant Workers Society in Hong Kong, tells me that her organization has had heated internal debates on precisely this issue. On the one hand, they felt a need to push for an eight-hour maximum, so that foreign resident workers would be treated on par with Hong Kong workers. On the other hand, they recognized that many domestic workers would oppose this policy because many work 14 to 16 hour days and they fear they would price themselves out of the market if they cut that by half. The Mission for Filipino Migrant Workers decided not to take a stand on this issue of maximum work hours. Personally, I can't say I blame them. Like all political actors, they must work within certain constraints and settle on less-than-ideal solutions. Yes, it means that much lies at the discretion of the employers, but it doesn't mean nothing can be done. Perhaps you can fund an NGO to print pamphlets for employers with suggestions on decent treatment of domestic workers – treatment that goes beyond the law. This kind of pamphlet could also educate employers regarding eating practices, sleeping arrangements, respectful forms of address, it could provide detailed examples of 'good' employers, it could suggest 'reasonable' standards for bonuses, and so on. Even the most comprehensive set of legal regulations couldn't cover every important issue that bears on the well-being of domestic workers. Consider, for example, the issue of trust between employer and employee. One of my interviewees couldn't stand the fact that her employer was suspicious of her every move; her employer went so far as to count the number of grapes she had bought for her family to make sure her employee hadn't eaten any. Besides, most of the interaction with domestic workers takes place within the 'privacy' of the home, where it's difficult if not impossible to enforce legal regulations. That's why the attitude of the employer is particularly important, and educative pamphlets that encourage good employment practices would go far towards improving foreign domestic workers' welfare in Hong Kong.

DEMO: Aren't there such pamphlets now?

VILLANUEVA: No, nothing at all! In this respect, even Singapore – which is widely regarded as having the most restrictive and repressive policies on foreign labour in Asia (Medel-Anonueva *et al.*, 1989) – is ahead of Hong Kong. Of course, there aren't any independent NGOs in Singapore that fight for the interests of foreign domestic workers; but the government prints pamphlets for employers, and these go beyond simply pointing out the need to respect the formal rights of employees. They aim to promote a harmonious working relationship between employer and employee through cultural understanding, open communication and mutual respect (Tan, 2002). Having said that, such pamphlets are counteracted by officially-sanctioned private agencies that offer very different forms of advice. Here, look at the section of 'prayers' from a pamphlet distributed by Advance Link Private Limited (2000, p.35):

1.    You are discouraged to bring your White Prayer Uniform along. This is because the Employer does not want this Uniform to scare their children. Most of the employers dislike their domestic helpers to pray while working in

their house. This condition has been stated earlier and we as your agent have agreed on your behalf in order to be able to secure you a job.

2.   Another thing due to various reasons such as a conflict between two Gods, employer does not want to have different kinds of prayers in their house, does not understand the domestic helper's religion, etc.

3.   But if you are lucky, you may be allowed to pray in the morning before your employer and the family members have gone to sleep.

4.   Subject to Employer's Approval. If this should happen, please pray in your heart and you may make it up when you return to your country.

5.   Thus, you should have an attitude by thinking that you are lucky to be able to work here whereas your friends are still in the village waiting for employment.

Of course, it's hard to enforce any of this and much depends on the attitude of the employer. Fortunately, some employers do seem to go out of their way to practice 'multiculturalism' in the household. One Mormon employer allows her domestic worker to drink coffee in her home; she tolerates her domestic worker's behavior even though it violates her religious code (Cheung and Mok, 1998, pp.198-9). That's what I mean about the importance of informal rules of engagement within the home. If the concern is to improve the welfare of foreign domestic workers, such rules are often just as fundamental, if not more so, than the set of rights guaranteed by law.

DEMO: Mmh, maybe so, but I'm constrained by my mandate. I'm supposed to fund pro-democracy forces in civil society, and NEHRD defines democracy as equal citizenship in the legal sense. So let's stick to legal issues, if you don't mind.

VILLANUEVA: No problem. At the moment, pro-domestic worker NGOs in Hong Kong are campaigning against proposals to cut the minimum wage by HK$500 per month and raise a levy on employers for that same amount, in a bid to raise money for the government (as you know, the Hong Kong government has a serious deficit problem). It's the third time that such proposals have been floated by political parties and employers' interest groups since the economic crisis of 1997. In 1999, the government cut the minimum wage for foreign domestic workers by 5 per cent. In early 2002, the government fortunately resisted pressure for further cuts. The government will soon decide on the latest proposal to cut the wages of Hong Kong's lowest paid and hardest working employees, and it doesn't look too promising…(short pause)…Another prominent issue for NGOs has been opposition to the 'two-week rule' that prohibits migrant workers who break their contracts from staying in Hong Kong more than two weeks. This rule effectively means that domestic workers must put up with exploitative conditions since it's difficult for them to find an alternative employer on such short notice. There's no other legal regulation that's as damaging to the interests of foreign domestic workers. NGOs in Hong Kong have suggested going back to the pre-1987 system: foreign domestic workers were given six-month renewable visas, which meant that they usually had more time to find alternative employers if things went sour.

DEMO: Of course such issues are important, but I'm not sure if I could justify funding NGOs if their struggles have nothing anything to do with democracy. I don't want to criticize those NGOs, but I wonder if they're focusing on the right issues. Surely the deeper problem lies with the fact that foreign domestic workers aren't actual or potential citizens. Their material condition is unlikely to improve except by altering their political status. If they're put on the road to citizenship, it would be easier to fight for their own interests.

VILLANUEVA: To repeat, I suggest that we look at this from the perspective of the domestic workers and their NGOs. The demand that domestic foreign workers should be given equal rights is rarely put forward in public debate, it's not seen as the most pressing issue.

DEMO: Mmh, maybe it's because citizenship itself doesn't have much value in non-democratic Hong Kong.

VILLANUEVA: I wouldn't say that. Citizenship – in the sense of permanent residence – entails a wide range of benefits, such as access to subsidized schools, health care and housing, valued travel documents, a certain degree of political representation, and so on. Yet the relevant NGOs aren't pressing for equal citizenship rights for foreign domestic workers. It's not seen as the most important issue, or even as something that would ultimately benefit domestic workers.[3]

## Does Democracy Benefit Foreign Domestic Workers?

DEMO: But Hong Kong doesn't have *political* democracy, even in the minimal sense of free and fair competitive elections for political leaders. That's the key difference between the West and Hong Kong. I don't understand why foreign domestic workers aren't taking up the struggle for democracy, along with pro-democracy forces in Hong Kong. Surely that's what counts the most.

VILLANUEVA: Actually, the benefits of democracy aren't so obvious for foreign workers. For one thing, most of them have left democratic countries – the Philippines and Indonesia – to find work in less-than-democratic but wealthier countries. Also, Korea and Taiwan are democratic in the 'minimal' sense, yet migrant workers do not fare as well in those countries as in Hong Kong. The minimum wage for domestic workers is much lower in Taiwan, for example, and the laws and practices on migrant workers are more restrictive and repressive.[4] In Korea, foreign workers were sent back en masse when the economy turned sour after 1997, which hasn't happened in Hong Kong. Most significantly, the proportion of migrant workers is far greater in Hong Kong than in Korea and Taiwan, that is, Hong Kong offers more opportunities for foreign domestic workers. Only Singapore comes close. And although the Singapore government can make a much stronger claim that its political leaders are chosen by the people, it turns out, however, that foreign domestic workers are better protected in undemocratic Hong

Kong than in somewhat more democratic Singapore. On balance it's widely recognized that Hong Kong is both freer and better paid, and that's why the large majority of foreign domestic workers prefer to work here, given the choice.

DEMO: And why do you think the conditions are relatively favorable here?

VILLANUEVA: One important factor is that domestic workers in Hong Kong are free to organize self-help groups and public protests to secure their interests. There may be fewer voting rights in Hong Kong, but civil liberties such as the freedom of speech and the right to associate are relatively secure. Only last week, 3000 domestic workers took to the streets to protest proposals to cut their minimum wage. More than twenty NGOs cater to the interests of domestic workers in Hong Kong, compared to three severely constrained NGOs in Singapore. In fact, there haven't really been any truly independent pro-foreign domestic workers NGOs since 1987, when several Christian members of a crisis centre for Filipina domestic workers were detained under the Internal Security Act (in a crackdown on alleged 'Marxist Conspirators'). What all this means is that the Hong Kong government feels much greater pressure to respond to mobilized pro-worker groups.

DEMO: Sounds plausible. But where's the argument against democracy? All you're suggesting is that civil rights are important for securing the interests of migrant workers, no democrat would disagree.

VILLANUEVA: Hold on. I don't like saying this, but we must face the facts. As I see it, the relative lack of political democracy in Hong Kong may not be harmful – and may in fact be beneficial – to foreign domestic workers in the territory. There are obviously many areas of potential and actual conflict between employers and their workers. If employers can vote for their community's decision makers, they will likely favor policies that work to the detriment of their domestic workers in cases of conflict. Politicians, for their part, may be tempted to pander to the interests of employers; at least, they won't forcefully argue on behalf of disenfranchized domestic workers.[5] That may explain why opposition parties in Singapore haven't campaigned to increase the wages of domestic workers; they can't get any political capital out of this issue.[6] Even in Hong Kong, to the extent that recent political reforms do represent a tiny step towards democracy, it's working against the interests of domestic workers. The new Executive Council includes two leaders of the Democratic Alliance for the Betterment of Hong Kong and the Liberal Party – political parties with substantial public support – and they have both spoken out in favor of the proposal for salary cuts. In the past, meritocratically selected and non-accountable civil servants would have played a greater role, and they would have been more likely to consider the interests of foreign domestic workers.

**Should Foreign Domestic Workers be Given Equal Rights?**

DEMO: As I see it, Singapore and Hong Kong are radically imperfect regimes. I still think the long-term goal should be Western-style liberal democracy. In any case, the problem now is that foreign domestic workers aren't entitled even to the limited rights available to locals – no matter how long they stay, foreign domestic workers can't be put on the road to equal citizenship. This basic injustice should be remedied! At the very least, they should be given the same set of rights as other long-term residents. You still haven't provided any arguments against this position.

VILLANUEVA: Look, we need to recognize certain realities. Of course it would be ideal for foreign domestic workers to be given the same rights as other long-term residents. But the counter-arguments also have merit, and the answer isn't so easy.

DEMO: What counter-arguments? I assume you're aware that the UN adopted the International Convention on the Protection of the Rights of All Migrant Workers and Members of their Families. According to article 54, governments can't discriminate against migrant workers who should be entitled to the same labour rights as locals.

VILLANUEVA: I can assure you that this charter hardly features in political debates in Hong Kong or Singapore. Neither government has ratified this document, so they don't feel bound by it. Actually, only sending countries have ratified this document, no receiving country has done so. That tells you something about the relevance of this document. I don't think such legalistic approaches will get very far if the aim is to protect the interests of migrant workers.

DEMO: OK, let's stick to the moral issues. How can governments justify permanent unequal rights?

VILLANUEVA: The most obvious argument is that domestic workers chose to come here. Many domestic workers have university degrees, but they chose to work as domestic workers abroad because their salaries are much higher. As the Philippine Labour Secretary put it, they 'make a choice for more money but less prestige'.[7] A domestic worker in Hong Kong earns much more than a teacher or middle-ranking civil servant in the Philippines. Many of the workers are mothers who seek relatively high-paying jobs abroad so that their children can be better educated and lead more comfortable lives. Basically, they sacrifice a few years of their lives to help their children. Of course it's tragic that they can't make a decent living in their own countries, but given their circumstances, I'm not about to condemn their choices.

DEMO: The problem with the argument of consent is that every plausible moral view sets limits to consent. For example, no liberal democratic state permits people to sell their organs or to sell themselves into slavery. Maybe it's true, given the conditions in the world today, that many immigrants would readily agree to severe restrictions on their rights, even including terms of indentured servitude. But consent alone can't legitimate that sort of arrangement. There are standards of fairness and justice beyond actual consent for assessing the ways in which states treat their own citizens and others (Carens, 2001, p.24).

VILLANUEVA: I don't think you can compare the plight of foreign domestic workers to 'indentured service'. In some cases, it's true that they must take out high-interest loans from private agencies, and much of their salary goes to pay off their loans. One domestic worker told me that she didn't get to keep any of her salary the first six months she worked in Singapore – and she never had a day off. But these are abuses of the system, and the relevant governments can and should crack down on unscrupulous agencies of this sort.[8] If the system works as it's supposed to, the choice is between low-paying jobs (or unemployment) at home and (relatively) high-paying jobs as foreign migrant workers. Moreover, they can return home whenever they want, so the comparison with indentured servitude isn't quite accurate. At the end of the day, it can't be denied that foreign domestic workers consent to an unequal rights regime because they conclude that the benefits of this arrangement outweigh the costs.

DEMO: But they consent to *what*? Such arguments may be sufficient to justify market transactions, but they can't justify the subjugation of foreign resident workers. For one thing, foreign workers don't simply sign contracts with their employers; they have another 'boss' – the state in which they live and work (Walzer, 1983, p.58). And the problem is that the state doesn't stick to the terms of their agreement. It has the power to unilaterally change the terms of its contract – for example, by cutting the minimum wage of foreign domestic workers.

VILLANUEVA: That's right, but on the other hand I'm not sure if foreign domestic workers would prefer contracts where all parties are indefinitely bound by original consent. They may discover new possibilities, learn about unexpected problems, compare their situation with migrant workers in other countries, and realize that they were given a raw deal that needs to be challenged. This helps to explain why, for example, many domestic workers' NGOs in Hong Kong are campaigning for an end to the 'two-week rule' and more severe punishment for employers who mistreat domestic workers. It's also possible that they may campaign for *increases* in salaries in inflationary and/or economic boom times. In other words, we have good reasons to doubt that domestic workers consent to the exact terms that have brought them to Hong Kong and Singapore – many discover upon arrival that the state can and should do more to improve their conditions.

DEMO: Well then why not ask for equal rights? That's what 'guest workers' in Western Europe did, and they've won many of their struggles.

VILLANUEVA: As I said, you have to look at this from the domestic workers' perspectives. Yes, they're the victims of many injustices, and yes, they're actively campaigning for better working conditions, but it rarely goes further. They may not be satisfied with the *status quo*, but they don't publicly ask for political equality. At some level, domestic workers really do consent to unequal rights.

DEMO: Is it real consent? I'd say coercion must play a role. They're forced to accede to current arrangements and are fearful about articulating or even contemplating an alternative. In a just world, free from coercion, they'd be pushing for equal rights and the state would be morally required to grant their demand.

VILLANUEVA: I certainly agree that coercion plays a role in Singapore; foreign domestic workers can't freely organize and publicly articulate their demands. But I think the situation in Hong Kong is more complicated. Hong Kong is a small, crowded territory where the cost of living is very high – not an ideal location for establishing long-term 'homes'. Even the locals frequently move abroad when they have the means to do so. Whereas most immigrant workers in, say, the US or Canada aim to establish roots in their new 'homeland', the large majority of foreign domestic workers here plan to return home once they've earned enough money. As one of my interviewees put it, 'I'm not interested to stay in another place. I love my country'…(short pause)…Another key difference is that guest workers in Europe are given longer visas for certain jobs and are allowed to bring their families. Their children often learn the language and culture of their host country and develop the desire to stay there. Even if their parents consent to return home, the consent of parents can't be construed as the consent of the children. No doubt, many parents want to stay in their new country for the sake of their children. In contrast, foreign domestic workers come to Hong Kong without their families and rarely make an effort to learn the local culture and way of life, though a few do pick up some Cantonese.

DEMO: I still find it hard to believe that coercion doesn't play any role when domestic workers 'consent' to unequal rights. More rights are better than less, and it seems irrational not to want more.

VILLANUEVA: I wonder about that. In the family, for example, the introduction of too many rights can be inappropriate if it leads members to often view themselves as subjects possessing rights upon which they make claims against their partners. Rights can motivate us to see other members' interests more as limitations on ours than as interests we wish to promote (Chan, 1999, p.220). Family relationships should be informed by love and caring, not by calculations of self-interest.

DEMO: But we're talking about relationships between domestic workers and their employers, which is ultimately a market relationship, it can't be compared to relations between family members.[9]

VILLANUEVA: I think there's also a familial aspect, and excessive focus on rights can undermine that. For example, one of my interviewees praised her former

Singapore employer for providing shampoo and other toiletries. Such 'little' gestures were deeply appreciated because they went beyond formal legal obligations, and they strengthened bonds of trust between employer and employee. If the employer had provided toiletries because it was specified in the contract, it likely would not have had the same beneficial effect on the relationship between employer and employee. Besides, most of the interaction between employer and domestic worker takes place in the 'privacy' of the home; it would be difficult if not impossible to enforce such detailed regulations even if they were specified in the contract.

DEMO (impatiently): You're not getting my point. I'm not talking about relatively trivial issues like the 'right' to shampoo. I'm talking about the right to permanent residence and to be treated as an equal member of the political community. It would be irrational not to want that right, other things being equal. Given the choice, some foreign domestic workers might well choose to settle in Hong Kong, just as some foreign professionals settle here.

VILLANUEVA: Perhaps. I'm entitled to permanent residence after seven years, like other foreign lecturers in Hong Kong universities, and I may well apply when the time comes, even though I plan on returning to the Philippines eventually.

DEMO: That's what I mean. Even those who plan to return home because of emotional ties to family and native land may prefer to be given the choice of membership on the basis of equal rights. So why not ask for equal rights?

VILLANUEVA: In the real political world, struggling for what seems like the ideal solution may lead to worse outcomes than settling for the second best. The simple fact of the matter is that locals would never agree to the demand for equal rights for foreign domestic workers and it may be counterproductive to even raise it. Urban areas in Hong Kong are already among the most crowded on earth (only the Gaza strip is more densely populated). Land is expensive and decent housing is beyond the reach of most people; the government provides heavily subsidized housing for more than half the population. There's a waiting list of five to seven years that would extend even further if foreign workers were given equal rights and allowed to join the queue. This would be an obvious source of discontent among locals.

DEMO: Well, that's just too bad. If justice is on the side of the domestic workers, it's just a practical question of how to overcome the 'discontent among locals'.

VILLANUEVA: There are also questions of fairness. As one of my interviewees put it, 'there are so many mainland Chinese waiting in the queue'. She was referring to the recent controversy over 'the right of abode'. To control population growth and prevent Hong Kong from being 'flooded' with relatively impoverished mainland Chinese 'compatriots', there are strict border controls between Hong Kong and China – the functional equivalent of an international border.

DEMO: I know. It's a real pain to cross over to the mainland. I had to pay HK$500 for a visa and then it took two hours to cross the border to Shenzhen.

VILLANUEVA: Right. Although the majority of the population in Hong Kong arguably benefits from this arrangement, some families in Hong Kong can't sponsor their own family members as immigrants. For example, the children of mainland Chinese academics working in Hong Kong don't have an automatic right of residence here. One of my Chinese colleagues can't get his daughter to live with him; in that sense, I'm better off, because I can bring my children. This seems like a flagrant injustice, but the Hong Kong government has been fighting hard to prevent mainland Chinese not born in Hong Kong, even if they have close relatives in the territory, from getting residence rights. From the perspective of Hong Kong residents with relatives on the mainland, it would seem unfair if the Hong Kong government were to grant permanent residence to foreign domestic workers who have no relatives here, even if only a minority actually took up the offer.

DEMO: Just because an injustice is being committed against one group, it doesn't justify an injustice to another. The Hong Kong government shouldn't discriminate against either mainlanders or migrant workers.

VILLANUEVA: Once again, the situation is more complex. It's not just a question of injustices. The fact that the door to equal rights is closed does have one benefit – it means that there are more doors open for temporary workers. The only reason that so many foreign domestic workers are allowed to work in Hong Kong – and Singapore – is that all sides assume they will eventually return home. In Canada, by way of comparison, foreign domestic workers can become permanent residents after two years, but the government can afford to be relatively 'generous' because it allows only a few thousand such workers every year – in 1996, for example, only 1,710 were admitted under the Live-in Caregiver program. The choice, it seems, is between few legal openings for migrant workers with the promise of equal citizenship and many openings for migrant workers without the promise of equal citizenship. So foreign domestic workers in Hong Kong who 'benefited' from the latter system generally refrain from raising the demand for equal rights because they know it's a non-starter. Were they to raise this issue, 'populist' politicians would propose replacing them with contract domestic workers from other countries. That's already happening in the 'minor' struggle against pay cuts – employers' groups point out that Filipinas can be replaced with contract domestic workers from mainland China if they complain too much. The Hong Kong government has also hinted at such possibilities.

DEMO: But Filipinas have the relative advantage that they usually speak English well, and – correct me if I'm wrong – that's what Hong Kong parents want their children to learn.

VILLANUEVA: We have to be realistic. Many Hong Kongers also want their children to learn Mandarin. Hong Kong's economy is growing more and more dependent on the mainland's, and there will be growing demand for Mandarin-speaking domestic workers. I think the main reason the government is resisting this option is that it would be relatively easy for mainland domestic workers to go 'underground' once their visas expire, given their cultural familiarity with the place[10]...(slight pause)...For Southeast Asian domestic workers in Hong Kong, the feasible alternatives to unequal rights are considerably worse.

DEMO (losing patience): Look, it comes down to basic justice. The institutionalization of second-class membership – permanent unequal rights for a group of residents – is a violation of fundamental liberal-democratic principles and should never be allowed, no matter what the circumstances. No decent government will compromise on these principles.

VILLANUEVA (pause): OK, let's assume, for the sake of argument, that policy makers in Hong Kong and Singapore are persuaded by this view. The laws are changed, and all foreign resident workers are automatically entitled to equal citizenship following a period of, say, seven years. All domestic workers are permitted to settle down in Hong Kong and Singapore and are given the same rights as locals. What would be the likely effect of this policy switch?

DEMO: You seem to know the answer, so please go ahead.

VILLANUEVA: Consider the impact on the Philippines. It's almost certain that the door to further immigration from the Philippines would be officially closed. I say 'officially', because this policy may well open the door to substantial illegal migration from the Philippines. Filipina domestic workers may still come to Hong Kong and 'choose' to work in even more exploitative conditions without any legal protection whatsoever. As it stands, there are few illegal migrants from the Philippines in Hong Kong.[11] But that may change if the legal doors to immigration are closed. Judging from the experience in the United States and Canada – where illegal employment of domestic workers from the Third World is widespread – one can expect that people from impoverished countries will migrate to rich countries with or without the legal rights to do so. Canada, for example, effectively cut back on the number foreign domestics legally entitled to work in the country, and this led to an increase in the number who work illegally (Bakan and Stasiulis, 1997, pp.19-20). The same is true in Asian countries. Following the 1997-98 economic crisis in South Korea, the government announced a moratorium on admitting low-skilled migrant workers, but this led to a large influx of illegal workers (Milly, 2000, p.310).

DEMO: What you say still doesn't bear on the normative point that justice requires equal rights for all residents.

VILLANUEVA (frustrated): But we need to consider the feasible alternatives! There are two choices right now, and the liberal-democratic way may not be the best way. From a normative standpoint, it's not obvious that formal equal rights for all workers combined with high rates of illegal employment of foreigners is preferable to reliance on large numbers of contract workers with legal protection but without the hope of equal rights. In the West, the political culture places higher priority on the justice of legal forms, and there may be relatively greater willingness to accept substantial harm in the social world for the sake of preserving laws that conform to liberal-democratic principles. That may not be the case in Hong Kong and Singapore. Their governments prefer to enact illiberal laws that allow for huge numbers of foreign domestic workers to (temporarily) engage in legally protected work in their territories. And from the perspective of the good of the Philippines, I'm not sure that they're wrong.

DEMO: This whole argument is premised on the assumption that illegal work by immigrants can't be controlled. But in Hong Kong and Singapore – small, relatively crowded territories, as you repeatedly point out – it shouldn't be so difficult to crack down on illegal migrant labor.

VILLANUEVA: OK, fine, let's assume that illegal immigration can be controlled. It's then worth considering the effect on people in the Philippines of granting equal rights to Filipina domestic workers in Hong Kong and Singapore (the situation would be similar in other sending countries such as Indonesia and Thailand, but let me focus on the Philippines here). The most likely effect would be to close off further emigration. This would mean that many young Filipinas would lose the opportunity to work abroad to support themselves and family members. The country's economy as a whole would suffer as well – Hong Kong's Filipinas make the fourth biggest contribution of remittances to the Philippines, a total of US$116 million in the year to October 2000.[12] That's why they're so appreciated by the Philippine government, even though the state isn't supposed to officially promote overseas employment as a means to sustain economic growth and achieve national development (Gonzalez, 1998, p.78). In 1988, President Aquino, speaking to a group of domestic workers in Hong Kong, coined the term 'national heroes' for overseas workers, a term that has been frequently invoked in national rhetoric since then (Law, 2002, p.208). The government recognizes that domestic workers experience hardship and loneliness abroad for the sake of earning money for their families, and their remittances help to sustain the whole Philippines economy.[13]

DEMO: Does this system really benefit the Philippine economy? Such a waste of talent – so many teachers, nurses, and other highly educated women working as domestic workers – may actually limit the possibility of economic development in the long-term. If they stayed at home working for lower salaries, that might ultimately do more good for the Philippines' economy.

VILLANUEVA: So what do you suggest? Force all migrant workers to return home, assuming that this will 'ultimately' benefit the Philippines? I doubt the outcome would be as positive as you suggest, but even if you're right I'm not sure we'd be justified in sacrificing the interests of the current generation of foreign domestic workers for the long-term good. Once again, I'd suggest looking at this issue from the domestic workers' perspective. They wouldn't endorse your proposed solution.

DEMO (shifting in chair): Huh, I wasn't saying they should all be sent home, I was just throwing out ideas. But if the goal is to promote the economic development of the Philippines and other sending countries so that their economies provide sufficient decent-paying jobs for their workers, there are better ways than relying on the export of migrant workers.[14] The situation wouldn't be so dire if, for example, Hong Kong and Singapore increase foreign aid to the Philippines so as to develop that country's economy.

VILLANUEVA: Maybe so, but there's no reason at all to expect that this will happen. According to the World Bank, the worldwide remittances of foreign workers are second only to the earnings of crude oil trading and bigger than all the combined developmental aid combined, so it doesn't look like the migrant labour system is about to disappear.[15] Certainly the experience of other countries doesn't provide grounds for optimism. Canada has recently increased its standards of education and experience for foreign domestic workers, with the consequence that the poorest and least-skilled have fewer opportunities to come in, but this hasn't been accompanied by increased aid to affected countries. Even if Hong Kong and Singapore were to increase foreign aid, this wouldn't necessarily or even probably translate into an improvement of the Philippine economy to the point that its people wouldn't need to work abroad. It's far from certain that channeling foreign aid to often corrupt government officials would do more to benefit the people of the Philippines than direct remittances from family members abroad.

DEMO (pause): I still think the liberal-democratic solution is the best. And I think it would be best if others became persuaded of this view. At the end of the day, it's just a practical matter of finding the political will to make the reality consistent with the ideal of free and equal citizenship.

VILLANUEVA (sighs): Well, I don't think you'll persuade the domestic workers. Let's try to think of a 'just' liberal-democratic solution to this problem, one that doesn't seem too far removed from the real world. In the foreseeable future, we won't be able to do away with the fact that workers from poor countries will seek to find their fortunes in the rich industrialized world. Nor does it seem likely rich countries are about to offer full citizenship rights to huge numbers of migrants from poor countries. One proposal, consistent with liberal democratic principles, might be to limit work visas for foreign domestic workers to, say, six years. That way, they won't have stayed long enough to be morally entitled to equal citizenship rights. But is that the right solution? If the choice is between Hong Kong-style work visas that can be renewed indefinitely without the hope of equal citizenship and six-year non-renewable work visas that are more consistent with liberal democratic principles, no sane foreign domestic worker would choose the latter. If the concern is to help foreign domestic workers, I strongly suggest that you consider the possibility of modifying or setting aside your ideals.

DEMO: Well, it's not really up to me. The problem is that I'm constrained by the NHERD. Remember, I work for a pro-democracy foundation whose mission is to promote political rights.

VILLANUEVA: There seems to be a conflict between the ideals of your organization and the actual needs and interests of domestic workers. I'm sure that pro-domestic worker NGOs would welcome support for their efforts to fight back attempts to cut their minimum wage, end the two-week rule, and so on; but they may be wary if that support hinges on prioritizing public advocacy of equal citizenship rights for migrant workers.

DEMO: I'm afraid I can't support NGOs that don't emphasize the democracy and political equality. Hopefully other foundations can help.

VILLANUEVA (looking at her watch): Well, that was interesting, thanks for your views. Hopefully we can pursue this conversation another time.


**The Role of Culture**

DEMO: Before I go, let me ask you one question. I'm not sure if this is your intention, but you seem to be suggesting that the Hong Kong-style foreign domestic worker system should be emulated by other countries....

VILLANUEVA (interrupting): No, no. I've already told you that the system can and should be improved. Foreign domestic workers should not be taxed, if this means reducing their salary. The two-week rule should be abolished. The government should get serious about cracking down on abusive employers, exploitative private agencies, and loan sharks. And that's only the legal side of things. As I mentioned, employers should be educated to treat their workers with more decency and respect.

DEMO: But you favor the system of long-term residency without hope of equal citizenship. You say this system allows for huge numbers of migrant workers, who can use these opportunities to help their families and their country's economy. You seem to be saying this system has some advantages relative to the Western liberal-democratic practice of small numbers of legal openings foreign domestic workers who can be put on the road to equal citizenship.

VILLANUEVA: It's something to be tolerated, not celebrated. The whole system of migrant labour is founded on global injustice. My view is that the global economy is unjust, that's it's unfairly skewed towards the interest of rich countries, and that it perpetuates poverty in the Third World.[16] I look forward to the day when global inequalities can be eliminated, or at least reduced to the point that decent work opportunities are available for all human beings. Unfortunately, that day doesn't seem to be forthcoming, and meanwhile we need to think about other ways of dealing with Third World poverty, and the export of contract migrant workers is one way. I worry about this liberal democratic prioritization of equal citizenship for all resident workers because it may have negative implications for people in poor countries. In the case of foreign domestic workers in Hong Kong and Singapore, putting them on the road to citizenship may well worsen their overall situation – if not for domestic workers currently working in those territories, then for people in sending countries, who would be denied the opportunity to improve their living standards. What I mean, in short, is that unequal rights between citizens and foreign resident workers may be tolerated if this arrangement (1) works to the benefit of foreign resident workers (as decided by the workers themselves); (2) creates opportunities for people in relatively impoverished societies to improve their lives; and if (3) there are no feasible alternative ways to serve the ends identified in (1) and (2).

DEMO: Feel free to qualify your claims, but at the end of the day you're justifying the system of unequal rights for domestic workers. You think that it's better, or maybe less hypocritical, than the liberal democratic defense of equal rights... (sarcastically)...Do you think I should go back and tell my fellow citizens in the United States that they open their homes to contract domestic workers from the Third World?

VILLANUEVA: Actually, I'm not sure that would be effective. There may be cultural particularities in East Asia underpinning the whole system, and these may not be shared in the West. One of my interviewees – a volunteer at the Hong Kong NGO called 'Helpers for Domestic Helpers' – noted that Asians have a longer history of living in homes with many extended family members, and there may be greater acceptance of domestic workers living in one's home and caring for children. Given the choice between at-home care for children and day-care, most people seem to prefer the former. In East Asia, the day-care system is relatively undeveloped, even in relatively wealthy societies such as Japan, Korea, Hong Kong and Singapore. No doubt there are many factors at work, but one important obstacle seems to be the reluctance to commit one's children to anonymous carers in publicly-funded institutions. Most employers in East Asia would rather hire domestic workers who can provide family-like care for their children.

DEMO (laughs): That's pure speculation! How can you, as an academic, buy into that stuff! For one thing, many Western expatriates in Hong Kong and Singapore are forced to hire domestic workers to care for their children. They can't send their kids to day-care even if they want to, because there isn't any!

VILLANUEVA: Maybe so, but the lack of public demand for decent day-care in developed East Asian societies is rather striking. Notwithstanding the few childcare centers available in Hong Kong, the average waiting period for crèches is only 1.6 months (Tam, 1999, p.266).

DEMO (raises voice): But how can you attribute any of this to 'culture'! There can be many explanations. What evidence do you have for your claims about the importance of culture?

VILLANUEVA: Not a lot, in this case. It's usually hard to 'prove' that culture plays an important role. But sometimes there's little doubt that cultural differences affect the way that people deal with each other. Consider the treatment of domestic workers. If you ask domestic workers, they will tell you that, for example, different sorts of employers act in very different ways, depending on their background and set of cultural expectations. Western employers, for example, generally treat domestic workers differently than Chinese employers.

DEMO: What's that supposed to mean? Such claims are purely impressionistic; they wouldn't stand up to social scientific scrutiny.

VILLANUEVA: Actually, some academics have investigated this phenomenon. Two social scientists at the Chinese University of Hong Kong administered a questionnaire to Filipina domestic workers in Hong Kong, and they came up with interesting results. The domestic workers were generally more satisfied with their Western employers, who allow them more personal space and are more likely to treat them on equal terms. The authors of this study suggest that Chinese and Western employers may have different conceptions of the Filipina domestic worker as a human being (Cheung and Mok, 1998, pp.191).

DEMO (getting more curious): Can you elaborate?

VILLANUEVA: The authors of the study don't go into further detail. It's hard to avoid crude generalizations. My own view is that the Christian tradition that we're all equals before God, irrespective of one's social status, informs the 'Western' practice. I'm a Christian myself, no doubt my views are colored by this fact.

DEMO: If the aim is to promote the interests of domestic workers, why not preach Christianity to the non-Christian employers?

VILLANUEVA (laughs): Don't be silly. Let me tell you something else that's interesting. The best employers do more than treat domestic workers with respect; they also treat them as valued members of the family. The authors of the aforementioned study provide a good example of how family-like treatment might occur. One Filipina domestic worker had special praise for her Chinese employer's parents because she was treated as the daughter they had never had. Consequently, the ties between employee and employer's family were based on mutual concern and caring, not simply contractual exchange.

DEMO: How did that show itself, in concrete terms?

VILLANUEVA: Simple things. The employer and the worker would watch TV together. They would tease each other. Her employer would show sincere concern for her biological family in the Philippines (Cheung and Mok, 1998, p.184). One of my own interviewees had similar things to say about her Chinese employers. The domestic 'worker' was made a Godmother of the employer's child and they would go to church together. Her biological family in the Philippines made regular visits to her employer's home in Hong Kong. Also, she expected that her employer's family will visit her in the Philippines when she returns....

DEMO (interrupting): You mention the fact the 'best' employers are Chinese, but does that really make any difference?

VILLANUEVA: Of course Western employers can also treat domestic workers as family members. But this Hong Kong study found that Western employers were more homogenous as a group compared to Chinese employers. My own interviewees said that Western employers often treat domestic workers with respect and fair-mindedness, but it doesn't typically go beyond that. Good treatment means paying beyond the minimum wage and giving more free time to employees, but the affective component may not be as prominent. That's not necessarily a bad thing, by the way. The claim that the domestic worker belongs to the family can be used as an excuse to impose extra burdens on the worker, for example, asking her to work during public holidays (Bakan and Stasiulis, 1997, p.11). That's why some domestic workers will refuse to address their employers by their first names, even if they're asked to. They prefer to use such labels as 'Sir' and 'Ma'am' because they don't want to get too close to their employers. Still, the benefits of being treated as a valued member of the family – feeling loved and trusted – usually outweigh the costs. Now once again, I'm speculating, but cultural factors may bear on the issue. There may be something about Confucianism that makes this kind of family treatment more likely, or at least more deeply entrenched when it happens. From what I know about Confucianism, there's a firm distinction between family insiders and non-family outsiders, but ethical relationships grow when family-type labels and norms are applied to non-family members (Liang, 1987, chapter12). When this happens with domestic workers, it might arguably be an ideal arrangement. I'm not sure how to encourage this, but it's worth thinking about.

DEMO: Don't you think we should also *challenge* cultural norms? You mention Confucianism, and aren't you uncomfortable endorsing this patriarchal tradition?

VILLANUEVA: Of course that aspect of Confucianism should be challenged.

DEMO: Well, how about the domestic worker system? The fact remains that it's regarded as women's work, shouldn't that aspect be challenged too?

VILLANUEVA: Yes and no. The system also has advantages for women. Most obviously, it frees women in the recipient countries from household duties and allows them to develop their talents in the 'public' sphere.

DEMO: But they're just being replaced by women from poor countries, how can you regard that as progress?

VILLANUEVA: I'm not saying that. But consider the fact that sending countries aren't rigidly patriarchal societies (countries like Pakistan won't send their women for work abroad, no matter what the potential economic benefits). The Philippines is relatively egalitarian compared to other Asian countries, and that's one of the factors explaining the trade – women must be regarded as free agents to a certain extent if they're 'allowed' to work abroad. While most overseas domestic workers go abroad to earn money, many are also seeking adventure, freedom, and independence (Momsen, 1999b, pp.10-11). Also, the export of domestic workers is transforming the way that child-rearing has been conceived in the Philippines. Given that mothers are often working abroad, many Filipino fathers have become the primary child-minders, notwithstanding the ideology that mothers should be responsible for the emotional care of children (Parrenas, 2001). It's hard to predict what kind of change this will lead to, but it may help to further challenge sexist stereotypes...(pause)...Ideally, of course, neither parent would be separated from their children.[17] Which reminds me, my five-year old daughter expects me home about now, so....

DEMO: Well then I won't keep you! It was a pleasure to meet you.

[Demo and Villanueva shake hands, and Demo departs from Villanueva's office; Villanueva turns on her computer, sees eighty-two new email messages, and sighs.]

### Notes

1    Another version of this paper appears in Eisgruber and Sajo (2005).
2    'Reflections on Racism', *Migrant Focus Magazine*, Jan-Mar 2001, vol.1, no.3, p. 11.
3    The next two sections draw on Bell, 2001.
4    'The Union Makes the Difference', *Migrant Focus Magazine*, April-June 2001, vol.1, no.4, p.25.
5    In the Singapore case, however, it could be argued that a more democratic government would be more responsive to the wishes of citizen-employers, and since most employers would not favor the levy on foreign domestic workers, this levy would be abolished, which might benefit foreign domestic workers because employers would have more to pay for their wages (I thank Sor-hoon Tan for this point). On the other hand, since most Singaporeans are not employers, they might actually prefer a levy that goes into government coffers to benefit all Singaporeans, so a government that responded to the majority will on this particular policy might actually keep this levy.
6    The Singapore Democratic Party, however, has recently criticized public policies governing the treatment of foreign domestic workers in Singapore.
7    'Maid Wage Cut a Political Football', *South China Morning Post*, 23 December 2001.
8    The Hong Kong government has recently established a commission, including the participation of pro-domestic worker NGOs, to investigate such abuses and prosecute rogue agencies (*South China Morning Post*, 4 January 2003).
9    See David Miller's (1999) argument that the family and the market should be

governed by different principles of social justice. The application of Miller's argument to the employment of domestic workers within the family is complicated by the fact that different modes of relationship interact and overlap with each other.

10 Instead, the government appears to be encouraging, if not condoning, the hiring of Indonesian domestic workers in Hong Kong. Compared to the Filipina domestic workers, the Indonesian workers tend be less well-educated and less well-organized, and their government does not offer the same level of support, with the consequence that relatively high-proportions of Indonesians are underpaid and abused (Asian Migrant Centre, 'Racial Discrimination in Hong Kong', 8 November 2001, p.2; http://www.december18.net/paper33Hongkong.htm.

11 The situation is more complex in Singapore, where the large majority of Filipina domestic workers come as 'tourist workers' without work permits from the Philippines, an arrangement that is legal in Singapore but is not considered so by the Philippine government. The purpose of this arrangement appears to be that of circumventing the regulations in the Philippines designed to protect the interests of migrant workers and therefore allowing for relatively exploitative work conditions for Filipina domestic workers in Singapore (Yeoh *et al.*, 1999, 131-2).

12 *South China Morning Post*, 7 May 2001.

13 The remittances of Filipinos living or working overseas account for nearly 8 per cent of the country's gross national product.

14 Noeleen Heyzer and Vivienne Wee (1994) suggest using the trade in migrant labor in a way that would end it : 'remittances should be garnered carefully as seed money to generate economic development that will enable workers to be employed as gainfully at home, as they are abroad [instead of remittances being 'squandered on unproductive consumption]. Only then will there be an end to the international trade in human labor'. The problem with this suggestion is that it would mean confiscating or taxing substantial parts of the remittances that would otherwise be sent to support family members at home. This would obviously be opposed by the migrant workers themselves. Moreover, it may be difficult to morally justify sacrificing their interests for the sake of the long-term economic development of their country.

15 'The Lucrative Business That Is Labour Export', *Migrant Focus Magazine*, Oct-Dec. 2000, vol.1, no.2, p.5.

16 See for example, the *New York Times* series of editorials, 'Harvesting Poverty', published throughout 2003.

17 Joan Tronto (2002) argues that the practice of hiring 'domestic servants' to accomplish child care work is unjust and furthers inequality, and that remedying this injustice ultimately requires 'radical reforms' in the form of publicly-supported child-care facilities and 'revolutionary changes' that entail collective rather than 'individualized' caring for children. If such changes entail separating children from their parents, however, the costs may outweigh the benefits.

## References

Advance Link Private Limited (2000), *Maids Handbook: An Essential Guide to Hiring and Keeping a Foreign Domestic Helper*, Raffles, Singapore.

Bakan, Abigail B. and Daiva Stasiulis (1997), 'Introduction', in Abigail B. Bakan and Daiva Stasiulis (eds.), *Not One of the Family: Foreign Domestic Workers in Canada*, University of Toronto Press, Toronto, pp.3-28.

Bell, Daniel A. (2001), 'Equal Rights for Foreign Resident Workers? The Case of Filipina Domestic Workers in Hong Kong and Singapore', *Dissent*, vol.48 (Fall), pp.26-34.

Carens, Joseph H. (2001), 'Citizenship and Civil Society: What Rights for Residents?' (paper on file with the author).

Chan, Joseph (1999), 'A Confucian Perspective on Human Rights for Contemporary China', in Joanne R. Bauer and Daniel A. Bell (eds.), *The East Asian Challenge for Human Rights*, Cambridge University Press, New York, pp.212-40.

Cheung, Tak Sing and Bong Ho Mok (1998), 'How Filipina Maids Are Treated in Hong Kong – A Comparison Between Chinese and Western Employers', *Social Justice Research*, vol. 11, pp.173-92.

Constable, Nicole (1997), *Maid to Order in Hong Kong: Stories of Filipina Workers*, Cornell University Press, Ithaca.

Eisgruber, Christopher and Andras Sajo (eds.) (2005), *Global Justice and the Bulwarks of Localism: Human Rights in Context*, Brill, Leiden.

Gonzalez, Joaquin L., III (1998), *Philippine Labour Migration: Critical Dimensions of Public Policy*, Institute of Southeast Asian Studies, Singapore.

Heyzer, Noeleen and Vivienne Wee (1994), 'Domestic Workers in Transient Overseas Employment: Who Benefits, Who Profits', in Noeleen Heyzer, Geertje Lycklamaa Nijehort and Nedra Weerakoon (eds.), *The Trade in Domestic Workers*, Asian and Pacific Development Centre, , Kuala Lumpur, pp.31-101.

Law, Lisa (2002), 'Sites of Transnational Activism: Filipino Non-Government Organizations in Hong Kong', in Brenda S.A. Yeoh, Peggy Teo, and Shirlena Huang (eds.), *Gender Politics in the Asian-Pacific Region*, Routledge, London, pp.205-22.

Liang Shuming (1987), *Zhongguo Wenhua Yaoyi* [Essentials of Chinese Culture], Sanlian Shudian, Hong Kong.

Medel-Anonueva, Carolyn *et al.* (1989), 'Filipina Domestic Helpers in Hong Kong and Singapore', in *Trade in Domestic Helpers: Causes, Mechanisms and Consequences*, Asian and Pacific Development Centre, Kuala Lumpur.

Miller, David (1999), *Principles of Social Justice*, Harvard University Press, Cambridge.

Milly, Deborah J. (2000), 'The Rights of Foreign Migrant Workers in Asia: Contrasting Bases for Expanded Protections', in Michael Jacobsen and Ole Bruun (eds.), *Human Rights and Asian Values: Contesting National Identities and Cultural Representations in Asia*, Curzon, Richmond, pp.301-21.

Momsen, Janet Henshall (ed.) (1999a), *Gender, Migration and Domestic Service*, Routledge, London.

Momsen, Janet Henshall (1999b), 'Maids on the Move', in Momsen, 1999a, pp.1-20.

Parrenas, Rhacel Salazar (2001), 'Mothering from a Distance: Emotions, Gender, and Inter-Generational Relations in Filipino Transnational Families', *Feminist Studies*, vol.27, pp.361-90.

Tam, Vicky (1999), 'Foreign Domestic Helpers in Hong Kong and Their Role in Childcare Provision', in Momsen, 1999a, pp.263-76.

Tan, Jean (2002), 'Report Maid Abuse to MoM or Police', *The Straits Times*, 30 January.

Tronto, Joan C. (2002), 'The 'Nanny' Question in Feminism', *Hypatia*, vol.17, pp.34-51.

Walzer, Michael (1983), *Spheres of Justice*, Blackwell, Oxford.

Williams, Ceri (1998), 'Workers Starting at 8 am are Stopping at 9 pm, Grumbles Councilor; 16-hour Day for Maids Urged', *South China Morning Post*, 9 November.

Yeoh, Brenda S.A. *et al.* (1999), 'Migrant Female Domestic Workers: Debating the Economic, Social and Political Impacts in Singapore', *The International Migration Review*, vol.33, pp.114-36.

# Chapter 5

# The Globalization of Citizenship

## Barry Hindess

Citizenship is commonly regarded as a matter of internal relations between individuals and the state to which they belong and between those individuals themselves. Standard accounts of its modern development describe it as appearing first, along with the modern state itself, in parts of Western Europe and subsequently developing both to incorporate a range of civil, political and social rights and to include within its reach all but a small minority of the state's population. It is seen as developing elsewhere as the modern system of states expanded to rule over the greater part of humanity. Citizenship in this sense is also regarded as a good thing, something to be defended and possibly deepened within the states where it exists and perhaps even to be extended into the international sphere.

This chapter approaches the significance of citizenship in the modern world from a rather different direction, essentially by considering the part it plays at a supra-national, or rather supra-state, level. Here I argue that citizenship can be seen as part of a regime of government which operates both by promoting the rule of territorial states over populations and by deploying a range of devices to regulate the conduct of states and the populations under their control. If there is an important sense in which all states are equally sovereign within this regime, there is another no less important sense in which some states are considerably more equal than others (Clark, 1989). We shall see that the inequalities involved here, especially those associated with globalization and liberal internationalism, have important implications for the character of citizenship in the world today.

I begin with a brief defence of my use of the word 'government' to refer to aspects of the system of states and especially to the modern partitioning of humanity into citizens of states and a significant minority of migrants, refugees, and stateless persons. I then move on to consider the emergence and subsequent globalization of the system of states, focusing especially on the manner in which, following the dismantling of direct imperial rule in the nineteenth and twentieth centuries, citizenship changed from being the condition of a small minority of the world's population to become the condition of the overwhelming majority. The shift from direct imperial rule to independent statehood provides us with a frame in which the character of modern citizenship can best be understood.

## Government

Aristotle's *Politics* (1279a27) uses the term 'government' primarily to denote 'the supreme authority in states', which suggests that government should be seen as emanating from a single centre of control, and modern political analysis has generally followed this usage. Aristotle (1278b37-8) also writes of the government 'of a wife and children and of a household', the government of a slave, and a government that one exercises over oneself. In his own discussions of government Michel Foucault (2001, p.341) notes that, for all the many differences between them, these otherwise distinct practices all share a concern with 'the way in which the conduct of individuals or of groups might be directed...To govern, in this sense, is to structure the possible field of action of others', or indeed of oneself. Thus, while it will often act directly to determine the behaviour of individuals, government also aims to influence their actions indirectly by acting on the manner in which they regulate their own behaviour and the behaviour of others.

While he promotes this more general understanding of government, Foucault (2001, p.206) also acknowledges that, from the beginning of the modern period, one form of government has been seen as having a quite distinct status: namely, 'the particular form of governing which can be applied to the state as a whole'. He observes, for example, that those who wrote of the art of government in the early modern period 'constantly recall that one speaks also of "governing" a household, souls, children, a province, a convent, a religious order, a family' (Foucault, 2001, p.205), but he also notes that they treat these 'other kinds of government as internal to the state or society' (*ibid.*, p.206), thereby always giving the government of the latter a superior status. This modern understanding of government thus follows the classical view not only in assuming that the government of a state should have 'regard to the common interest' (Aristotle, 1279a17) but also in treating the state as 'the highest of all' (*ibid.*, 1252a5) forms of community. Government, in this special sense, is clearly focused on the state as a whole but, Foucault insists, the work of governing the state extends well beyond the institutions of the state itself. It need not be seen as emanating from a single centre of control and it will often be performed by elements of what is now called civil society – by religious organizations, employers, financial institutions, legal and medical professionals, voluntary associations, and also, less directly, by markets and other institutionalized patterns of interaction.

Influential figures in the disciplines of public administration and international relations have used the term 'governance' to describe such forms of governing 'without government', suggesting that the work of governing within states is increasingly being conducted by public-private partnerships and by formal and informal networks involving a variety of state and non-state agencies while, in the international sphere, states and other actors are regulated by an expanding web of conventions, treaties, and international agencies, all of which operate without the backing of an overarching Hobbesian power.[1] For all their differences, these various literatures all suggest that activities within states and in the spaces between them are governed in ways that cannot properly be grasped by the state-centred view of government with which I began this section.

We shall see that this suggestion has important implications for our equally state-centred understanding of citizenship. My own view is that, if government in its most general sense is a matter of structuring the possible fields of action, then the organization of citizenship within the modern system of states can itself be seen as a regime of government, albeit one that operates, like civil society and the market, with no controlling centre. However, it is of no particular importance for my argument here whether we use 'government', 'governance', or some other term to refer to this aspect of the modern system of states. What matters, rather, is that we acknowledge the presence of significant elements of design in the modern partitioning of humanity into citizens of states and a small minority of others. There are, in fact, many such elements of design in the modern system of states and some of them will play an important part in the discussion that follows.

**The Modern System of States**

Systems of states have appeared in many parts of the world - in the Americas, China, Europe, South Asia, the Malay Archipelago and Western classical antiquity – but, for reasons which need not concern us here, the system dominated by the modern West is the first of these to have become truly global in scope. This system has its origins in seventeenth-century European attempts to contain the political problems arising from the existence of powerful religious differences between Catholics, Lutherans, and Calvinists by granting territorial rulers supreme political authority within their domains, leaving it to rulers and their subjects to reach some accommodation in matters of religion. These political arrangements were designed to pacify warring populations but they also had the effect of transforming political conditions in the Western part of Europe, essentially by assigning populations which had been subject to a variety of overlapping and conflicting sources of authority to sovereign states which were themselves acknowledged as having the primary responsibility for the government of the populations within their territories.[2]

Where the classical view of politics treats the state as 'the highest of all' forms of community (Aristotle, 1252a5), the development of the modern system of states reflects the emergence of a more complex form of political reason. The state clearly retains its privileged position with regard to its own population, but there are also important governmental contexts in which the 'international community' – the order represented by the system of states – is now regarded as 'the highest of all'. My argument is that the development of modern citizenship within this order has fundamental consequences for its role in the world today.

We can begin by noting that the Westphalian system of states operates as a regime of population management by assigning responsibility for the government of populations to a plurality of independent sovereign states and further that, as we have already seen, the government of these states is expected to have 'regard to the common interest' (Aristotle, 1279a17) – the common interest, that is, of its own citizens. Citizenship, in this respect, is clearly divisive in two rather different respects, separating the citizens of a state not only from the citizens of other states but also from the non-citizen residents who occupy a lesser status within the state itself (Isin, 2002). This chapter focuses on the first of these divisions. In effect, the institution of citizenship requires each state to be particularly responsible for looking after its own citizens – a view which has underpinned the development of welfare states in the prosperous societies of the modern West – and promotes a correspondingly exclusive sense of solidarity among the citizens themselves. Some discussions treat the kind of national sentiment involved here as resulting from a natural tendency to feel more responsible for those who are closer to us: to members, first, of the family or household, then of the local community or region, then of the state or nation, and only then to people in other parts of the world (Miller, 2000). I prefer the contrary view, which sees such sentiments as products of institutional arrangements, not as their 'natural' (and therefore final) causes: the formation of such national sentiments is itself a consequence of the governmental partitioning of humanity into the populations of discrete and independent states.

The view that each state is primarily responsible for looking after its own suggests also that it does not have the same responsibility for looking after others. Thus, while acknowledging that we may all have responsibilities towards the populations of other states, it treats these as being of secondary importance at best. It suggests to the rest of the world that the people of states such as Afghanistan, Burundi, or Bangladesh should be regarded as having primary responsibility for their own condition and that if their states fail them – especially if they do so in a manner which appears to threaten the interests of other states – then it may be necessary for the international community to step in and sort them out. There is a remarkable denial of history and, indeed, of responsibility at work in this perception but the point I want to make here is a slightly different one. The assignment of responsibility for the regulation and the welfare of populations to the states to which they belong has clear positive effects, effects whose importance is demonstrated most dramatically in cases where states are unable to live up to this responsibility. But it also has important effects of a very different kind. In particular, it tells the people of each state that, while they might generously accept a few refugees from time to time, the welfare of other populations is not their primary responsibility – that, of course, individual members of these populations have human rights but, as the UN Declaration of Human Rights so eloquently insists, the responsibility for securing those rights ultimately rests with the states to which they belong. This is precisely the brutal and demeaning vision which dominates the treatment of refugees and many other actual or would-be migrants in the world today.

We can note that where contract theory tends to present the state as constituted internally, by real or imaginary agreements between its members – as do many of the contributions to this volume – the account of the system of states presented here suggests that the sovereignty of a state is in part a function of its recognition as a state by other members of the system (Weber, 1995). Government of the state is not restricted to the activities of the state itself or to developments within its borders: it also appears in the organization of relations between states. The rights of states to manage their own affairs, for example, have always been heavily qualified (as rights commonly are) by a corresponding set of responsibilities to what is often called the 'international community', that is, to the overarching system of states to which they belong.

This point gives a very different twist to the Aristotelian view of the citizen as both ruler and ruled. Not only are there important respects in which citizens are not the collective rulers of the state to which they belong – as in fact has always been the case – but to the extent that they do rule, this serves to reinforce their subordination to agencies and forces over which they have little real control.[3] Thus, while all contemporary states, even the most powerful, are to some degree subject to the general supervisory mechanisms of the enlarged system of states – to a variety of international conventions, treaties, a developing framework of international law on the one hand, and the 'civilizing' effects of international trade on the other – a clear majority of the new states that emerged from the twentieth-century end of empire, along with many non-Western states in territories which had never been colonized, also find themselves subject to the supervisory mechanisms of the more specific international regime of development. Some of these states (with more than a little help from their friends) have played the development game with a notable degree of success while others have tried to play by radically different rules, usually with unhappy results, but most have fallen somewhere between these extremes.

The normative force of the contractarian account of the state has never been based on a claim to historical realism. Accordingly, we should be careful not to read too much into this discrepancy between contract theory and the actual history of the system of states. Contract theory is concerned less to *understand* the character of modern states than it is to *justify* (and in some respects to limit) their claims to supreme authority over their own citizens and territory. It is this normative imperative which produces the view that citizens should engage with their own state as if, whatever its actual history, it had emerged through formal or informal agreements amongst numerous individuals who then became its subjects.[4] The normative implications of the contractarian view thus tend to reinforce the governmental thrust of the modern system of states by promoting the belief among citizens that, in Aristotle's words, the state is 'a body of citizens sufficing for the purposes of life' (1275b21-2). It is this view of the state which underlies the modern understanding of citizenship as a matter of relationships between individuals and the state to which they belong and between these individuals themselves. It suggests not only that sovereignty is essentially a matter of the internal relations between a state and its citizens on the one hand, and of the capacity of a state to defend itself against outsiders on the other, but also that the state in turn has a particular responsibility for securing the welfare of its own citizens.

A third implication is that effective government within the member states of the Westphalian system is predicated on political conditions that operate above the level of the individual states themselves. This suggests not only that the order secured within the more successful states depends in part on the order which prevails in the relations between states but also that much of the disorder within less successful states may also be a product of this latter order. The European system of states and the sovereignty which that system secured for participating states provided conditions which made possible the internal development of citizenship which Marshall (1950) described as involving the emergence, in roughly this order, of three sets of rights: the *civil* rights to liberty and equality before the law; the *political* rights to vote and to participate in the political process; and the *social* rights to participate fully in a way of life that is shared by the citizens as a whole. Recent commentators have disputed many aspects of Marshall's argument but their criticisms have rarely engaged with the strictly intra-state focus of his analysis (Bulmer and Rees, 1996).

Finally, at least in its early stages, the Westphalian states system was specifically European, covering territories and populations in parts of Europe by means of treaties and understandings between participating states. It imposed few constraints on the conduct of these states towards those who inhabited territories not covered by these agreements, who were seen as possessing no sovereign states of the European kind (Schmitt, 1996). Thus while European states were consolidating their rule over their own populations – in part through the development of the civil and political rights of citizenship – some of them were also engaged in imperial adventures elsewhere. This brings us to the globalization of the system of modern states, with its consequences for the subsequent globalization of citizenship.

## The Expansion of the System of States

The subordination of substantial non-European populations to rule by European states was clearly a central feature of European imperialism, but a second feature was no less important for our purposes: the incorporation of those populations and the territories they inhabited into the European system of states. In a different but related development, the remainder of the non-European world was brought into the system of states indirectly: through the deployment by European states of a standard of civilization in their dealings with independent states elsewhere (Gong, 1984), the imposition of elaborate systems of capitulations which required the latter to acknowledge the extra-territorial jurisdiction of Western states (Fidler, 2000), and what Gallagher and Robinson (1953) have called 'the imperialism of free trade'.

Direct or indirect imperial domination was the form in which the European system of states first became global in scope, but this process of incorporating non-European populations into the European system of states was followed, more or less rapidly, by a second stage in the globalization of the European states system. The achievement of independence throughout much of the Americas during the nineteenth century, and its achievement or imposition elsewhere during the twentieth, dismantled one aspect of imperial rule while leaving the state and the institutions of citizenship within it as, in Michael Hardt and Antonio Negri's words (2000, p.135), 'the poisoned gift of national liberation'. This imperial legacy has consequences for citizenship at a number of different levels.

We can begin by noting that the second twentieth-century wave of independence marks the point at which citizenship became an almost universal human condition. However, the citizenship that developed through the transition from imperial rule to independent statehood followed a radically different trajectory than the one traced by Marshall and other sociologists for modern Western states. One consequence is that the condition of citizenship in postcolonial states is seriously constrained by the governmental institutions and practices inherited from the colonial period, most of which were predicated on a view of the subject population as considerably less civilized than their rulers. While we might expect such a view of the bulk of the subject population to be held by the political/administrative class in all modern states, it was more pronounced, or at least more freely expressed, in the case of populations subject to direct imperial rule. Colonial rule by Western states involved a clear distinction between citizens and subjects and a systematic development of what eventually became known, in the case of Britain's African possessions, as indirect rule – a form of government which worked through institutions that relied on what were thought to be indigenous customs and structures of authority.[5]

Precisely because they adapted what were thought to be indigenous practices to the demands of administrative convenience, the detailed character of these ersatz governmental arrangements varied from one colonial administration to another. Their overall effect, however, was to institutionalize a differentiated pattern of relations between the colonial state and sections of the subject population which reinforced or even created divisions between them (Appadurai, 1993) and promoted forms of localized authoritarian rule, a regime which Mamdani (1996) aptly describes as one of 'decentralized despotism'. While independence has displaced the colonial distinction between citizen and subject, the laws and administrative practices inherited from the period of indirect rule have often continued to limit the civil and political rights of citizenship.

A second consequence of this trajectory relates to the argument of Marshall and many social policy analysts in the West that the role of the state's social policy was to ensure that citizens were not in fact excluded from participation in the life of their society by reason of poverty, ill-health, or lack of education. This sociological literature focuses on the prosperous (and predominantly Western) states of the OECD, but it is worth noting here since its insistence on the role of the state in securing the social rights of citizenship serves to mark another significant difference between citizenship in the West and citizenship elsewhere. While these social rights are comparatively well-established in most Western states – in spite of considerable neo-liberal pressure – they have barely had a chance to develop in the majority of other states. Third, the imperial legacy of communal division suggests that the challenge to citizenship posed by ethnic, linguistic, religious, and other group memberships within the state or cutting across its boundaries, should not be seen simply as a product of late twentieth-century developments. On the contrary, there is an important sense in which this challenge has been a condition of postcolonial states from the beginnings of citizenship itself.

At a rather different level, the growth of political independence in the modern sense both expanded the membership of the system of states and inaugurated a radically new way of bringing non-Western populations under the rule of that system (Seth, 2000). These populations thus found themselves governed both by modern states of their own and by the overarching system of states within which their own states had been incorporated. I noted earlier that, as with other regimes of government that possess no controlling centre – the workings of an established market or of civil society for example – some members of the modern system of states are clearly more equal than others. Like the modern states that have been established in territories that were never directly colonized, the newly independent states are recognized as members of the international system of states but few have been admitted to its more exclusive inner circles. As a result, they are subject to regulation by international financial agencies which are clearly dominated by Western concerns and, in particular, by an updated version of the European 'standard of civilization' which requires them to demonstrate their fitness to participate in various international arrangements (OECD, GATT, and its successor WTO, providing the most obvious examples), and which dominates the rhetoric of intervention by the 'international community' (Cooper, 1996; Kaplan, 2000).

I noted earlier that the idea of a 'standard of civilization' played an important part in the conduct of relations between Western states and independent states elsewhere during the imperial period. Like the 'civilizing mission' of Western imperialism, the standard of civilization treated the greater part of humanity as being in considerable need of improvement and, in particular, as unable to properly manage its own affairs. Governmental programs of improvement or development remain influential in the postcolonial world but the discourse of improvement has taken a radically different form – in part, no doubt, because its earlier imperial versions can hardly be voiced in public without offending the leaders and citizens of independent states.[6]

It would clearly be a mistake to treat this project of improvement as if it were simply imposed on the rest of the world by Western states. It is also pursued – as it was during the colonial period – by influential groups in the ex-imperial domains themselves. Nevertheless, the most powerful forces behind this project of improvement are to be found in the liberal West itself. The old imperial divisions between citizens, colonial subjects, and non-citizen others have been displaced by a post-imperial globalization of citizenship, and indirect rule within imperial possessions has been superseded by an even less direct form of decentralized rule, reminiscent in many respects of the older system of capitulations, in which the inhabitants of postcolonial successor states are governed through sovereign states of their own (Fidler, 2000). This is also to say, of course, that they are ruled through states which are themselves governed by the regulatory regimes of the modern system of states and, in particular, by international financial institutions and that fundamental liberal instrument of civilization, the market. Indeed, it is tempting to suggest that the use of markets to regulate the conduct of states has become increasingly prominent as we move further away from the decolonizations of the mid-twentieth century. This reflects the concern of the 'international community' to tighten supervision over what it regards as weak and poorly performing states.

International financial institutions and development agencies are now promoting 'good governance' within states, which is seen as involving the implementation of basic human rights and democracy. Governments of states are expected to be at least minimally responsive to the wishes of their citizens and the citizens in turn are expected to 'own' or at least to go along with the policies of their government: the language of 'ownership' now plays an important part in development discourse. Joseph Stiglitz, while still Vice-President of the World Bank, described the Bank's proposed Comprehensive Development Framework as involving 'a new set of relationships, not only between the Bank and the country, but within the country itself…Central is the notion that the country (*not just the government*) must be in the driver's seat' (Stiglitz, 1999, pp.22-3, emphasis added; see also Wolfensohn, 1999; Palast, 2003, chapter 4). The point, in other words, is to get the citizens themselves to accept responsibility for implementing the conditions imposed by the Bank. The promotion of reforms designed to limit governments' freedom of action and therefore citizens' ability to influence their actions, goes hand-in-hand with the promotion of democracy as a central component of good governance.

## Conclusion

I began this chapter by observing that citizenship is generally regarded as a good thing and, rather than challenge this view directly, I have tried to suggest that citizenship should be seen, like other human arrangements, as something that often cuts both ways. Thus, for the inhabitants of any state it is usually preferable to be a citizen of that state – or a wealthy, well-connected foreigner – than it is to occupy a lesser status. In this respect at least, the possession of citizenship is clearly beneficial and its beneficial effects are considerably increased if one is fortunate enough to be a citizen of one of the prosperous (and overwhelmingly Western) states of the OECD, most of which have secured some approximation to the civil, political, and social rights which Marshall regards as necessary for the full development of citizenship. These rights are poorly developed in many postcolonial successor states, but even in these cases it is usually far better to be a citizen than not.

On the other side of the ledger, we have seen that there is an important sense in which citizens are never the only rulers of the state to which they belong and, further, that their participation in rule serves also to reinforce their subordination to agencies and forces over which they have limited control at best. This last point applies to the citizens of any state but it can be especially consequential for those who belong to states subject to supervision by international financial agencies and the international development regime. That citizen's rule is subject to significant external constraints is not the primary cause for concern here – quite the contrary in fact. What should concern us, rather, is the grossly unequal character of the international order from which these constraints derive.

I noted also that the institutions of citizenship are divisive in two rather different respects. In the first, which has been the focus of my discussion, citizenship provides a state with a means of distinguishing between those who belong and those who do not and, more importantly perhaps, with entirely legitimate grounds for excluding, if it so chooses, the latter from some or all of the benefits it accords to citizens, including the right to reside in the state's territory. Since states are expected to look after their own and most of the world's citizens in fact belong to its less advantaged states, we might say that the international citizenship regime plays a part in protecting the privileges of the wealthy. There are good reasons for resisting attempts – whether by states or by political theorists – to present citizenship as one's primary political identity and the state as one's principal focus of loyalty. Commitments which cut across national boundaries may well threaten the role of citizenship within the larger system of states, and possibly even the design of the system more generally, but their development is surely to be encouraged.

Finally, lest this last point be seen as lending support to the idea of cosmopolitan citizenship, I should perhaps conclude by returning briefly to the second sense in which citizenship can be seen as divisive, namely, in separating the citizens of a polity from those of its inhabitants who are regarded as occupying a lesser status. Cosmopolitan citizenship is clearly intended to undermine the divisiveness which sets the citizens of one state against those of another, and in this respect its universalism is something to be welcomed. Unfortunately, however, its relationship to this second kind of divisiveness is more problematic. The cosmopolitan figures of the European Enlightenment rarely found any difficulty in combining their universalism with the view that much of humanity was not yet – and in some cases might never be – able to properly manage its own affairs. Such elitist universalisms clearly underlay both the 'civilizing missions' of Western imperialism and the 'standard of civilization' which Western states deployed in their relationships with independent states elsewhere. Steven Lukes (2003) argues that universalism need not be ethnocentric. Perhaps so – but we may nevertheless remain suspicious of the universalisms proclaimed by the imperial powers. It is far from clear, for example, whether contemporary Western cosmopolitanism has entirely escaped the elitist universalisms of its Enlightenment and colonial predecessors. Nor is it clear that a concern for the welfare of humanity is best pursued through the Western idiom of citizenship.

## Notes

1    There is a substantial literature in both fields, for example, Rhodes, 1997; Rosenau and Czempiel, 1992.
2    There is an extensive literature on the emergence of the Westphalian system and its geo-political effects. For example, Held, 1995; Hirst, 1998; Schmitt, 1996; Spruyt, 1994; Walker, 1993.
3    There are many other reasons for this condition too, of course. I have argued elsewhere that the institutions of representative government – which reflect the predominant modern understanding of democracy – are clearly designed to ensure that citizens play a strictly circumscribed role in the government of the state to which they belong (Hindess, 2000).
4    Cf. Kant's insistence, in *The Metaphysics of Morals*, that 'for all practical [i.e. moral] purposes' the origin of sovereign power 'is not discoverable by the people who are subject to it...The subject ought not to indulge in speculations about its origin...as if its right to be obeyed were open to doubt' (Reiss, 1970, p.143).
5    The most influential British statement of the case for indirect rule is Lugard, 1923. However the practice of working through what were believed to be indigenous institutions was a pervasive feature of Western imperial administration (Malinowski, 1929; Mamdani, 1996).
6    What may be said in private is often a different matter. A brief prepared by Australian government departments for a 1997 meeting of Economic Ministers of the Pacific Islands Forum described the leaders of member states in the following terms: 'Used to ambitious but unrealized development plans, they may balk at settling for modest but

achievable objectives'; 'have generally shirked hard decisions'; 'he is boastful and vain – having spent heavily on grandiose monuments – can irritate others'; 'Temperamentally volatile, he is still given to Third World posturing against Western colonialism' (http://166.122.164.43/archive/1997/August/08-04-11.htm). Rather than question the content of this brief, Australian media reports focused on the diplomatic blunder involved in allowing that content to be made public.

# References

Appadurai, Arjun (1993), 'Number in the Colonial Imagination', in Carol A. Breckenridge and Peter van der Veer, *Orientalism and the Postcolonial predicament. Perspectives on South Asia*, University of Pennsylvania Press, Philadelphia, pp.314-39.

Aristotle (1988), *The Politics*, Cambridge University Press, Cambridge.

Bulmer, Martin and Anthony M. Rees (eds.) (1996), *Citizenship Today. The Contemporary Relevance of T. H. Marshall*, UCL Press, London.

Clark, Ian (1989), *The Hierarchy of States: Reform and Resistance in the International Order*, Cambridge University Press, Cambridge.

Cooper, Robert (1996), *The Post-Modern State and the World Order*, Demos, London.

Fidler, David P. (2000), 'A Kinder, Gentler System of Capitulations? International Law, Structural Adjustment Policies, and the Standard of Liberal, Globalized Civilization', *Texas International Law Journal*, vol.35, pp.387-413.

Foucault, Michel (2001), 'Governmentality' in James D. Faubion (ed.), *Power, Essential Works of Foucault*, Allen Lane, London, vol.3, pp.201-22.

Gallagher, John and Ronald Robinson (1953). 'The Imperialism of Free Trade', *The Economic History Review*, vol.VI, pp.1-15.

Gong, Gerrit. W. (1984), *'The Standard of Civilization' in International Society*, Oxford University Press, Oxford.

Hardt, Michael and Antonio Negri (2000), *Empire*, Harvard University Press, Cambridge.

Held, David (1995), *Democracy and the Global Order: From the Modern State to Cosmopolitan Governance*, Polity, Cambridge.

Hindess, Barry (2000), 'Representation Ingrafted upon Democracy', *Democratization*, vol.7, pp.1-18.

Hirst, Paul (1998), 'The international origins of national sovereignty', *From Statism to Pluralism*, UCL Press, London.

Isin, Engin (2002), *Being Political: Genealogies of Citizenship*, Minneapolis, Minnesota University Press.

Kaplan, Robert D. (2000), *The Coming Anarchy*, Random House, New York.

Lugard, Frederick D. (1923), *The Dual Mandate in British Tropical Africa*, Blackwood, Edinburgh.

Lukes, Steven (2003), 'Is Universalism Ethnocentric?' in *Liberals and Cannibals*, Verso, London.

Malinowski, Bronislav (1929), 'Practical Anthropology', *Africa*, vol.2, pp.22-39.

Mamdani, Mahmood (1996), *Citizen and Subject: Contemporary Africa and the Legacy of Late Colonialism*, Princeton University Press, Princeton.

Marshall, T. H. (1950), *Citizenship and Social Class*, Cambridge University Press, Cambridge.

Miller, David (2000), *Citizenship and National Identity*, Polity, Malden.

Palast, Greg (2003), *The Best Democracy Money Can Buy*, Plume, New York.

Reiss, Hans (ed.) (1970), *Kant's Political Writings*, Cambridge University Press, Cambridge.

Rhodes, Roderick A.W. (1997), *Understanding Governance*, Open University Press, Buckingham.

Rosenau, James N. and Ernst-Otto Czempiel, (eds.) (1992), *Governance without Government: Order and Change in World Politics*, Cambridge University Press, Cambridge.

Schmitt, Carl (1996), 'The Land Appropriation of a New World', *Telos*, no.109, pp.29-80.

Seth, Sanjay (2000), 'A "Postcolonial World?"' in Greg Fry and Jacinta O'Hagan (eds.), *Contending Images of World Politics*, Macmillan, London, pp.214-26.

Spruyt, Hendrik. (1994), *The Sovereign State and Its Competitors: An Analysis of Systems Change*, Princeton University Press, Princeton.

Stiglitz, Joseph (1999), 'Participation and Development: perspectives from the Comprehensive Development Paradigm', World Bank, Seoul.

Walker, R.B.J. (1993), *Inside/Outside: International Relations as Political Theory*, Cambridge University Press, Cambridge.

Weber, Cynthia (1995), *Simulating Sovereignty: Intervention, the State and Symbolic Exchange*, Cambridge University Press, Cambridge.

Wolfensohn, James D. (1999), *A Proposal for a Comprehensive Development Framework*, World Bank, Washington.

# Chapter 6

# Active Citizens or an Inert People?

James E. Tiles

> Those who won our independence believed...that the greatest menace to freedom is
> an inert people; that public discussion is a political duty; and that this should be a
> fundamental principle of the American government.
>
> Justice Louis D. Brandeis, concurring,<br>Whitney v. California [274 U.S. 357 (1926), 375]

Recognizing that at her trial there had not been an adequate rebuttal of the
evidence that Charlotte Whitney's efforts to organize a branch of the Communist
Labour Party posed a 'clear and present danger' to California, Justice Brandeis
acquiesced in upholding her conviction under that state's Criminal Syndicalism
Act.[1] Nevertheless, in an opinion joined by Oliver Wendell Holmes Jr., Brandeis
lectured the other seven justices on the point of protecting free speech and
declared that a greater menace to freedom lay in an inert people. An indication of
the extent of the 'menace' at the time Brandeis's opinion was released (16 May
1927) appears in a passage of a book published by John Dewey in the same year,

> The number of voters who take advantage of their majestic right is steadily
> decreasing in proportion to those who might use it. The ratio of actual to eligible
> voters is now about one-half. In spite of somewhat frantic appeal and organized
> effort, the endeavor to bring voters to a sense of their privileges and duties has so far
> been noted for failure...Skepticism regarding the efficacy of voting is openly
> expressed, not only in the theories of intellectuals, but in the words of lowbrow
> masses: 'What difference does it make whether I vote or not? Thing go on just the
> same anyway. My vote never changed anything' (1927, pp.308-9).

Voter apathy and alienation in the United States and many other nominally
'democratic' societies has certainly not decreased in the intervening years.

## Civic Republicanism

The belief that an 'inert people' is a symptom of something wrong with our
political order is a product of understanding what 'democracy' should be in terms
that draw on the traditions of civic republicanism.[2] A republic is not in itself an

intrinsically democratic organization. Aristotle, whose discussion of citizenship laid the foundations of civic republicanism, held a republic (*polis*) to be an organization of equals who possess common interests and who take turns to govern themselves and their affairs with a view to promoting their common interests. Those who are eligible for this role, the citizens or ruling class, may be the whole of the adult population (as in a democracy) or a relatively small minority (as in an oligarchy). Any number of citizens, from one to a sizable proportion of the citizen body, may take turns to exercise at any one time all or some part of the authority to govern.

It is crucial, Aristotle adds, if a republic is to be straight rather than deviant (*orthos* rather than *parekbasis*, 1279a28-31) that when exercising authority, those who govern do so in the interest of the whole of the citizen body rather than of themselves or of some other proper part of the whole. Those who exercise rule in their own interests over others are not citizens but masters (*despotai*). Aristotle also distinguishes the rule of citizen over citizen from that of husbands and fathers over wives and children. The latter is rule over inferiors even if exercised in the interests of those inferiors; citizens by contrast take it in turn to rule over equals. Aristotle would clearly not have recognized as 'political' (that is, republican) in his sense a society governed, as Confucians desired, on the model of a family, nor for that matter a feudal society, one structured on the relations of loyalty owed by inferiors to those stationed above them in a stable hierarchy.[3]

The prevailing conception of a modern 'democracy' shares some features of the civic republican ideal. It is assumed that in a 'democracy' all adults (except possibly convicted felons) are allowed to participate in the institutions of government and to have their voices heard. If any are excluded or silenced, this calls for remedy or reform, but it is unclear what if any remedy is called for under the prevailing conception of 'democracy', if only a few careerists are able and willing to fill public office and if the electorate can neither be bothered to turn out to choose between the candidates available for election nor inform themselves on the issues at stake. In this the prevailing conception displays relatively weak civic republican sensibilities, for this lack of even minimal participation on the part of large segments of the population, who are otherwise free to participate, should appear no more satisfactory than if some were being actively excluded or silenced.

Those inclined to take a more relaxed attitude find comfort in the fact that, if the political careerists to whom it has fallen to govern do not perform well, they can be thrown out of office at the next election. That the electorate is not involved in the issues and that turn-out for elections is low are signs that our political class is doing a satisfactory job. If individuals feel frustrated at not being able to change anything with their votes, they just have to realize that in a democracy those in the minority must wait until the majority comes around to feeling as they do. If it is pointed out that the electorate is not given effective choice in matters relating to health care, corporate responsibility, or environmental regulation, the response is that all who live in a 'democracy' are at liberty to try to infect their fellow citizens with their concerns. There are those who worry that when their concerns reach crisis point, it will either be too late to do anything about it (reverse degradation of the environment) or that untold suffering may occur (to those without adequate health care) before our institutions can be wrested from the hands that currently control them. These anxious souls are told to take their worries to the market-place of ideas to see if they can find any buyers. Pointing out that the market in which ideas must compete is brokered by well-established media-interests is greeted with a shrug of the shoulders.

Those who are not merely comfortable with but have invested in the *status quo* resist the civic republican ideal by claiming that the demands entailed by its conception of citizenship are simply too great for people whose lives are already fully occupied with family commitments, leisure pursuits, and employment. Our careers do not leave us with enough leisure both to participate actively in public life and still maintain a fully rounded private life. To point out that much of our private time is occupied by entertainments of no quality and no consequence will be met by accusations of snobbery; to suggest that through education we should encourage individuals to take an interest in and become involved in public affairs will be said to smack 'of paternalism. By incorporation into this kind of civic regime the individual suffers a loss of personal freedom, autonomy and the power of fully independent critical thought. So speak the opponents of the republican school...' (Heater, 1999, p.73). So speak those who believe that autonomy and the power of fully independent critical thought do not normally need the stimulus of education nor the sustenance of a social environment where critical thought is common.

To find the *status quo* unsatisfactory, indeed threatening, one need not subscribe to the idea sometimes advanced by civic republicans that it is only in active political participation that individuals realize their true freedom: autonomy and independence of judgment. For those who regard this carrot of personal fulfilment as illusory, the product of what Heater (1999, p.73) refers to as 'philosophical sleight of hand', Quentin Skinner (1989, pp.202-19) has pointed to a stick in the form of arguments drawn from Machiavelli's *Discourses*, that individuals who do not exercise active citizenship will find themselves made into subjects without real opportunities to exercise autonomy and independence. There are always those among us with the ambition to dominate (*ambizione di dominare*), their efforts devoted to maintaining as much personal liberty as possible for themselves and avoiding any intervention in their own affairs even on behalf of legitimate public interests (Skinner, 1989, p. 205). The only way to keep such people from monopolizing power is for all people to retain a firm hold on whatever leverage active citizenship gives them to restrain the monopolizers.

Heater (1999, p.73) also reviews more sympathetic criticisms of civic republicanism, 'It would not be so bad if the civic republicans could interpret participation in public affairs more loosely and flexibly than has normally been the case. But theirs has been the grand design of citizenly participation in the politics of the state, the Aristotelian *polis*, naturally, being the model'. The specific implications of this are said to be that citizenship becomes an elite activity, while a range of civic society's activities (pressure groups, trade unions, charities) are left out of the picture and, furthermore, that as men find it easier and more congenial than women to involve themselves in formal politics, the whole thrust of civic republicanism is distasteful to feminists (Heater, 1999, pp.73-4). These criticisms at least can be met by joining to civic republicanism the more synoptic vision of a democratic society offered by John Dewey, although the result will not make the task of realizing a 'democratic society' any less daunting.

## A 'Democratic Society'

The analytical framework that Dewey devised is not designed to tell us much about the functioning of actual political institutions, and for this reason it has not found favour with political scientists, but it has the advantage of offering a way of seeing beyond familiar institutional boundaries and of glimpsing possibilities that cut across them. Dewey defined 'state' (1927, p.260) as a public organized to deal with the interests that constitute it (as a public) and 'government' as the instruments of that organization – 'the equipment of the public with official representatives to care for the interests of the public' (Dewey, 1927, p.259). The foundational notion, that of 'the public', draws on the idea that when two or more people get together as private individuals to conduct some enterprise, there are often effects on third parties. All the people, for whom these indirect consequences are 'extensive and enduring' and on whose behalf these effects need to be managed, constitute 'the public' (Dewey, 1927, pp.245-6). There is good reason, however, to doubt whether one can use a definite article with this notion of public. The people indirectly affected by the commerce between A and B may not be the same as those affected by the commerce between C and D. If A and B and C and D are involved in the same kind of commerce, the sum total of those affected by this kind of commerce may not be the same people as those affected by some other kind of commerce. If we add together all people who are indirectly affected by the private activities of anyone else, we may well find, especially in this global age, that our public comprehends far more than is or can be catered for by any individual state.

These implications would not be unwelcome to Dewey, for he offered his framework as a way to understand why and in what respects modern states appear dysfunctional. Modern states are historical products, often imposed on people in order to further the personal interests of those who would hold or control authority, rather than to care for the interests that constitute a public. Dewey's framework can nevertheless be taken as identifying a function for something called a 'state' in response to the question, 'why is there a need to retain any semblance of such historical products?' People who live together will always need a way of controlling the wider effects of their private interactions; instruments of government can achieve that. The problem is how to refashion the institutions we have to better serve this function.

This may well, however, define the notion of public on too narrow a basis. One senses that Dewey framed the concept of a public as he did in order to occupy high ground overlooking those who were urging an excessively *laissez faire* approach to the indirect effects of conducting privately owned business activities. A group of people may find that they have a common need to care for more than merely the side-effects of other people's private enterprise. A group of farmers living near a river may need to control its flow in order to irrigate their crops; the owners of condominiums in a tower block need to maintain the fabric of their building so as not to lose the value of the apartments they have purchased. Even Dewey's example of a frontier community who combine to build a school-house and hire a teacher for their children does not fit comfortably under phrases like 'extensive and enduring indirect consequences of the actions of private individuals or groups' (1927, pp.305-6). Common interests are created by the possibility of realizing goods and warding off evils that individuals acting separately cannot realize or ward-off. This includes, but is not exhausted by, the need to control the indirect consequences of privately conducted affairs. A public in other words may be constituted by a common interest that is wider than that of controlling the indirect effects of private activities.[4]

A people who have a common interest and do not perceive it are in Dewey's language 'an inchoate public' (1927, p.317). This allows the identification of one important problem that political thinkers need to address: how to get an 'inchoate' public to recognize itself through recognizing the 'extensive and enduring' indirect consequences that affect its members as well as the possibilities of controlling those consequences – or, if we apply the more generous notion of public based on common interest, to recognize the possibility of achieving some good and the need for collective action to realize it. Another problem – one that has already been mentioned and which has grown along with the complexity of our society – is that, from this perspective, the use of the definite article may beg important questions. 'There are too many publics and too much of public concern for our existing [institutional] resources to cope with' (Dewey, 1927, p.314). There are potentially as many publics as there are subsets of the population; some are exclusive, some overlap, some include others. It would be unthinkable for all potential publics to organize themselves; that would create more problems than it would solve. The continual challenge is to invent or adapt the instruments of government to facilitate as many of the plural publics and their multiple goods as possible.

Examples may help to show why our thinking should not be constrained by existing political or institutional boundaries. Imagine a trade or profession plagued by rogue operators whose inept and unscrupulous activities have a severe dampening effect on the prosperity of competent and honest practitioners. We have what Dewey identifies as a public as soon as and to the extent that the competent and honest practitioners perceive the indirect consequences on their trade of the inept and unscrupulous and see the possibility of combining in an organization that will guarantee the expertise and *bona fides* of its members. To be effective the organization may have to be seen to discipline its members, possibly by having them (in the language of the British Medical Association) 'struck-off' a register of approved practitioners if they damage their trade or profession – if they (to switch to sports language) 'bring the game into disrepute'. This little 'public' becomes a *res publica* by acquiring instruments of government and thereby, to adapt Dewey's language, constituting itself as a mini-state. Standards may be needed not only for dealing with clients or customers, but for dealings between and among those engaged in an enterprise. Pre-modern European merchants held formal hearings of their own to settle disputes among themselves and to sanction trade or financial practices. Western mercantile law is an important historical example (admiralty law is another) of activities conducted across or beyond national boundaries initially governed by customs that solidified into law before being incorporated into national law—an example of law that was not imposed from above.[5]

Not all of Dewey's publics, in other words, are the populations of nation-states; nor has he refined his definition of 'state' so that its extension coincides with that of 'modern nation'—or even with the constituencies (states, provinces, municipalities) of a modern nation. His framework applies to significant portions of what is known as civil society, and if that diminishes its utility for political science, it nevertheless helps to strengthen the hand of those who argue that a vigorous civil society must be involved in the remedy for an 'inert people'. Above all it clarifies what kind of civil society, what characteristics its culture must have, if it is to support a democratic society. A mini-state, just like a proper state, may be constituted as a fiefdom or a republic, and a republic may be governed exclusively (as an oligarchy) or inclusively (as a democracy). Fiefdoms and oligarchies are incompatible with the active participation of all members, and if the bulk of a membership participates only passively – turns out to socialize, to be entertained, to be led and will not take a turn in planning, guiding or leading – it is at best a *de facto* oligarchy. No people who expect to retain control of the instruments of the more comprehensive levels of government can expect to succeed if they have not practiced – have not honed their habits of expectation and the critical edge of their judgments – on public affairs in their immediate vicinity.

In response to the criticisms Heater aired about the narrow and inflexible view of public affairs commonly taken by civic republicans, we can place in the hands of these theorists a more comprehensive notion of 'public' under which the civic republican ideal is anything but elitist, far from confined only to affairs in the government of cities, provinces, and nation-states, and in no way needing to be governed by methods which are thought of as traditionally 'male oriented'. Dewey's publics are more numerous and interwoven than publics traditionally conceived; their crying need under his analysis is for them to find themselves and find better instruments for furthering the interests that constitute them. There are many ways to conduct deliberations, and we need active citizens equipped with mastery of a wide variety of ways to reach consensus; for sound judgment about what is to be done often requires sound judgment regarding the best way in the circumstances to go about determining what is to be done.

That a group's deliberations should be as inclusive of the interests of its members as possible is only one side of Dewey's ideal of 'democracy' (1927, pp.327-8). All individuals benefit from membership in many groups, many publics; they cannot otherwise be full multi-dimensional human beings. A group that pursues its collective good at the expense of others not only beggars its neighbours, it impoverishes its own members by damaging their opportunities for participating in and reaping benefits collectively accessible in other dimensions of social life. It is entirely possible that it should come to pass that 'What is good for the country is good for General Motors and vice-versa', but it is highly implausible that the harmonization of the two goods can be achieved by individuals whose dominant personal interests are bound up entirely with General Motors.[6]

The problem is not just to organize publics in ways that serve equitably all their members, the problem is to coordinate publics in ways that mutually support rather than obstruct one another. Citizens must learn not only to represent narrow collective interests in wider arenas, they must learn to be representatives of wider collective concerns when defining and pursuing local goods. This is the task which must be accomplished, if the benefits to be realized through organized publics – however they are organized – are not to cancel one another. Citizenship is not well understood as responsible membership in one comprehensive organization; a superior understanding is that of membership in multiple organizations that brings with it a comprehensive responsibility.

## Agenda

In response to the criticism rehearsed by Heater, it has been acknowledged that the civic republican idea of democracy should indeed be joined to a more inclusive and pluralistic notion of the publics which active citizenship is to constitute and serve. We then need to confront the intellectual challenge which this entails: how to harmonize interests so that neither are comprehensive goods lost in the competition between single-minded advocates of local interests nor are local interests sacrificed entirely to more global interests. Achieving this will take a lot more honest thought and intense discussion than is currently being invested and it is towards this responsibility that our inert people have been most seriously derelict. It may be most efficient for policy that reconciles interests to be formulated by a few, but for ownership of the policy to be widely distributed, it has to be shaped and refined in numerous satellite forums.

Active citizenship in a thoroughly democratic society is undeniably very demanding. It does not, however, mean that we the people all have to be engaged in the day to day running of the affairs of our nation-states. Such affairs are indeed complex and do require professional management, but management should be distinguished from governance. Even Rousseau (1762, III.1, p.49), who feared 'representatives', allowed a sovereign people to hire agents (the government) to manage public affairs. What a people has to do to retain sovereignty over its affairs is what any public has to do to see that its hired agents look after its interests, which is to maintain firm control over the determination of the policies its managers will carry out on its behalf, as well as a close eye on their performance in doing so – for these are the public servants who will most readily become, first their own masters and then, the people's masters.

Exercising close scrutiny over one's employees may not always be easy, but it does not appear intractable until one asks who, when the employer is a public of any significant size, is to frame policy and exercise oversight? There are after all undeniable limits on the size of a body of people that can conduct deliberations effectively. Even legislative bodies of moderate size (for example, boards of directors of companies and non-profit concerns) seek efficiencies and divide their labour by delegating work to committees. Here we appear caught between, on the one hand, the constraints of minimal efficiency in carrying out oversight and the formation of policy and, on the other hand, the fear of the common interest being hijacked by those delegated to act on its behalf. Rousseau (1762, III.15, p.75) was unequivocal, 'the moment a people gives itself representatives, it is no longer free'.[7] More recently Hannah Arendt has expressed the view that relying on legislative representatives has encouraged the formation of a political elite so that 'once more the business of government has become the privilege of the few'.[8]

A division of the labour of oversight and policy formation is however plainly inevitable; the problem is how to select those who will carry out these tasks and keep them from being suborned by the very interests they have been assigned to deal with disinterestedly. The long history of the corruption of the legislative process by what are nowadays referred to in the United States as 'special interests' has so obscured the function that legislative representatives should perform under a civic republican conception – the promotion of the interests of the whole – that the performance of representatives is measured almost exclusively by the benefits their constituents receive, the size of the slices of pig-meat sent home from what in the United States is referred to as the Congressional pork-barrel.[9]

It is not a large step from this understanding of the function of 'democratic' representatives to accepting – under the general principle, 'he who pays the piper calls the tune' – that the constituents who contribute most to electing successful representatives are the constituents who deserve to be served first and most fully. Our representatives do not tend to become our masters; they simply become the servants of other masters. Thus does the idea that citizens are equal and equally represented melt away in the heat generated by an electoral system fuelled by campaign contributions, and adding to this heat is the habit of treating any move towards free markets as another triumph for 'democracy'. We are all free and equal in the market, distinguished only by what we can afford to purchase. Can we blame citizens with one vote and little disposable income for becoming inert?

There are numerous reforms that have been proposed to counteract the tendency of private interests to subvert the functioning of the people's representatives and through the subversion of their oversight the functioning of the people's agents. It is well worth pursuing anything that compensates for the leverage that wealth gives in exerting political influence (campaign finance reform) or the shaping of public opinion (regulations, now sadly being abandoned, to prevent media conglomerates from dominating the market of ideas). So also are measures to break the hold that careerists have on the legislative process (term-limits). On a smaller scale are efforts like those to open conferences on matters of public concern (such as nuclear safety) to wider participation by not charging registration fees that discourage the public, by announcing meetings in a timely manner and by ensuring that those who attend have access to relevant information.[10] Even if these and numerous similar measures were to be comprehensively applied, it would not bring about the sea-change that is required. What is needed is for a democratic application of the civic republican idea of governance throughout the sphere of the public in the expanded sense of 'public' set out by Dewey.

Consider the absence of democracy in the many microcosms that make up the business world. Management reports to the board of directors, the representatives of the stockholders. The stockholders of large modern corporations are, with rare exceptions, inert; they have no interest in how the company is run; they care only about their dividends and even more about the value of their stock on the market. These are the measures of performance to which boards of directors tie management remuneration and then give management a free hand to use their employees, the environment, and the political process in any way conducive to success so measured. If the public created by the activities of such a corporation were to be represented adequately in its governance, the board of directors would have to represent the employees, the customers and anyone else affected by the conduct of its activities. Company policy would have to be carefully formulated to ensure that what is deemed by General Motors to be good for General Motors is really good for the country.

The same, of course, applies to the AFL-CIO and its constituent unions, to the Ford Foundation, the United Way, and the Sierra Club. A democratic polity cannot exist where the conduct of affairs in civil society is not sufficiently democratic. One may grant this and balk at the inclusion in civil society of major players in the market. The deepest assumption of our political culture is that the economic (market) sphere is closer to the private sphere and is not properly included in the public, is not part of civil society. This assumption is explicit in Figures 6.1 and 6.2. More than anything we need to re-examine this assumption about where the line between the public and private sphere is to be drawn. In Figure 6.2, far more of the circle on the right ('the market sphere') needs to be regarded as properly 'public' (unshaded).

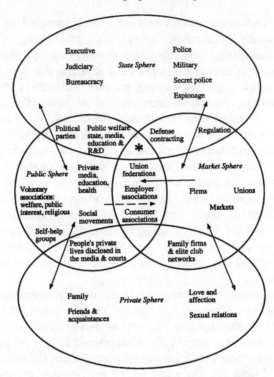

*Public law corporations with tripartite control

**Figure 6.1   The public and private spheres that locate civil society**

*Source*: Janosky, 1988, p.13

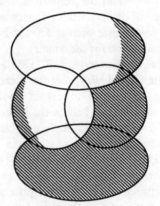

**Figure 6.2   The public (unshaded) and private (shaded)**

*Source*: Janosky, 1988, p.16

For at least a century now the most significant players in the markets have not been private individuals investing, risking, using their own private capital, but 'public' companies, that is corporations that raise capital in publicly accessible markets.[11] To treat union federations, employer associations and consumer pressure groups as part of civil society (and public) and all instances of this corporate formation as outside of civil society (as Janoski does) serves only to insulate the oligarchical foundations of political power from public reach.

No specific policy of regulating either the sphere of civil society or the market sphere is being advanced here, although some such regulation may be required to realize the expectation that all groups of significant size and impact on the lives of our communities should function democratically.[12] If in our daily lives, when we work, when we seek recreation, when we find association outside our families, we are either feudal lords or oligarchs on the one hand or inert subjects on the other, we cannot expect our nation-states to govern and be governed democratically.

## Notes

1   For background on this and the related *Gitlow* case, see Irons, 1999, chapter 22.

2   Quotation marks will be attached to this word throughout, because, although in the past century and a half it has acquired 'new, quite positive, associations with popular sovereignty and political equality' and indeed as a *'value'* has become 'transcendent, its *meaning* [has been] lost in the cacophony of competing interpretations...' (Hanson, 1989, pp.68-9). It will be obvious that the sense of 'democracy' favoured by civic republicans is at variance with the concept of democracy currently prevalent throughout the world. Civic republicans will view claims that the masses are incapable of doing more than choosing between candidates who should govern them, or that modern society is too complex for more wide-spread involvement in governance, as feeble excuses offered for the convenience of those eager to govern and eager to persuade those they govern not to scrutinize their performance too carefully.

3   Those owing duties to superiors in a feudal hierarchy and holding rights on the basis of their position in the hierarchy are referred to as 'subjects' rather than 'citizens'. It is clear that the notion of citizenship under consideration in this paper is that which is nowadays commonly referred to as 'active citizenship'. The residual notion of 'passive citizenship' defined in terms of duties owed to, and rights held against, a state by those regarded as legal members of the state is very close to that which defines a feudal subject, and is for this reason of only subsidiary interest to a civic republican democrat.

4   Circles of private individuals (families, friends, business associates) are also held together by common interests. If clarification of the distinction between private and public interactions is needed we can begin with Aristotle's (1156b1) characterization of imperfect friends as those who wish to spend their [working] days or [domestic] lives together for the sake of the pleasure or the utility they afford one another. It is sometimes more helpful to think of a public as constituted of households or business

partnerships rather than of individuals. Dewey is clearly offering a stipulative definition of 'public' which requires us to pay closer attention to the complex structure of what goes on outside of what are normally thought of as private affairs, as well as requiring us to question continually where the line between public and private should lie. It is not obvious that in replacing our present ways of conceiving the public sphere, we lose anything of value that is not covered by the more comprehensive 'publics' that Dewey's theory will evidently require us to recognize.

5       Tigar, 2000, pp.55-6 and *passim*. It was assumed correctly by the participants in the Singapore conference that the approach taken here would respond to 'legitimation' questions in a manner similar to that currently taken by the proponents of 'deliberative democracy' and therefore stood in opposition to the thesis advanced by Catherine Audard in the next chapter. The legitimacy of decisions reached by deliberative bodies is a matter now commonly regarded as constrained by constitutional instruments (Bills of Rights), but how to construct and interpret these instruments is in turn treated as a matter to be settled by a (different) deliberative body. To seek in opposition to this principle to ground legitimation in the non-public identities of individuals would require deferring to subjective certainty in face of a long experience, beginning with Descartes, of failure to secure in a convincing way the validity of such certainty. A better way to keep deliberative democracy from oppressing dissenting individuals (to keep it 'liberal') is to conduct deliberations within the (pragmatists') spirit of fallibilism and not regard any decision reached by a deliberative body as possessing a certainty that justifies its imposition on the unwilling except where clear and compelling public interests are at stake.

6       Philip Green (1985, p.15) attributes this remark to Charles Wilson, United States Secretary of Defence-designate in 1952.

7       Rousseau on 'slaves': 'The English people believes itself to be free. It is greatly mistaken; it is free only during the election of the members of Parliament. Once they are elected, the populace is enslaved; it is nothing. The use the English people makes of that freedom in the brief moments of its liberty certainly warrants their losing it' (1762, III.15, p.74).

8       Arendt (1965, p.237-8) quoting from Jefferson's correspondence: 'The result is that the people must either sink into "lethargy, the forerunner of death to the public liberty" or "preserve the spirit of resistance" to whatever government they have elected, since the only power they retain is the "reserve power of revolution"'. The first two quotes are found in a letter to William S. Smith, Paris, 13 November 1787 (Jefferson, 1984, p.911). Arendt does not indicate where to find the third.

9       A member of the student senate at the university where I teach recently replied to allegations that he had sponsored the diversion of a sizable sum of money from common funds for student activities to pay for equipment in his own academic department. He responded not by denying the allegation but by asserting that this only showed what an effective representative he had been. The exposure of this appropriation had included an observation about the student senate being 'the springboard into the legislature', and while student senator in question professed ignorance of this career track, he allowed, 'I guess I will find out if it is true, as I am running for the Hawai'i State House of Representatives as a Democrat in 2002. Should I get elected and if I am able to bring home funding to my district as I did for my department, I would be one of the most effective legislators in the State Capitol' (*Ka Leo O Hawai'i*, 22 January 2002, p.4.).

10    Having pressured the United States Nuclear Regulatory Commission to institute these reforms, Lochbaum (2002, p.8) declares 'Next on my "To Do" list is making the NRC [Nuclear Regulatory Commission] more responsive to public input. Right now, the agency lacks a formal mechanism for reporting how they consider public input'. Mention should also be made of the innovative use of 'policy juries' or 'consensus conferences' by the Loka Institute of Amherst, Massachusetts (based on Danish models) and of similar devices ('science shops') in Denmark, Holland and elsewhere (Rampton and Stauber, 2001, pp.308-10).

11    For the early stages of the history of this transformation see Sklar, 1988; and for a classic study of its effects during the early part of the twentieth century, see Berle and Means, 1933.

12    According to the history traced by Hurst (1970, pp.58-111), concern to regulate how modern corporations were governed internally was supplanted during the 1920s by efforts to regulate corporate activities externally according to criteria of 'utility'. The suggestion here is that in leaving the corporate culture to follow and develop the 'oligarchical tendencies' encouraged by the growth of the power of directors (Horwitz, 1992, p.74), we have left in our midst a powerful force that will naturally seek to suborn our political institutions. What is needed is what Kutner (1996, pp.189-190) refers to as 'stakeholder capitalism'. We will not realize the republican ideal of freedom as non-domination (Pettit, 1997, *passim*) if the governance of our most powerful economic institutions is left in the hands of those who have given freest reign to the *ambizione di dominare* (Skinner, 1989, p.209)

## References

Arendt, Hannah (1963), *On Revolution*, Penguin, Harmondsworth.

Aristotle (1922), *The Politics*, H. Rackham (trans.), Loeb Classical Library, Cambridge.

Aristotle (1926), *The Nicomachean Ethics*, H. Rackham (trans.), Loeb Classical Library, Cambridge.

Berle, Adolf A. and Gardiner C. Means (1933), *The Modern Corporation and Private Property*, Macmillan, New York.

Dewey, John (1927), *The Public and Its Problems* in Jo Ann Boydston (ed.), *John Dewey, The Later Works, 1925-53*, Southern Illinois University Press, Carbondale, vol.2, pp.235-372.

Green, Philip (1985), *Retrieving Democracy: In Search of Civic Equality*, Rowman and Allanheld, Totowa.

Hanson, Russell L. (1989), 'Democracy', in Terence Ball, James Farr, and Russell L. Hanson (eds.), *Political Innovation and Conceptual Changes*, Cambridge University Press, Cambridge.

Heater, Derek (1999), *What is Citizenship?* Polity, Cambridge.

Horwitz, Morton (1992), *The Transformation of American Law 1970-1960*, Oxford University Press, New York.

Hurst, James Willard (1970), *The Legitimacy of the Business Corporation in the Law of the United States 1780-1970*, The University of Virginia Press, Charlottesville.

Irons, Peter (1999), *A People's History of the Supreme Court*, Penguin, Harmondsworth.

Janoski, Thomas (1998), *Citizenship and Civil Society*, Cambridge University Press, Cambridge.

Jefferson, Thomas (1984), *Writings*, selected by Merril D. Peterson, The Library of America, New York.

Kutner, Robert (1996), *Everything for Sale*, University of Chicago Press, Chicago.

Lochbaum, David (2002), 'Nuclear Democracy', *Catalyst*, vol.I, p.8

Pettit, Philip (1997), *Republicanism: A Theory of Freedom and Government*, Clarendon, Oxford.

Rampton, Sheldon and John Stauber (2001), *Trust Us, We're Experts*, Tarcher/Putnam, New York.

Rousseau, Jean-Jacques (1762), *On the Social Contract*, Cress, Donald A. (trans.) (1987), Hackett, Indianapolis.

Skinner, Quentin (1984), 'The Idea of Negative Liberty: Philosophical and Historical Perspectives', in Richard Rorty, J.B. Schneewind and Quentin Skinner (eds.), *Philosophy in History*, Cambridge University Press, Cambridge, pp.193-221.

Sklar, Martin J. (1988), *The Corporate Reconstruction of American Capitalism, 1890-1916*, Cambridge University Press, Cambridge.

Tigar, Michael (2000), *Law and the Rise of Capitalism*, Monthly Review Press, New York.

# Chapter 7

# Socratic Citizenship:
# The Limits of Deliberative Democracy

Catherine Audard

## Introduction

I would like to examine the claim that public deliberation as such can be a legitimization process for principles and norms governing our collective democratic life, that 'popular sovereignty is a procedure' (Habermas, 1999, p.35). I will challenge this claim in the name of a conception of citizenship that values critical thought and reflective conscience as sources of normativity and that echoes a kind of 'Socratic citizenship' of the sort advocated by Dana Villa in his book *Socratic Citizenship* (2001, pp.248-9): 'a genuinely critical conception of citizenship, one based not on the morally dubious foundations of shared values or absolute truths, but rather on scepticism, intellectual honesty and the will to avoid injustice'.

My question will therefore be where is the space, in our conception of citizens' participation, for reflective and critical thinking and also for the protection of moral integrity. We tend to identify 'good' citizenship with participation; but this should be qualified. Not all cases of abstention are apathy. Not all discussions are tolerant and positively accept dissent. I will show that deliberative models of democracy need to include a conception of moral individuality and integrity, based on critical thought and judgement. I will find elements for such a conception in some of the writings of Hannah Arendt as well as in a reinterpretation of John Rawls' famous 'original position' as an opportunity for critical thinking.

## Popular Sovereignty as Procedure

But let us start, first, with a fantasy...Imagine that this is France, 20 April 2002, the day preceding one of the major electoral consultations: the direct election of the French President. Instead of the citizens being as usual ill-informed, ill-prepared, slightly fascinated by the political 'funfair', but mostly cynical and irresponsible, imagine that France has developed a new electoral system wherein citizens are invited to participate in public deliberations with fellow-citizens, politicians, journalists, experts, *et cetera*, on 'Deliberation Day' a week before casting their ballot (Ackerman and Fishkin, 2002). Imagine also, that this is not a new practice, but a 'new tradition', not a one-day event, but one actively prepared by public debates all over the country at local and national levels, over a long period of time. Imagine that France has become the land of an active deliberative democracy...

We have good reasons to believe that the citizens will be in a much better position to vote, having gained access to new information and to new arguments that they were not previously aware of. They will understand their civic duty as a public and morally significant gesture, as having the ability to enhance, blight, or harm other people's lives. They will cease thinking that this is mostly a question of mere preferences, of taste even. We would have moved from a conception of democracy as consumer-preferences-driven to the recognition of its strong normative content.

The ideal of deliberative democracy, which has dominated most theoretical and practical debates on political and social alienation in liberal democracies for the last decade, is obviously very attractive. 'Deliberation is, at different levels of government and in various political contexts, the most legitimate way of resolving conflicts about social justice...the decision which results from the deliberation between free and equal citizens is the most defensible form of justification' (Gutmann and Thompson, 1996, p.343). Its obvious merits are that of combining 'strong' democracy with the protections of constitutional rights and liberties (Barber, 1984; Young, 2000). It shows how it may be possible to overcome both populism and elitism, the two plagues of contemporary democratic governments.

I will now examine in greater detail the claims made for the use of public deliberation to democratize political will-formation and decision-making processes, as well as to legitimize first principles of justice.

Let us draw a contrast with the most common form of democratic regime: representative or electoral democracy. Representative democracies consider negotiation among particular interests and voting as the main political process; but this is a long way from what democracy should be. The limitations of the representative model have been classically expressed by Jean-Jacques Rousseau: 'the English people believes itself to be free; it is gravely mistaken; it is free only during the election' (Rousseau, 1762, III.15, p.141). This competitive and elitist view of democracy has been famously developed by Joseph Schumpeter (1976, p.269) and is still relevant. It understands democracy as a method of government rather than a normative ideal. The development introduced by the deliberative model, in parallel with John Rawls's *Theory of Justice* (1971), has seemingly changed all this and put the normative ideal again at the forefront.

The first and most impressive claim is that, through public deliberation, citizens will be able to change their preferences in two directions. Epistemically, preferences thus become more 'informed', articulate and rational. Presenting our reasons in public may force us to change our outlook and to refine our arguments, for fear of not being understood or listened to. Listening to other people's views and information can enlarge our understanding of the problems at stake. We are on a learning curve.

Morally, citizens will progressively become more public-spirited. The obvious reason for this mechanism is the publicity condition. It acts as a sort of filter for openly self-centred views. It becomes quasi-impossible to express directly selfish interests in a public debate on the common good. The practice of public discussion creates then the 'moral point of view' suitable for finding the best answers and decisions.

Here, two trends separate. For the first one, illustrated by John Stuart Mill and Alexis de Tocqueville, electoral democracy remains a disastrous method of government and decision-making. But it has indirect benefits in the sense that the practice of public deliberation, though useless for making correct decisions, is beneficial in creating public-spirited individuals. For Habermas (1996, Postscript V), a similar indirect educative value is gained through the exercise of rights to discussion that change the use of our communicative freedoms and put them at the service of the public interest.

However, according to a second stronger 'epistemic' claim, deliberative processes are better, in the end, than mere negotiations for reaching the 'right' decision. The reason has been brilliantly explained in the famous Condorcet Jury Theorem. The chances of arriving at a satisfactory decision are greater when the people involved in the process are more numerous. 'If voters are better than chance on some yes/no question, then under majority rule the group will be virtually infallible on that question if only the group is not too small' (Estlund, 1999, p.185). Fairness and efficiency can cohere in leading us to the best results.

I will now leave these general issues to concentrate on one central claim presented more clearly by Habermas that public deliberations can generate the legitimacy of their outcomes if a democratic procedure is followed. 'The legitimacy of legislation is accounted for by a democratic procedure that secures the autonomy of citizens. Citizens are politically autonomous only if they can view themselves as the joint authors of the laws to which they are subject as individual addressees' (Habermas, 2002, p.71). In other words, it is the democratic process, the will-formation and decision-making processes themselves, which generate the legitimacy of the law and the legislative power.

Habermas's ambition here is quite remarkable. He is trying to overcome the traditional divide between on the one hand republicanism and popular sovereignty as the source of legitimacy, and on the other hand, liberal constitutionalism and the rule of law as the only standards of legitimate power and rule. He claims that: 'The democratic procedure for the production of law evidently forms the only post-metaphysical source of legitimacy...Consequently, a discursive or deliberative model replaces the social contract model' (Habermas, 1996, pp.478-9) The overt ambition of this project is to overcome the philosophy of the subject, present both in liberal and republican thinking, and to replace it with an inter-subjective paradigm, more fitting for a complex and decentred society. 'Deliberative politics remains a component of a complex society...that regards the political system neither as the peak nor the centre...but as just *one* action system among others' (Habermas, 2002, p.251).

One should note how far we have moved from the previous objectives of the deliberative model. We have reached a 'first' principle of legitimacy: '(D) Only those norms can claim validity that could meet with the acceptance of all concerned in practical discourse' (Habermas, 2002, p.41). The ambition is obviously similar but opposed to the Rawlsian project: 'Here the 'acceptance' (*Zustimmung*) achieved under conditions of rational discourse signifies an agreement (*Einverständnis*) motivated by epistemic reasons; it should not be understood as a contract (*Vereinbarung*) that is rationally motivated from the egocentric perspective of each participant' (Habermas, 2002, p.42). The agreement on first principles of justice is the outcome of practical discussions in ideal communicative conditions.

This outcome is based on the truth-value of moral norms, defined not through an independent standard, but through the rational and universal acceptability of the arguments presented. 'Whereas rational acceptability merely *points to* the truth of assertoric propositions, it makes a *constructive* contribution to the validity of moral norms' (Habermas, 2002, p.38). In other terms, the best we can expect from these debates is validity and legitimacy, not truth or justice. 'Discursive agreement justifies the claim that a norm is worthy of recognition and thereby itself contributes to the fulfillment of its conditions of validity' (Habermas, 2002, p.38).

Is rational agreement enough to overcome the difficulties of a correspondence-truth theory as a model for deontological validity? Here we must briefly introduce the main idea of communicative ethics. 'Since communicative processes and forms of life have certain structural features in common', we can suppose a basis for shared, even universal moral norms. We can 'rely on the "neutral" fact that each of us participates in *some* communicative form of life which is structured by linguistically mediated understanding' (Habermas, 2002, p.40). Does this not lead us to a contextualist view of the universality of norms? The difference between what is 'justified in our context' and what is 'justified in any context whatsoever' is overcome, thanks to 'a *weak idealization* of our argumentative processes...When we assert "$p$", and thereby claim truth for "$p$", we accept the obligation to defend "$p$" in argumentation – in full awareness of its fallibility – against all future objections' (Habermas, 2002, p.37).

The latter point raises an immediate objection. The very decision made by citizens to enter argumentative communication, not to remain at the basic level of daily clashes of life forms and conceptions of the good, is a precondition for this legitimization; but this decision needs to be justified. This leads to a sort of infinite regress. The unsatisfactory answer, at this stage, is that some conditions should be met to protect the 'weak idealization' already mentioned. These conditions are the following (Habermas, 2002, p.44):

1.  Publicity of the exchanges: no one should be prevented from entering the debate.
2.  Equality of communicative rights: all must have a fair and equal chance to participate.

3.  Truthfulness of the exchange: participants should be able to express what they really think.
4.  Absence of coercion and external or internal constraints: freedom of communication should be guaranteed.

The main objections I would raise against such an 'extended' version of the deliberative model are as follows:

First, the question of the citizens' *decision* to enter into argumentative procedures is never properly examined. Is it a regulative political *ideal*, a horizon for any democracy, or is it simply a *transcendental* necessary condition for any language game? Should we not presuppose an initial agreement whereas participants in these language games accept the normative responsibilities for their exchanges? The very decision citizens make to enter public deliberation under specific conditions of equality, fairness, and liberty has to be justified and explained, not simply posited. The 'moral point of view' is not an outcome, but a prerequisite for deliberative practices, which is embedded in a conception of moral individuality as capable of a sense of justice as well as a conception of the good.

Second, the hope that public deliberations will lead not only to equitable and effective decisions, but also to legitimacy and reconciliation within the polity, depends on factors external to the procedure itself. It is only *indirectly* that public deliberations will affect the political sphere and redirect the general will in the direction of justice and the common good. Communicative processes are not directly constitutive of the validity, the rightness of outcomes as they can always be distorted by external factors such as rhetoric and the tyranny of majorities.

Third, the main concern is with the source of normativity. If, as claimed by Habermas, justice is constituted by rational acceptability in specific conditions, there is no room left for a sense of injustice, for resistance and criticism of what is generally deemed to be rationally acceptable. 'Validity' is not a satisfactory category to describe the nature of political agreement. Such an agreement is of a more substantive nature. It is based on recognition of the fairness of the procedure assessed against a set of personal moral beliefs or 'considered judgements' (Rawls, 1995). It is the anti-individualist stance in Habermas's position, which seems to be at odds with his desire to restore dignity to citizenship and public engagement.

## The Ideal of Socratic Citizenship and the Limits of Deliberative Democracy

In order to suggest a more vivid formulation of my objections, I will now turn to a celebrated example: the paradox and enigma presented by Socrates, the lauded 'model' citizen, nevertheless condemned by the city whose very laws he still recognized.

On the one hand, Socrates is the model of the committed, public-spirited citizen. He is not only concerned with respect for the laws of Athens, but he wants to explain to his fellow-citizens why they are justified and should be obeyed. He is *par excellence* the practitioner of deliberative democracy. His use of *dialectics* is aimed at stimulating argumentative communication, energizing public consciousness, his appeal to *maïeutics* at changing citizens' preferences and outlooks. All this is in line with what I have described as the primary ambitions of the deliberative model. This aspect of Socrates, the citizen, has been well described by Hannah Arendt in various essays, especially, 'Philosophy and Politics', commented upon by Dana Villa (2001, pp.259-65). Contrary to the classical interpretation, Socrates for Arendt was never detached from the polity. On the contrary, he had a richer and more demanding vision of citizenship than most.

However, because of this exacting vision, Socrates seemed to be separated from the rest of his fellow citizens and his death sentence was not unexpected. Why so? Because of the tight connection he established between the welfare of the city and the individual's concern for his or her moral and intellectual integrity. He could not therefore accept the claim that the democratic deliberative process would necessarily produce the *right* result, no matter what the circumstances, as in Rousseau's 'general will' which is always right as long as it is general, not particular. In the name of Athens' moral welfare, he claimed the right to discuss popular sovereignty, to dissent and to retreat. But in contrast to Plato, he did not do that in the name of philosophers' superiority and access to truth beyond *doxai*. He belonged to the city, but in a critical, indirect, and reflective manner, one which sets the limits to any deliberative model of democracy.

Inspired by Socrates, but mostly by her observation of Eichmann in Jerusalem, Arendt (1984, pp.7-8) asks herself: 'Does our capacity to judge, to distinguish right from wrong depend on our capacity for thinking? Do an inability to think and the disastrous failure of what we call the voice of conscience coincide? Could the powers of thought as such, the practice of examining and reflecting, be such that they would condition us against evil?' Following Socrates' lesson, she sees intellectual and moral integrity as indissoluble, even if, in other texts, she worries about the dissolving effects of critical thinking upon the cohesive nature of the polity. This concern for truth and justice constitutes the other dimension of citizenship, besides participation in the search for the common good. 'Socrates wanted the city to be more truthful thanks to a liberation, a revelation of each citizen's truth...Dialectics do not destroy truth, but reveal *doxai*'s truthfulness...' (Arendt, 1990, p.81). In her insistence on the ability of each citizen to reach truth or justice through his/her own thought processes, she re-evaluates the primacy of deliberation and restores the tension we saw in Socrates' position.

Thus the 'moral point of view' is to be found neither in the deliberative process as such nor in the ethical life forms shared by the citizens, but in their critical examination, in the reflection on the dilemmas and tensions existing between both. It is only *indirectly* that public deliberation can lead to 'truth', when citizens cease to be under the pressures of the political *agon*, the necessities of urgency and decision, and can reflect. This is part of the answer to my second objection, that reflective thinking cannot take place directly within the public sphere, but affects it only *indirectly* (Villa, 2001, p.xii, p.262).

Another unexpected advocate of 'Socratic citizenship' would be John Rawls in both his conceptions of the person and of the 'original position' or the social contract. Let us look at the political conception of the person presented in *A Theory of Justice* (1971) and *Political Liberalism* (1996). Moral individuality for Rawls is divided between the personal, historical attachments and commitments that define it and the power to distance oneself from these commitments, the capacity for change. This has been misunderstood by communitarians such as Michael Sandel, as a 'disencumbered' view of the Self. My interpretation is that this internal division between the public and the non-public identities creates the potential for thinking and reflective participation.

The durable practice of civil and political liberties has created a new reality, a new relationship between the Self and its commitments. Far from being detached and uncommitted, available for anything or utterly indifferent, the modern democratic Self is deeply committed, but in a different way. The burden of freedom means that responsibility for choices, decisions rests on the Self and cannot be passed on to another: the community, religion, the State, or other groups. The fact that Rawls (1996, pp.31-2), in order to illustrate his view on freedom, chooses the example of Saul of Tarsus on the way to Damascus and to becoming Paul the Apostle, shows us the tragic dimension, the moral depth of this capacity to examine and change one's deepest commitments. I see the source of normativity in this deep intra-personal struggle, not as an outcome of public deliberations (Korsgaard, 1996, p.91).

It is in the intra-personal tensions experienced between one's public and non-public identities, the personal and the impersonal points of view, that thinking takes place, that negotiations and choices have to be made, not under the pressures of public/political debates. As Thomas Nagel (1991, p.14) says, 'In most people, the coexistence of the personal standpoint with the values derived from the initial judgement of the impersonal standpoint produces a division of the self'. This represents part of the answer to my first objection, that the decision to take part in the deliberative process is the result of intra-personal debates and is not explained by the process itself, for fear of a sophism of infinite regress.

Nowhere is this potential for thinking and resisting, for criticizing the laws of the city in a Socratic manner, clearer than in the device of the 'original position' in Rawls. The search for justice is both the search for a well-ordered society, but also for a well-ordered Self, one that has reached a new moral and political identity, where both personal interests and impartiality, the ability to think in the place of other people, are not reconciled, but ordered: the priority of the Just over the Good means the priority of liberty and responsibility over welfare and personal utility.

Both Habermas and Rawls see the Constitution, the choice of first principles of justice as the 'citizens' project' (Rawls, 1996, p.401). For Habermas, as I have shown, the Constitution has to be understood as an ongoing social process, 'open and unfinished', as an exercise of the citizens' political autonomy. It is the expression of popular sovereignty. For Rawls, too, the Constitution is an ongoing process as historically shown in the constitutive power of the people at certain stages of their history when the first principles have to be constantly revised and put in 'reflective equilibrium' with our considered convictions. But this is a personal, reflective process, not simply a social public one. The thought experiment, in the 'original position', has then to be included in some ways into the deliberative process as a source of validation and legitimacy. This is part of the answer to my third objection that justice cannot spring simply from deliberative processes.

My critique of deliberative democracy leads me to a variant of the theory. Preconditions are necessary to protect the free, unhindered and equal exercise of our right to political participation and public discussion. These preconditions are first principles, which regulate our search for the good, our collective survival. We have to decide, before we engage in problem solving exercises according to political will-formation and decision procedures, what these principles should be. The primacy of the agreement and of the choice expresses the primacy of reflection over public deliberation and argumentative practices. It is a result of thought and questioning in the Socratic sense, as commented upon by Arendt and rediscovered in Rawls. This is part of the answer to my second objection that the preconditions of a free and equal deliberative process have to be agreed upon before the process can start, in that sense they are procedure-independent.

## Conclusion

Deliberative democracy and the new institutions that should embody it represent a great chance for ending decades of political alienation and citizens' apathy, for overcoming both elitism and populism. But a space must be created, within its conception and practices, for moral individuality as the source of normativity, for reflective agreement and dissent, for scepticism and abstention. The newfound dignity of the public realm must not be bought at the cost of citizens' moral and intellectual integrity. My view is that, without the full recognition of the worth of the *'travail de la pensée'*, deliberative democracy runs a serious risk of providing only a non-critical defence of dialogical virtues, forgetting that the sources of normativity are to be found in moral individuality, dialogically constructed as I have suggested. But I recognize that the arguments in favour of such a conception of moral individuality as part of democratic citizenship should be provided, which is beyond the scope of this chapter (Audard, 2000).

## References

Ackerman, Bruce and Fishkin, James (2002), 'Deliberation Day', *The Journal of Political Philosophy*, vol.10, pp. 129-52.
Arendt, Hannah (1984), 'Thinking and Moral Considerations' *Social Research*, vol.51, no.3.
Arendt, Hannah (1990), 'Philosophy and Politics' *Social Research*, vol.57, no.1.
Audard, Catherine (2000), 'Citizenship and Moral Individuality', in Zdenek Suda and Jiří Musil (eds.), *The Meaning of Liberalism –East and West*, CEU Press, Prague, pp.29-46.
Barber, Benjamin (1984), *Strong Democracy*, University of California Press, Berkeley.
Bohman, James and Rehg, William (eds.) (1999), *Deliberative Democracy: Essays on Reason and Politics*, MIT Press, Cambridge.

Estlund, David (1999), 'Beyond Fairness and Deliberation', in Bohman and Rehg, 1999, pp.173-204.

Gutmann, Amy and Thompson, Dennis (1996), *Democracy and Disagreement*, Harvard University Press, Cambridge.

Habermas, Jürgen (1996), *Between Facts and Norms*, William Rehg (trans.), Polity Press, Cambridge (*Faktizität und Geltung*, Frankfurt, Suhrkamp, 1992).

Habermas, Jürgen (1999), 'Popular Sovereignty as Procedure', in Bohrman and Rehg, 1999, pp.35-65.

Habermas, Jürgen (2002), *The Inclusion of the Other*, James Bohman and Ciaran Cronin (trans.), Polity Press, Cambridge (*Die Einbeziehung des Anderen*, Frankfurt, Suhrkamp, 1996).

Korsgaard, Christine (1996), *The Sources of Normativity*, Cambridge University Press, New York.

Nagel, Thomas (1991), *Equality and Partiality*, Oxford University Press, Oxford.

Rawls, John (1971), *A Theory of Justice*, Belknap Press of Harvard University Press, Cambridge.

Rawls, John (1995), 'Reply to Habermas', *Journal of Philosophy*, vol. 92, in Rawls, 1996, pp.372-434.

Rawls, John (1996), *Political Liberalism*, 2nd edition, Columbia University Press, New York.

Rousseau, Jean Jacques (1762), *The Social Contract*, Maurice Cranston (trans.) (1968), Penguin Books, London.

Schumpeter, Joseph (1976), *Capitalism, Socialism and Democracy*, 5th edition, Allen and Unwin, London.

Villa, Dana (2001), *Socratic Citizenship*, Princeton University Press, Princeton.

Young, Iris Marion (2000), *Inclusion and Democracy*, Oxford University Press, Oxford.

# Chapter 8

# Liberalism, Identity, Minority Rights

## Alan Montefiore

The question that I address is that of the rights of those (more or less) non-liberal minority communities or sub-groups who have become recognizably established as such within the boundaries of a liberal democratic society. Modern liberal democracies are, I take it, societies that profess as one of their central values a respect for the freedom of autonomous individuals to live their own lives in whatever way may seem best to them, provided only that their choice does not unavoidably infringe on the autonomous free choices of other individuals, all of whom are taken to be, in this sense at least, equal to each other in the validity of their claims to such respect. However, liberals also typically see themselves as committed to a maximum toleration of diversity so far as the existence and dissonant customs of social sub-groups are concerned, provided only, once again, that the exercise of these customs does not unavoidably infringe on the equally cherished rights and customs of other groups, whether minority or majority. So the question is: can these two potentially conflicting commitments be rendered compatible? In other words, or more fundamentally no doubt, can a consistent liberal really make proper sense of the very idea of respect for groups as such? Is liberalism in the end a genuinely self-consistent position?

I shall here try to sketch an outline framework for a coherent liberal approach towards dealing with such a question. A coherent approach is *not* to be taken for a would-be theoretical formula somehow automatically applicable to all and every particular case; no serious moral or political (or even, indeed, legal) principle can dispense its possessor from the need for the unformulatable wisdom of practical judgment. In this chapter, I am concerned only to work out an appropriate framework within which to seek an answer to this particular question. In doing so I hope to be able to indicate something of the interlocking complexity of the conceptual web in which the different elements of this framework have their roots. I shall not attempt to justify this liberal framework as providing the only ultimately viable way of looking at the world; indeed, in the last resort, liberals have both to accept that their faith is none the worse for being just that – the faith by which they stand – and also that they have in the end to acknowledge certain limits to their individualism. After all, in seeking to live together, liberals too effectively constitute their own form of community.

In seeking to follow through the many ramifying threads of the different types of argument here involved, it would be only too easy to find oneself led into exceeding by far the limits of one mere chapter. For present purposes, therefore, I shall restrict myself to a set of connected affirmations, leaving out most of the infrastructure of what I take to be their supporting argument and making no attempt at a properly scholarly set of references to the surrounding literatures.[1]

Liberals of all persuasions, whether or not they are happy to use the word 'autonomous', can scarcely fail to agree that their liberalism, whatever else it may commit them to, commits them to respect for the right of individuals to live their own lives free from direction or interference by others. The question here, of course, is that of what exactly it may be for an individual to determine his or her own life in this way. To put it briefly and very roughly, we may say that individuals are following their own self-determined courses through life if whatever it is that causes or leads them to go this way rather than that derives from 'within their own selves' rather than from 'without'. Where and how to situate the line between this 'within' and 'without' – whether indeed any such line should be taken to exist in any clearly determinable sense – are notoriously contestable issues in the history of the on-going debates concerning the nature of the relations between causation and free will. It is not always noticed that in these debates the stakes for liberalism are very high. If there is nothing that might be identifiable as distinctively 'within', then it is hard to see what clear sense there might be to the very notion of an individual self-directing agent. If, on the contrary, one can properly talk of such an 'inner' source of at least relatively autonomous or self-determining choice, then it is this 'within', however exactly it may have been formed, that is to be thought of as constituting the core of each particular individual's capacity for autonomy or self-determination. In an earlier tradition, this alleged inner core would have been referred to as 'the real self'; in much more recent discourse it is more frequently referred to as that which constitutes *the very identity of the self*, that which characterizes each individual self as the particular self or individual that he or she is.[2]

To use the language of identity in this way has, as such, nothing to do with any sort of commitment to what is known as identity politics. What is going to be of crucial importance for liberals is the question of whether the constitution of this 'within', this 'real self' or this 'personal self-identity' is to be thought of as allowing for an in principle wholly unrestricted power of self-determination or whether such individual autonomy has to be recognized as subject to certain internal self-limitations – in particular the limitations stemming from the fact that all individual identities are at least in part (and whether the individual in question likes it or not) necessarily functions of the communities to which the individuals in question may properly be held to belong and of the roles which they may be thought to occupy in virtue of their community membership(s). This is one of the main questions that I shall try to confront.

Very often, of course, an enquiry about someone's identity is simply a (most probably practical) request to pick out one particular individual from among all others. In answer to such questions passports, identity cards, birth or death certificates may be offered as supporting evidence, or some quasi-biblical placing of an individual on some family map. Alternatively, the question may be one concerning membership of some relevant class to which, *qua* class, other particular individuals may also in principle belong. (In the case of classes which are by definition closed, the number of other possible members will of necessity be finite; more typically, however, this is either not, or at least not known to be, the case.) I myself, for example, may according to the context of enquiry be variously and correctly identified as, say, an Old Cliftonian, a philosopher, a Jew (brought up in the tradition of Reform Judaism), an Englishman, a Londoner both by origin and by present domicile, an opponent of anti-outsider nationalism of whatever sort it may be or, as indeed I sometimes am, as one of my grandfather's grandsons; and this is but a sample list of perfectly proper identifications.

However, although I may correctly be identified as belonging to any of these different classes, as indeed to many more, it does not follow (according to the normal usages of contemporary English-language discourse) that I should be prepared to 'identify myself with' all or any of them. This would depend on circumstances and on what was at stake. To acknowledge myself as belonging (de facto) to a given class of description is one thing, to 'identify myself' with that class is another. Still less can each and all of these descriptive or classificatory 'identifications as' be taken as necessarily forming any part of what today might very widely be referred to as my 'identity'. It is in this latter sense that the term appears in such expressions as, for example, 'national or cultural identity', 'identity crisis', 'sense of identity', and so on.

In his 'The Problem of Ego Identity', the psychoanalyst Erik Erikson (1956) explained:

> First a word about the term 'identity'. As far as I know Freud used it only once in a more than incidental way...when he tried to formulate his link to the Jewish people [and] spoke of an 'inner identity' which was less based on race or religion than on a common readiness to live in opposition and on a common freedom from prejudices which narrow the intellect [Freud, 1926]. Here the term 'identity' points to an individual's link with the unique values, fostered by a unique history, of his people...It is this identity of something in the individual's core with an essential aspect of a group's inner coherence which is under consideration here; for the young individual must learn to be most himself where he means most to others – those others, to be sure, who have come to mean most to him. The term 'identity' expresses such a mutual relation in that it connotes both a persistent sameness within oneself (self-sameness) and a persistent sharing of some kind of essential character with others...
>
> At one time, [the term 'identity'] will appear to refer to a conscious sense of individual identity; at another to an unconscious striving for a continuity of personal character; at a third, as a criterion for the silent doings of ego synthesis; and, finally, as a maintenance of an inner solidarity with a group's ideals and identity...

This passage is interesting in the way that it points to many of the themes and forces that find expression in the discourses of identity to-day. The use of this language is thus both highly charged and persistently elusive.

Another widely influential writer with a long-standing concern for questions of personal, cultural, and national identity is Charles Taylor. Near the beginning of *Sources of the Self*, he has the following significant passage: 'To know who I am is a species of knowing where I stand. My identity is defined by the commitments and identifications which provide the frame or horizon within which I can try to determine from case to case what is good or valuable, or what ought to be done, or what I endorse or oppose. In other words it is the horizon within which I am capable of taking a stand' (Taylor, 1989, p.27).[3]

In all this, Taylor is working against the background of his elaboration of a theme proposed by Harry Frankfurt.[4] Taylor himself distinguishes between ordinary or normal evaluative assessments and that which he characterizes as radical evaluation. When engaged in radical evaluation, one reviews one's whole existing range of first-order evaluations and, comparing them to other possible constellations of values, makes a deep existential choice between them. In so doing one determines or re-determines one's own self-identity. Taking these two lines of argument together, then, one may say that, for Taylor, individuals, as in principle always potential radical evaluators, are by the same token always in principle possessed both of the possibility of and the responsibility for deciding where to take their own stand as to whom they identify with, of which group they see their own membership as being – for better or for worse – inescapable.[5] After all, a group may perfectly well be constituted by a number of 'essentially' autonomous individuals coming together to constitute it in the knowledge that 'united they stand' while separately they are each of them in danger of falling. (This makes, of course, for a very different sort of group from one the members of which see their very self-identity as being ineluctably bound to their sense of themselves as given members of that group and as bearers of its traditions.)

Liberals, then, will naturally tend to regard (and in practice to treat) individuals as capable of deciding, and entitled to decide, for themselves whether to join or to continue in membership of any given group and to be bound by its conditions, that is, as free to determine their own self-identities. Any other attitude would be a betrayal of their own liberal principles. Of course, when the issue is one of the purely de facto membership of an essentially descriptive class, it will usually make no sense to take this as being open to individual choice. It might be nice if, for example, I could effectively choose no longer to belong to the class of those who, in a given year, have already long passed the statutory age of retirement; but that I do belong to this class is something which I simply have to accept. Similarly, it would make no truth-respecting sense for me to deny my given membership of the branch of the Montefiore family into which I was born.

At the same time, seen from a properly liberal point of view, I remain entirely free to determine for myself whether or not to assume any, all, or none of the responsibilities and obligations that may be or have been thought by anyone else to go with, even to form part of, such an indisputably de facto family membership; that is to say, in Erikson's terms, to determine whether or not such values form any part of my own 'core identity'. And if the 'more traditional' family members seek to impose on me the observance of any of these obligations against my manifest will, strict liberals will, as a matter of principle, defend my right to determine my own stance in the matter – even if they themselves happen personally to disapprove of where I choose to take my stand.

So what might or should be the liberal attitude towards the rights of minority groups, families, or wider associations with their own traditional claims upon their own members that find themselves settled within the overall framework of a strictly liberal democratic state? If liberalism is a doctrine of maximum toleration of diversity so far as the existence and customs of social sub-groups are concerned, provided only that the exercise of these customs does not unavoidably infringe on the equally cherished rights and customs of others, everything will turn on exactly whom, for these purposes, is to be counted as 'other' to the social sub-group in question. In practice many of the most familiar problems arise when members of a younger generation, in particular the women, of a recently immigrant or hitherto relatively self-contained community start to demand freedoms of choice incompatible with the standing conditions of what the group as a an established whole takes to be its continuing identity. Those – typically but not necessarily the older and/or male members of the group – who are most profoundly attached to the community's traditional forms of identity may demand the right, whether implicitly or explicitly, to deal with what they see as offences by younger members of their own community in their own (often deeply unliberal) traditional ways.

To think of membership-identity as subject to the 'radically evaluative' self-determination of individuals, however, carries with it an acknowledgement of their right to take their own autonomous stand as one of a realignment of their identities by way of disentangling themselves from certain aspects of group membership with its traditional values and ties; and this independently of whether or not that stand meets with the approval of their elders, husbands, brothers, or sons. From this point of view, nobody – or at any rate no adult of right mind – is to be held to belong to a network of obligations and responsibilities if they have not accepted or endorsed it for themselves. Thus, those who 'radically' reject the norms and obligations of a given group in effect establish their identity as standing (at least partially) outside the group in question. From which it would follow - always from this liberal point of view – that they must figure among those others whose 'cherished rights and customs' are to be protected from infringement by the exercise of the customs of the social sub-group from which they have, as it were, autonomously (at least partially) dis-identified themselves.

Thus the liberal's characteristic commitment to respect diversity and the rights of minorities established within a liberal political domain cannot extend to recognition of any right, which a minority might claim, to determine who should be identified as belonging among its members in cases where the individual or individuals concerned explicitly identify themselves otherwise. As a matter of purely descriptive identification, there may be no disputing the fact that a given individual was born into a Jewish, or Muslim, or Catholic family, as the case may be; but it remains up to individuals, as citizen members of a liberal state, to decide whether, so far as their own values are concerned, to identify themselves with their given family or not and, in Taylor's terms, whether or not to take their stands with and alongside them.[6]

All this presupposes, of course, that the individual in question is in a position to take such radically evaluative decisions as amount to an establishment or re-establishment of his or her own personal identity; and this raises the familiar problem of knowing at what age or in the light of what sort of personality or mental fitness assessment people may properly be judged to be responsibly and autonomously capable of making such fundamental choices. Some very thoroughgoing liberals have famously maintained that even very young children should be given the responsibility of deciding whether or not to submit themselves to educational procedures; but whatever the pros and cons of treating them in this way may be – something which they will not of course have chosen for themselves, to do so is to treat them as already possessed of a primary liberal identity rather than that of a future full member of a less individualistic, traditional, perhaps more authoritarian society. Indeed, if offered the choice of whether to choose for themselves or to have someone else choose for them, many people, and not only children, might well opt for the latter alternative – even supposing that they would know what to do with such a meta-choice if offered it.

What all this shows, if my arguments are correct, is that from a strictly liberal perspective there is, in general, a consistent way of articulating the manner in which to address the problems presented by the existence within an overall liberal society of a non-liberal minority sub-group with a proper claim to respect for its rights as a group with its own group identity. This does not mean, however, that, over and above the difficulties posed by issues of contentious interpretation on one margin or another, there might not be circumstances in which liberals might find very good practical reasons for going slow in putting these particular principles into practice. Faced with the different forms of reluctance, resentment, and resistance with which a non-liberal minority might confront them, it might sometimes even seem more sensible and, in the long run, more in accord with the full range of their own (no doubt not entirely mutually self-consistent) principles, to allow the minority group a longer period of adaptation to the norms of the host society, even at the cost of refraining from intervention on behalf of those in the immediately current generation who would wish to dis-identify themselves from full membership of the minority group into which they had been born. All such matters inevitably call for difficult and often painful judgment. There are also certain theoretically limiting considerations to be taken into account.

First, however, it is worth stressing the way in which a number of prima facie different conceptual elements in the overall liberal perspective here come together in support of each other. We started by noting the pervasive importance of the role played by the contemporary discourses of membership and identity in debates concerning the rights of (traditionally non-liberal) minorities who find themselves embedded within some wider liberal society. Already it was clear how closely (if imprecisely) Erikson's conception of identity was tied to that of an individual self. With Taylor, the concept is even more clearly associated with those of autonomy, self-determination and their conceptual cousins. Again, while individuals' personalities, consciousness and general ways of relating to the world are to an important extent functions of the social, cultural, and linguistic contexts within which they grow up and evolve, it is a conceptual truth that they can only envisage the possibility of taking their own (possibly radical) evaluative stands in relation to their contexts of origin (or, if it comes to that, to those of their current insertion) in so far as they have learnt to operate with appropriate evaluative concepts – that is to say, concepts that obey or incorporate some version of the principle that has found one of its most famous (if not most strictly accurate) expressions in the slogan 'No "ought" from an "is."' To hold otherwise is to accept that there may be facts – of one's birth, of one's nationality, concerning the nature of the groups (and in particular the family) to which one belongs as a matter of descriptive classification, of one incontrovertible sort or another from which certain normative judgments, whether of value, obligation or duty, follow as a matter of conceptual entailment. In general, of course, this is not so much a matter of explicit doctrine as one of presuppositions written deep into the conceptual bases of one's language and thought. Moreover, for those for whom this is indeed a presupposition of their evaluative vocabulary, it functions not only as a necessary condition of their own evaluative autonomy, but also, like it or not, as a sufficient one; for them, as Richard Hare for one repeatedly insisted, there is in the end no logically coherent escape from personal evaluative responsibility.

This assumption of 'the autonomy of values' is equally a necessary, and probably also a sufficient, condition of conceiving of groups as consisting in nothing more than the set of complex relations holding between the distinct and in principle autonomous individuals who happen to compose them. If, on the contrary, values could in theory be unconditionally determined by facts, the individual members of a group might in principle be so marked by their membership of it as to continue to belong to its network of collective obligations and responsibilities simply by virtue of the fact of their membership roles and identities, whatever their own 'merely' personal preferences in the matter might be. They would be in no conceptual position even to conceive of themselves as protesting radical evaluators.

As has often been remarked, the principle of 'no "ought" from an "is"' – whatever the imprecision of its various formulations – is of strikingly individualist import. Facts confront individuals as fundamentally resistant to their preferences or powers of choice; if, therefore, it were possible validly to derive value-judgments from statements of fact (or if values, in particular moral values, could themselves plausibly be construed as constituting a special class of facts), individuals would be similarly constrained in their recognition of values and obligations. But if, whatever the facts that they are constrained to recognize, they are left necessarily free to determine their own evaluative attitude towards them, then, and then only, are they ineluctably free to determine their own values, commitments and self-identity.[7]

However, it goes without saying, the liberal view of these matters is not the only one in town – nor, as I should join many others in arguing, can it claim to be entirely coherent when pushed to unqualified limits. Even a liberal may have to admit that there is something one-sided in a view of personal identity (and *pari passu* of group membership) that focuses exclusively on individuals' own presumed power of determining their own identities. Indeed, when Erikson explained how he came to introduce the term, he insisted that the formation of what he called the youth's identity depended on what he made of his relations with others, on how he experienced himself as seen in their eyes and on the identifications that he made with his relevant membership groups. In addition to the various psychological and psychoanalytic accounts that are proposed of the social constitution of self-identity, there are also certain philosophical considerations which, though they may inevitably remain open to much detailed dispute, are, if correct, of indisputable relevance.

The most fundamental of these derive from the well-known anti-private language argument. For present purposes let it be taken for granted that, in some version or another, this argument can be successfully made out. If to learn a language is indeed to take upon oneself the basic 'public' commitments of the rules governing the use of its vocabulary and the formation of its concepts, it is clear that these are interpersonal normative commitments that have to be discovered, learnt, recognized, and respected as so many facts concerning the necessary constitutive conditions of reflective thought and communication. Once one has learnt a language, there will, of course, always remain a certain margin of free play for creative innovation, but only on the basis of what has already been learnt and accepted. Given the intimate dependence of the capacity for self-identification, (as, indeed, for the identification of anyone or anything else), on the terms and nature of the language through which the capacity is acquired, this interplay between a necessary respect for rules as given and the room that such rules may allow for their creative revision or extension, may well be taken to represent a roughly parallel interplay between what has to be taken as given and what is open for creative self-redefinition in respect of one's identity itself.

In fact, the very versatility and persuasive power of the language (or languages) of identity owes much to the way in which it manages to reflect so many deep but also deeply conflicting pulls and constraints. On the one hand there are the pulls towards individual autonomy and everything that goes (conceptually) with it; but on the other hand, there are in the end always the limiting constraints of the rules of reciprocal intelligibility and recognizability in the eyes of significant others, as well as the practical pressures of a given situation. It seems to me that no amount of argument can succeed, in our present discursive situation at any rate, in finally settling such questions, be they of theory or of practice, in favor of confining our thinking about identity and membership within the limits of either the pulls or the constraints. In the end each case must come down to some essentially contestable matter of judgement and an always challengeable decision as to where to take one's stand – which is, of course, a basically autonomist, liberal individualist conclusion to come to. But how, if the whole drift of my arguments are approximately correct, could it be otherwise? Always acknowledging, of course, the historically and personally variable limits within which any such decision must always admit itself to be constrained...

When faced, therefore, with the challenges of having to confront the problems posed by the existence within their societies of minority communities of stubbornly illiberal traditions, liberals have first and foremost to remember that such communities are, like any others, made up in the end out of the inter-relationships of individuals each with their own individual identities – however closely similar these may perhaps be to each other. It is clear that the dominant discourse of any such traditionally non-liberal group may allow no room for the operation of any such thorough-going distinction between facts and values as may make it impossible to derive value-judgments from any statement or ensemble of statements of fact with logically compelling force. If it did make such allowance, the group would already possess within the conceptual resources of its own discourse the full potential for its own self-transformation into a liberal society of autonomous individuals – a potential which it would be up to liberals of the wider society to exploit in cases of what they deemed to be needed. If, however, it makes no such allowance, then it is equally clear that its inability to recognize any such distinction, being, as it would be, such a fundamental feature of its discursive resources, must have played a determining structural part in the formation of the identities (the basic self-perceptions) of a preponderant proportion of its existing membership. Were this not the case, they would not so relate to themselves and to each other as together to make up the tradition-bound community of which they are its members.

Liberals may perceive any failure to acknowledge the basic distinction between facts and values and the logically sovereign freedom of each individual to come – in the face of whatever the facts may be – to his or her own personal value conclusions as a simple failure to recognize what should be evident to anyone of natural intellect and good faith. But what they have to remember is that this 'failure' or inability is nevertheless a controlling feature of the identity-formations of those still tradition-dominated members of the minority communities with which they have to deal. And since from their own liberal point of view they are committed to regard those tradition-minded members also, however conceptually misguided they may be, as individuals in principle fully capable of autonomous self-direction, they are equally committed to respect their life-commitments as they see them and to weigh their claims against those whom they may see as their bounden fellow community members, but who may themselves see themselves as radically free to dissent and in crucial respects to secede.

The challenge of having to weigh the competing claims of one set of individuals against those of another is, however, a constant of any liberal's moral or political experience of the world. Here, once again, they will have to rely on their best judgment – a judgment that has always to be acknowledged as in principle fallible and open to revision. As Kant put it in the section immediately preceding the Schematism in his Critique of Pure Reason, 'General logic contains, and can contain, no rules for judgment...Though understanding is capable of being instructed, judgment is a peculiar talent which can be practiced only, and cannot be taught...Examples are the go-cart of judgment; and those who are lacking in the natural talent can never dispense with them' (Kant, 1929, pp.177-8).

## PostScript: the Views of Joseph Raz

Though I have abstained from any attempt at a systematic trawl through the contemporary literature on the problem of how liberals might, most consistently with their own principles, set out to deal with the problems posed by the existence of non-liberal minority communities within an overall majority liberal society, it may help to clarify the suggestions in this chapter to set them alongside David McCabe's discussion of Joseph Raz's treatment of the issue, as he develops it in the final section of his recent paper 'Joseph Raz and the Contextual Argument for

Liberal Perfectionism'(2001). As McCabe puts it, 'Raz endorses in principle the "gradual transformation" of [non-liberal] communities on the grounds that their members require autonomy to prosper in the goals that characterize liberal society'(McCabe, 2001, p.521). This suggests strongly that, as McCabe quotes Raz, 'The perfectionist principles espoused in this book suggest that people are justified in taking action to assimilate the minority group, at the cost of letting its culture die or at least be considerably changed by absorption'(McCabe, 2001, p.520; Raz, 1986, p.424). But McCabe also quotes Raz's later affirmation that 'cultures cannot just be compared in terms of relative value [because, as Raz says] none of them can be judged superior to the others' (McCabe, 2001, p.520; Raz, 1994, p.183). This can only mean, McCabe goes on to argue, that 'Raz regards the non-liberal culture as inferior not intrinsically, but only insofar as it exists within a liberal society whose social forms reflect the prominence of autonomy. Raz's position appears to be that such a community, in not preparing its members for the goals they will face in liberal society, significantly damages their prospects for well-being'(McCabe, 2001, p.521).

If this is indeed Raz's position, it would seem to present a more immediately thoroughgoing threat to the survival of such traditionalist non-liberals as may find themselves embedded within an overall majority liberal social environment than would the attitudes advocated in this chapter. It is true that the transformation of non-liberal minority societies that Raz appears to recommend is 'only' a gradual one and true also that he recognizes that 'this is easier said than done' (McCabe, 2001, p.520). It is nevertheless difficult to see how a deliberate policy of even gradual transformation can be squared with the view expressed in Raz's later view (1994, p.174) that 'Multiculturalism requires a political society to recognize the equal standing of all the stable and viable cultural communities existing in that society...There is no room for talk of a minority problem or of a majority tolerating the minorities'. No doubt, my own suggestions also carry with it the threat – or promise? – of such an eventual transformation; but in this case the threat is not based on any real or alleged failure of non-liberal societies to prepare their members to maximize the chances of living a good and fulfilling life that are ipso facto open to their contemporaries in the wider liberal society to which they all belong. It is based rather on the commitment, incumbent on that wider liberal society, to support those of its individual members who, being members also of the narrower non-liberal society contained within it, wish to loosen their ties of identity with it in their own autonomously chosen respects and to their own autonomously chosen extent.

There are a number of reasons why a policy based on this, as I should argue, fundamental commitment on the part of liberal society to respect the individual autonomy of all its own members, whatever their social background, may present less of an immediate or potentially wholesale threat to the continuing stability of traditional minority sub-groups than one aiming at their transformation, however gradual, let alone at their eventual absorption, whether their individual members notice or chafe at the limitations imposed on their autonomy or not. Most importantly of all perhaps, the minority community retains the possibility – and the responsibility – of seeing to it that, as the generations succeed each other, all its members remain unconditionally satisfied that the traditional patterns of their lives provide them with such a full sense of fulfillment that they feel no overriding need to abandon them. So long as it does this, perhaps but not necessarily by somewhat modifying these patterns in view of the nature of their overall situation within the institutions of liberal society, this wider society will have no call to intervene.

In particular, only the most fanatical – and one might say the most illiberal of liberals – are going to insist on supporting such movements of apparent dissent as the very youngest members of the minority group may be taken to manifest – let us say, to draw a rapid and no doubt somewhat arbitrary line, those of primary school age. We have already noted that the most sensitive problems may be expected to present themselves first in the case of their older children and to be at their most acute during the periods of adolescence and young adulthood; and also, of course, in relation to the freedoms allowed or denied to their women members, especially, no doubt, the younger ones. I have already made the point that there is no quick or ready-made answer to the question of when and which such individual persons are properly to be judged to be autonomous and self-responsible agents in their own right. It is indeed certain that there may arise, perhaps even numerous, cases where liberal intervention on their behalf may lead to the serious destabilization of the traditional educational and family institutional patterns of a minority community; and that the knock-on effects of this destabilization may lead, more or less gradually or more or less rapidly as the case may be, to an all pervasive transformation of the minority community's traditional sense of identity. But, if the minority community is strong enough and sufficiently resourceful in sustaining a sense of satisfied and fulfilled well-being in the great majority of its own individual members, and if it shows itself capable of allowing its unsatisfied minority of nevertheless indisputably autonomous and self-responsible members to secede without undue recrimination or persecution, then liberal society should have no overriding reason to intervene.[8] Liberal tolerance and, beyond 'mere' tolerance, respect for cultural diversity may be maintained and exercised without that sense of inner tension and always potential inconsistency that anti-liberals are so ready to exploit in their efforts to undermine the liberal conscience.

Nevertheless, it has always to be repeated, a framework of guiding principles can never function as if it were an algorithm for the production of decisions in border line cases. No one, least of all liberals, should ever regard themselves as dispensed from the hard need to exercise hard and often controversial judgement.

## Notes

1    The Postscript will, however, contain a comparison between my own attempt at confronting this problem and what I take to be the line taken by Joseph Raz towards it. It will thus constitute one fairly substantial exception to my general policy of unscholarly abstinence.

2    To quote David Herman (2001, p.59): 'The key word here is "identity": how we construct an image of ourselves as individuals and as groups, and how damaging these identities can be for ourselves and for others'.

3    Taylor may here be understood as seeking both to articulate and to understand the origins of a sense of identity according to which people – both individuals and, indeed, groups – are to be respected as having a large share of more or less autonomous responsibility for the acceptance or re-making of their own identity and hence for the obligations to which their self-identifications may commit them.

4    This "hierarchical account of identity" was introduced by Frankfurt (1971) and modified in an attempt (Frankfurt, 1987) to meet some of the difficulties involved in his original account of the hierarchy. Jan Bransen (1996) takes the discussion further by presenting the argument, significantly enough, as turning essentially upon the appropriate choice of prepositions to go with the key terms: 'identification as' rather than 'identification with' and 'alternatives of' rather than 'alternatives for oneself'.

5    Bransen (1996) also remarks on the crucial ambiguity of the term 'determination' as it hovers between 'discovery' and 'resolve' or' decision', between 'laying bare' and 'laying down', and insists on retaining the ambiguity, rather than attempting to resolve it, as deeply reflective of the human condition.

6    One might very reasonably ask whether Taylor himself is – or has always been – altogether consistent in such matters.

7    Whether one experiences the possibility of making an always clear distinction between the factual and the normative as a personal liberation or rather, like Alasdair MacIntyre perhaps, as a disenchantment or impoverishment of the world, is, of course, another matter.

8    Here negotiations may obviously be called for between the minority community and the wider liberal society within which it finds itself as to the criteria by which any individual's capacity for autonomy and self-responsibility are properly to be judged.

# References

Bransen, Jan (1996), 'Identification and the idea of an Alternative of Oneself', *European Journal of Philosophy*, vol.4, pp.1-16.

Erikson, Erik (1956), 'The Problem of Ego Identity', *The Journal of the American Psychoanalytic Association*, no.4, pp.56-121.

Frankfurt, Harry (1971), 'Freedom of the Will and the Concept of a Person', *Journal of Philosophy*, vol.68, pp.5-20

Frankfurt, Harry (1987), 'Identification and Wholeheartedness', in Ferdinand Schoeman (ed.), *Responsibility, Character and the Emotions*, Cambridge University Press, Cambridge, pp.159-76).

Freud, Sigmund (1926), Address to the Members of B'nai B'rith.

Herman, David (2001), 'Jews, Jung and a new Politics', *The Jewish Quarterly*, no.182, pp.55-9.

Kant, Immanuel (1929), *Critique of Pure Reason*, Norman Kemp Smith (trans.), St. Martin's Press, New York.

McCabe, David (2001), 'Joseph Raz and the Contextual Argument for Liberal Perfectionism', *Ethics*, vol .111, pp. 519-22.

Raz, Joseph (1986), *The Morality of Freedom*, Clarendon Press, Oxford.

Raz, Joseph (1994), 'Multiculturalism', in *Ethics in the Public Domain*, Clarendon Press, Oxford.

Taylor, Charles (1989), *Sources of the Self: the Making of the Modern Identity*, Harvard University Press, Cambridge.

# Chapter 9

# Models of Multicultural Citizenship: Comparing Asia and the West

## Will Kymlicka

Several countries in Asia and the Pacific confront difficult challenges of ethnic conflict. Afghanistan, Pakistan, India, Burma, Sri Lanka, Indonesia, Philippines, Papua New-Guinea, and Fiji have all faced serious bouts of ethnic violence, even all-out civil war. In other countries, such as China or Malaysia, ethnic violence is seen as a serious possibility that can only be avoided by careful state control. The causes of these conflicts are disputed. Some scholars blame the lack of democracy; others argue that democratization is itself a major cause of ethnic conflict (Bell, 2002; Liddle, 1997; Ganguly, 1997; Wimmer and Schetter, 2002; Snyder, 2000). Proposals for resolving these conflicts are also contested. For some, the best hope lies in Western-style models of multiculturalism and minority rights. For others, these models are inappropriate, and the solution must instead be found in local models of ethnic accommodation.

This chapter will examine the possible relevance of Western models. Western ideas of multiculturalism and minority rights are becoming influential within the region, partly as a result of the increasing linkages between local minority groups/NGOs and larger international networks. Moreover, several international organizations – such as the United Nations, the World Bank, and the International Labour Organization – have started to formulate international declarations of minority and indigenous rights that Asian countries are expected to comply with. Such international declarations have typically been promoted by Western countries, often adopted over the resistance of countries in Asia, Africa, or Eastern Europe, and have sometimes been seen as embodying distinctly Western ideas of multiculturalism.

So there are various forces at work advocating the adoption of Western models of minority rights in Asia. It is too early to tell how widely such models will be adopted, or whether they would work in practice; but we can begin to identify some of the challenges involved. I will begin by outlining what I take to be the main features of 'Western' models of minority rights, and their strengths and limitations (sections 1-2). I will then turn to the Asian context, to consider some of the obstacles to the adoption of Western models, and the alternatives to them (sections 3-5).

## 1. Western Trends Regarding Ethnocultural Diversity

What do we mean by Western models of multiculturalism and minority rights? There have been dramatic changes in the way Western democracies deal with ethnocultural diversity in the last 30-40 years. I will focus on four important trends: *(a) minority nationalisms*; *(b) indigenous peoples*; *(c) immigrant groups*; and *(d) Metics.*[1]

The first trend concerns the treatment of substate/minority nationalisms, such as the Québécois in Canada, the Scots and Welsh in Britain, the Catalans and Basques in Spain, the Flemish in Belgium, the German-speaking minority in the South Tyrol in Italy, and Puerto Rico in the United States. In these cases, we find a regionally-concentrated group that conceives of itself as a nation within a larger state, and mobilizes behind nationalist political parties to achieve recognition of its nationhood, either as an independent state or through territorial autonomy within the larger state. In the past, all these countries attempted to suppress these forms of substate nationalism. To have a regional group with a sense of distinct nationhood was seen as a threat to the state. Various efforts were made to erode this sense of distinct nationhood, including restricting minority language rights, abolishing traditional forms of regional self-government, and encouraging members of the dominant group to settle in the minority group's traditional territory so that the minority becomes outnumbered even in its traditional territory.

However, there has been a dramatic reversal in the way Western countries deal with substate nationalisms. Today, all the countries I have just mentioned accept the principle that these substate national identities will endure into the indefinite future, and that their sense of nationhood and nationalist aspirations must be accommodated. This accommodation has typically taken the form of what we can call 'multination federalism': that is, creating a federal or quasi-federal subunit in which the minority group forms a local majority, and so can exercise self-government. Moreover, the group's language is typically recognized as an official state language, at least within their federal subunit, and perhaps throughout the country as a whole.

At the beginning of the twentieth century, only Switzerland and Canada had adopted this combination of territorial autonomy and official language status for substate national groups. Since then, virtually all Western democracies that contain sizeable substate nationalist movements have moved in this direction. The list includes the adoption of autonomy for the Swedish-speaking Aland Islands in Finland after the First World War, autonomy for South Tyrol and Puerto Rico after the Second World War, federal autonomy for Catalonia and the Basque Country in Spain in the 1970s, for Flanders in the 1980s, and most recently for Scotland and Wales in the 1990s. Amongst the Western democracies with a sizeable national minority, only France is an exception to this trend, although legislation has been adopted to grant autonomy to its main substate nationalist group in Corsica.

The second trend concerns the treatment of indigenous peoples, such as the Indians and Inuit in Canada, the Aboriginal peoples of Australia, the Maori of New

Zealand, the Sami of Scandinavia, the Inuit of Greenland, and Indian tribes in the United States. In the past, all these countries expected that indigenous peoples would eventually disappear as distinct communities, as a result of dying out, inter-marriage, or assimilation. Various policies were adopted to speed up this process: stripping them of their lands, restricting the practice of their traditional culture, language and religion, and undermining their institutions of self-government.

However, there has been a dramatic change starting in the early 1970s. Today, all the countries I just mentioned accept the principle that indigenous peoples will exist into the indefinite future as distinct societies within the larger country, and that they must have the land claims, cultural rights and self-government rights needed to sustain themselves as distinct societies. This is reflected in the constitutional affirmation of Aboriginal rights in the 1982 Canadian constitution, along with the land claims commission; the revival of treaty rights through the Treaty of Waitangi in New Zealand; the recognition of land rights for Aboriginal Australians in the *Mabo* decision; the creation of the Sami Parliament in Scandinavia, the evolution of 'Home Rule' for the Inuit of Greenland; and the laws upholding self-determination rights for American Indian tribes. In all these countries, a gradual decolonization is taking place, as indigenous peoples regain their lands, customary law, and self-government.

A third trend concerns the treatment of immigrant groups, that is, groups formed by the decision of individuals and families to leave their original homeland and emigrate to another society, often leaving their friends and relatives behind. It is essential to distinguish two categories of immigrants – those who have the right to become citizens, and those who do not. I will use the term 'immigrant group' only for the former case, and will discuss the latter case, which I will call 'metics', below. Immigrants, then, are people who arrive under an immigration policy which gives them the right to become citizens after a relatively short period of time – say, 3-5 years – subject only to minimal conditions (for example, learning the official language, knowing something about the country's history and political institutions). This has been the traditional policy governing immigration in the four major Western 'countries of immigration' – United States, Canada, Australia, and New Zealand.

In the past, these four countries had an assimilationist approach to immigration. Immigrants were expected to assimilate to the pre-existing society, with the hope that they would eventually become indistinguishable from native-born citizens in their speech, dress, and way of life generally. Any groups that were seen as incapable of this sort of cultural assimilation were prohibited from emigrating in the first place, or from becoming citizens. This was reflected in laws that excluded Africans and Asians from entering these countries for much of the twentieth century, or from naturalizing.

However, since the late 1960s, there have been two dramatic changes: first, the adoption of race-neutral admissions criteria, so that immigrants to these countries are increasingly from non-European (and often non-Christian) societies. Second, the adoption of a more 'multicultural' conception of integration, which expects that many immigrants will visibly and proudly express their ethnic identity, and which accepts an obligation on the part of public institutions to accommodate these ethnic identities. These changes have occurred in all the traditional countries of immigration, although there are important differences in how official the shift to multiculturalism has been. In Canada, Australia, and New Zealand this shift was marked by the formal declaration of a multiculturalism policy by the central government. Even in the United States, which does not have an official policy of multiculturalism at the federal level, we find a broad range of multiculturalism policies at lower levels of government, such as states or cities.

The fourth trend concerns those migrants who are not admitted as permanent residents and future citizens. This is a heterogenous category, including people who enter a country illegally (e.g., North Africans in Italy), or as asylum-seekers (e.g., Kosovars in Switzerland), or as students or 'guest-workers' who have overstayed their initial visa (e.g. Turks in Germany). When they entered the country, these people were not conceived of as future citizens, or even as long-term residents, and would not have been allowed to enter if they were seen as permanent residents and future citizens. However, despite the official rules, they have settled permanently. In principle, some face the threat of deportation if they are detected by the authorities, or if they are convicted of a crime. But they nonetheless form sizeable communities, engage in some form of employment, legal or illegal, and may marry and form a family. Borrowing a term from Ancient Greece, Walzer (1983) calls these groups 'metics' – long-term residents who are nonetheless excluded from the polis. Since metics face enormous obstacles to integration – legal, political, economic, social, and psychological – they tend to exist at the margins of the larger society.

The most basic claim of metics is to regularize their status as permanent residents, and to gain access to citizenship. They want, in effect, to follow the immigrant path to integration into the mainstream society, even though they were not initially admitted as immigrants. In the past, Western democracies have responded to this demand for access to citizenship in different ways. Some countries, particularly traditional immigrant countries, have grudgingly accepted these demands. Other countries, particularly those which do not think of themselves as immigrant countries, have resisted these demands, and hoped that metics will leave the country.

This approach is increasingly recognized as unviable. Metics who have lived in a country for several years are unlikely to go home, despite their precarious legal status. This is particularly true if they have married and had children in the country. At this point, it is their new country, not their country of origin, which has become their 'home'. Once they have settled, started a family and started raising children, nothing short of expulsion is likely to get metics to return to their country of origin. So a policy based on the hope of voluntary return is unrealistic. Moreover, it endangers the larger society. For the likely result of such a policy is to create a permanently disenfranchised, alienated, and racially or ethnically defined underclass. To avoid this, there is an increasing trend in Western democracies, even in non-immigrant countries, towards adopting amnesty programs for illegal immigrants, and granting citizenship to long-settled refugees, guest-workers and their children. In effect, long-settled metics are increasingly allowed to follow the immigrant path to integration.

In all four of these trends, we see shifts away from historic policies of assimilation or exclusion towards a more 'multicultural' approach that accommodates diversity. For our purposes, the first two trends regarding national minorities and indigenous peoples deserve highlighting. These trends help illustrate the extent to which Western democracies have moved away from older models of unitary, centralized nation-states, and repudiated older ideologies of 'one state, one nation, one language'. Today, virtually all Western states with indigenous peoples and substate national groups have become 'multination' states, recognizing the existence of 'peoples' and 'nations' within the boundaries of the state. This recognition is manifested in a range of minority rights that includes regional autonomy and official language status for national minorities, and customary law, land claims, and self-government for indigenous peoples.

## 2. Evaluating the Western Models

Are these models a 'success' or a 'best practice' to be celebrated, and perhaps even exported to other regions, such as Asia? Let me focus on the evaluation of multination federations, since they are probably the most controversial. Are multination federations in the West working well? In some cases, it is too early to judge their success. For example, the federalization of Spain and Belgium is comparatively recent, and devolution in Britain is only a few years old. However, if we look across the broad range of cases, we can identify their strengths and weaknesses. Multination federalism in the West has clearly been 'successful' along some dimensions, and equally clearly been a 'failure' along other dimensions.

Multination federalism has been successful along at least five dimensions:

1. *Peace and individual security*: these multination federations are dealing with their competing national identities and nationalist projects with an almost complete absence of violence or terrorism by either the state or the minority.[2]
2. *Democracy*: ethnic politics is now a matter of 'ballots not bullets', operating under normal democratic procedures, with no threat of military coups or authoritarian regimes which take power in the name of national security.
3. *Individual rights*: these reforms have been achieved within the framework of liberal constitutions, with firm respect for individual civil and political rights.
4. *Economic prosperity*: the move to multination federalism has also been achieved without jeopardizing the economic well-being of citizens. Indeed, the countries that have adopted multination federalism are amongst the wealthiest in the world.
5. *Inter-group equality*: by equality here I mean non-domination, such that one group is not systematically vulnerable to the domination of another group. Multination federalism has helped create greater economic equality between majority and minority; greater equality of political influence, so that minorities are not continually outvoted on all issues; and greater equality in the social and

cultural fields, as reflected for example in reduced levels of prejudice and discrimination between groups.

On these criteria, multination federalism in the West is a success. These multination federations have not only managed the conflicts arising from their competing national identities peacefully and democratically, but also secured a high degree of economic prosperity and individual freedom for their citizens. This is remarkable in view of the immense power of nationalism in the past hundred years. Nationalism has torn apart colonial empires and Communist dictatorships, and redefined boundaries all over the world. Yet democratic multination federations have domesticated and pacified nationalism while respecting individual rights and freedoms. It is difficult to imagine any other political system that can make the same claim.

However there are at least two respects in which multination federations have failed. First, the lived experience of inter-group relations is hardly a model of robust intercultural exchange. At best, most citizens in the dominant group are ignorant of and indifferent to the internal life of minority groups, and vice versa. At worst, the relations between different groups are tinged with feelings of resentment. Despite the significant reforms of state institutions in the direction of multination federalism, substate national groups still typically feel that the older ideology of the homogenous nation-state has not been fully renounced, and that members of the dominant group have not fully accepted the principle of a multination state. By contrast, members of the dominant group typically feel that members of the minority group are ungrateful for the changes that have been made and unreasonable in their expectations. As a result, inter-group relations are often highly politicized, as members of both sides are (over?)-sensitive to perceived slights, indignities, and misunderstandings. As a result, few people go out of their way to increase their contact with members of the other group. When contact does occur, it tends to involve crude forms of bargaining and negotiation, rather than any deeper level of cultural sharing or learning.

The result is sometimes described as the phenomenon of 'parallel societies', or of 'two solitudes'. Consider the Flemish in Belgium or Québécois in Canada. Multination federalism has enabled these national groups to live more completely within their own institutions operating in their own language. In the past, these groups often faced extensive economic, political, and social pressure to participate in institutions run in the dominant language. For example, the courts, universities, and legislatures were only conducted in the dominant language. Yet today, as a result of adopting multination federalism, these groups have built up an extensive array of public institutions in their own language, so that they can access the full range of educational, economic, legal, and political opportunities without having to use the dominant language, or without having to participate in institutions that are primarily run by members of the dominant group. In effect, multination federations allow groups to create 'parallel societies', co-existing alongside the dominant society, without requiring much interaction between them.

In short, increased fairness at the level of state institutions has not been matched by increased interaction at the level of everyday inter-group relations. The *state* has made itself accessible to all citizens, and affirms the important contribution that each group makes to the larger society; but from the perspective of individuals, the presence of other groups is rarely experienced as enriching.

Second, multination federations have not removed secession from the political agenda even though it may have reduced the actual likelihood of secession. Secessionist mobilization is a part of everyday life in many Western multination federations. Secessionist parties compete for political office, and citizens may even be given the choice of voting for secession in a referendum (as has happened in Puerto Rico and Quebec). To date, no such referendum on secession has succeeded in the West. This suggests that the adoption of federalism has reduced the actual likelihood of secession, since it is almost certain that one or more of these countries would have broken up long ago without federalism. Had Canada, Belgium, and Spain not been able to federalize, they might not exist as countries today. Still, secessionists are on TV, in newspapers, and compete freely for elected office. And secessionist political parties often get substantial support in elections: for example, 40 per cent in Quebec; 30 per cent in Scotland; 15 per cent in Flanders or the Basque Country or Catalonia; 5 per cent in Puerto Rico. This means that secessionists are present in parliament and on government commissions, and they use these platforms to articulate their views.

Given this balance sheet of successes and failures, it is potentially misleading to describe multination federalism as something to 'celebrate'. Celebration is hardly the spirit with which most Western citizens view multination federalism. And yet, beneath the reservations and ambivalence, there is also the sense that this is the best, and perhaps the only, way for liberal democracies to deal with substate nationalisms.

A similar ambivalent acceptance applies to the other forms of minority rights discussed earlier, such as self-government for indigenous peoples, citizenship for metics, and multiculturalism for immigrants. None of these raise the spectre of secession, and so tend to be less controversial. However, here too there are often feelings of disappointment, particularly regarding the strained quality of inter-group social relations. Indigenous peoples and immigrant groups in the West, like national minorities, tend to resent what they perceive as lingering hierarchies and to distrust the majority's commitment to true equality. Conversely, the majority tends to view indigenous peoples and immigrants as impossible to satisfy and ungrateful for the significant reforms that have been implemented. These feelings of resentment and distrust affect ethnic relations in many Western countries, despite the trend towards multiculturalism and minority rights. Yet most people accept that these policies have enabled Western democracies to manage their ethnocultural diversity within the constraints of peace, freedom, equality, democracy, and prosperity, and as such are worthy of support.

## 3. National Minorities in Asia

More could be said about the strengths and weaknesses of Western models of multiculturalism and minority rights; but let me turn to Asia and the Pacific, and ask whether it is feasible or desirable to adopt these models in the region.

The first question is whether the categories I have been using make sense outside the Western democracies. Can we speak about 'immigrants', 'indigenous peoples', 'substate national groups', and 'metics' in the Asian context, or do we need a different vocabulary? Some of these categories apply more readily to Asia than others. For example, the category of 'immigrants' as I have defined it is primarily applicable to the traditional Western countries of immigration, such as the United States, Canada, and Australia. Few Asian countries (as indeed few European countries) have policies to admit immigrants with the right to citizenship. However, there are examples of the other categories I have discussed. Let me focus on the case of national minorities, before briefly discussing indigenous peoples and metics in sections 4 and 5.

Cases of national minorities demanding greater autonomy in Asia include the Karens and Shans in Burma; the Baluchis in Afghanistan and Pakistan; the Tibetans and Uighurs in China; the Sikhs and Kashmiris in India; the Acehnese (and East Timorese, until recently) in Indonesia; the Bougainvilleans in Papua New Guinea; the Moros in the Philippines; and the Tamils in Sri Lanka. There are strong parallels between these minority nationalisms and those in the West. In both contexts, groups are seeking regional autonomy; in both contexts, this mobilization was often triggered in response to the threat posed by majority nation-building (e.g., imposing the Sinhalese language on Tamils in Sri Lanka; eliminating political autonomy in Tibet); in both contexts, this has generated demands to adopt federalism as a mechanism for accommodating minority nationalisms; and in both contexts, there is the threat of secession if this desire for autonomy is not met.

As Walker Connor notes, minority nationalism is truly universal:

> countries affected by it are to be found in Africa (Ethiopia), Asia (Sri Lanka), Eastern Europe (Romania), Western Europe (France), North America (Guatemala), South America (Guyana), and Oceania (New Zealand). The list includes countries that are old (United Kingdom) as well as new (Bangladesh), large (Indonesia) as well as small (Fiji), rich (Canada) as well as poor (Pakistan), authoritarian (Sudan) as well as democratic (Belgium), Marxist-Leninist (China) as well as militantly anti-Marxist (Turkey). The list also includes countries which are Buddhist (Burma), Christian (Spain), Moslem (Iran), Hindu (India), and Judaic (Israel) (Connor, 1999, pp.163-4).

We need to think creatively about how to respond to these conflicts, which continue to plague efforts at democratization and to cause violence around the world.

In the West, federal or quasi-federal forms of territorial autonomy are increasingly seen as the best solution to these conflicts. Where national minorities form clear majorities in their historic homeland, and particularly where they have some prior history of self-government, Western democracies have not found any alternative to territorial autonomy. Yet territorial autonomy is strongly resisted virtually everywhere outside the West, whether in Eastern Europe, Africa or Asia. As

Nandy (1992, p.39) puts it, 'Any proposal to decentralise or to reconceptualize the state as a truly federal polity goes against the grain of most postcolonial states in the third world'. Around the world, territorial autonomy is typically only granted as a last-ditch effort to avoid civil war, or as the outcome of civil war. Most states object to the very idea of empowering national minorities and have chosen to suppress rather than accommodate minority nationalisms.

We can see this dynamic in many countries of South and East Asia. Most Asian states have suppressed minority nationalisms. This has typically been justified on the grounds that (a) national minorities are likely to be disloyal; (b) the minority is backward and uncivilized and so needs to be brought into the modern world; and (c) the minority's territory contains land and resources needed for the country's economic development. This mixture of security concerns, paternalism, and desire for resources is ubiquitous in the treatment of national minorities in Asia (Weiner, 1997, pp.9-12, pp.23-24; Gurr, 1993; Siddle, 1996, pp.88-94; Kingsbury, 1999; Penz, 1992 and 1993; Guha, 1994; Ahmed, 1993).

Indeed, Asian countries have often used the same tools Western countries historically adopted to suppress minority nationalism. These include settlement policies designed to swamp national minorities in their historic homeland with settlers from the dominant group (e.g., government policies to promote ethnic Bengali settlement in the Chittagong Hill Tracts of Bangladesh; or ethnic Javanese settlement of East Timor or the Aceh area of Indonesia; or Christian settlement of the Moro areas of the Philippines; or ethnic Han settlement of Tibet and Eastern Mongolia in China; or Viet settlement of the Champa and Montagnard areas of Vietnam). Or consider the many cases in which minorities have been stripped of their traditional self-government, either through the centralization of power or the redrawing of boundaries (e.g., Baluchistan in Pakistan, Arakan and Kachinland in Burma/Myanmar, South Moluccas in Indonesia, East Turkestan in China, or Bougainville in Papua-New Guinea). Or consider the policies to impose the majority Sinhalese language on the Tamils in Sri Lanka; the Persian language on the Arabistans in Iran; the Dzongkha language on the Nepalese in Bhutan; the Burmese language on the Mons in Burma; or the Urdu language on the Sindhi in Pakistan.[3]

India is an exception to this trend, and so is worth considering. It is one of the few countries outside the West to have voluntarily federalized to accommodate minority nationalist claims.[4] The Indian National Congress endorsed the idea of a multination federalism along ethnolinguistic lines as early as 1920, and the freedom movement was itself organized in this way (Banarjee, 1992, p.48). This pre-independence promise of autonomy to ethnolinguistic minorities was not in itself unusual. Many national liberation movements in Asia and Africa made such promises as a way of broadening the base of popular support for independence. However, in most cases, these promises were merely strategic and were broken once in power.[5]

For a time, it appeared that India too would backtrack on promises of autonomy. After independence, Nehru resisted the idea of reorganizing states along ethnolinguistic lines, and said that he preferred a more 'rational' (and highly centralized) form of federalism which would be purely territorial, like the American or

German model, where the borders of the states are drawn so as not to enable minorities to exercise territorial self-government (Banerjee, 1992, p.56; Bhattacharya 1992).[6] However, faced with increasing restlessness amongst many ethnolinguistic groups, the Indian government accepted the linguistic reorganization of states in 1956. The system has been further refined since then – in 1960, 1962, 1966, and 1972 – to accommodate groups left out of the original reorganisation (Patil, 1998; Schwartzberg, 1985). Moreover, India has accepted the requirement for some form of *asymmetry* in the federal system, for example, the special self-government provisions for Kashmir in Article 370 of the Constitution (Kohli, 1997; Khan, 1997a; Dabla, 1998), the special provisions for other states in article 371, or the provisions in Schedule VI that provide special protections for the autonomy of tribal territories in Assam, Meghalaya, and Mizoram. Indeed, India seems to have had less difficulty accepting the principle of asymmetry than many Western multination federations.[7]

Therefore India has many of the hallmarks of a genuinely multination federalism. To be sure, there are aspects of federalism in India that limit its operation as a truly multination federalism. First is the frequent imposition of direct presidential rule on states by the central government, often for partisan reasons, or to suppress the expression of what are perceived to be inappropriate forms of minority nationalism (Khan, 1997; Dabla, 1998, p.232). A minority group may acquire a separate state, but it does not have genuine autonomy if the central government has virtually unlimited authority to dismiss state governments that it dislikes. More generally, many commentators argue that the Indian federal system is too centralized, and that this remains a source of grievance amongst many minorities (Hardgrave, 1993, p.60).

Second, there is the absence of any clear framework for dealing with as-yet-unfulfilled demands for new ethnolinguistic states, including demands for the creation of Gorkhaland in West Bengal; for Jharkhand in Bihar; for Bodoland in Assam; and for Uttarkhand in Uttar Pradesh.[8] Rather than establish any clear criteria or process by which such claims could be adjudicated, the central government's strategy seems, at times, to be to wait until these areas are engulfed in violence, and then to negotiate a settlement (Arora and Mukarji, 1992, p.9; Krishna, 1992, p.83).[9] Since the existing states in India are on average much larger than in any other democratic federal system, there would appear to be considerable room to increase the number of states, and/or to federalize the states themselves, that is, to create a multi-level federalism, or what Mukarji and Arora (1992, p.270) call 'cascading federalism: a federation of federations'. Rather than viewing the creation of new states (or new autonomous areas within states) as a last resort in response to violence, it can instead be seen as a chance to promote greater democratic participation and greater ethnocultural justice.[10]

A third problem concerns the existence of exclusionary practices within these ethnolinguistic states favouring the 'sons of the soil' in the provision of public employment, sometimes accompanied by 'street-level sanctions by way of harassment, intimidation and violence' against people perceived as 'outsiders' (Srinivasavaradan, 1992, p.148; Krishna, 1992, p.74; Weiner, 1998). It is one thing to say that ethnolinguistic minorities should be able to exercise territorial autonomy, and to use their language in public institutions – this is a defining feature of multination federalism. But it is quite another to say that such groups can ignore the basic civil or political rights of individuals living within the territory. This is a problem, not so much with the multination character of Indian federalism, but rather with its protection of liberal-democratic principles. A liberal-democratic form of multination federalism must ensure that *all* governments – whether at the central, state, or substate level – respect basic rights. How best to protect the rights of such 'internal minorities' is a fundamental challenge facing all multination federations.

In sum, it appears that India, like many Western democracies, has adopted a multination form of federalism that recognizes the rights of national minorities to self-government, and to maintain their own public institutions in their own language. I would argue that this experiment with multination federalism, as in the West, has generally been a success. Earlier fears that it would lead to the breakdown of the country have not materialized.[11] Most commentators now argue that it has helped to reduce violence and increase stability and some even describe it as a 'remarkable success' (Schwartzberg, 1985, p.177; Lijphart, 1996, p.263; Sisk, 1996, p.52; cf. Srinivasavaradan, 1992). One might expect the success of the Indian model to inspire other countries in the region to adopt federal or quasi-federal forms of territorial autonomy in response to national minorities' aspirations. One can find many academics who argue that federal or quasi-federal forms of territorial autonomy are the only viable solution for other states in the region facing the challenge of minority nationalisms, including Burma/Myanmar (Smith, 1997; Silverstein, 1997); China (Yan, 1996; Davis, 1999); Sri Lanka (Shastri, 1997; Krishna, 1999; Edrisinha, 2001); Pakistan (Ahmed, 1997); Indonesia (Anderson, 2004), and perhaps Afghanistan (Thier, 1999; cf. Wimmer and Schetter, 2002). Yet India (and the Federated States of Micronesia) remains the exception in the region. In most countries, the idea of federal autonomy for national minorities remains taboo. Many countries have chosen civil war rather than concede such autonomy, and have only been prepared to contemplate multination federalism when a military solution has become too costly.[12]

What explains this striking opposition to a model that has worked well in the West and in India? Some people attempt to explain this on purely practical grounds. It is sometimes said, for example, that ethnic groups in Asia are less territorially concentrated than in the West, or that poorer Asian countries cannot afford the extra costs of a federal system. Similar arguments are often invoked to explain the hostility to federalism in Eastern Europe. In my view, these arguments are misleading. In several of the most serious cases of minority nationalism in Asia, the minority groups are at least as territorially concentrated as comparable groups in the West. And it is simply not true that federal states are inherently more costly to administer.

What then is the real explanation for the resistance to multination federalism? One possible explanation is that the political culture in Asia is more 'communitarian'. As a result, ideas about the sanctity of the state and the unity of the nation are more powerful in the region, and are invoked to pre-empt movements for multiculturalism and minority rights. This has been argued by some commentators, such as Baogang

He, who claims that the Confucian heritage of East Asia has a strong sense of communitarianism that conflicts with Western liberal ideas of minority rights (He, 1998 and 2004). But that is at best part of the story. For the fact is that even liberals in Asia are more likely to oppose multination federalism than their liberal counterparts in the West. Liberals in the West assume that substate national groups will exercise their territorial autonomy in accordance with the basic principles of liberal constitutionalism, so that devolving power from the central state to a self-governing region does not threaten individual rights and democratic freedoms. This indeed is what we see throughout the Western multination federations. In other regions, by contrast, many liberal-democrats worry that such substate autonomies will become petty tyrannies that flout the rule of law, deny human rights, and oppress internal minorities (Bell, 2001).

Similarly, communitarians in Asia are more hostile to multination federalism than communitarians in the West. The latter have grudgingly accepted that their dreams of constructing a united community within uncontested borders are unrealistic. Attempts to preserve the ideology of 'one language, one nation, one state' through the assimilation or exclusion of minority groups have proven futile. Minorities are too numerous, and too politically conscious of their rights, to disappear. In Asia, by contrast, many communitarians cling to the hope that minority nationalism will fade away. They believe that substate nationalism is a transient by-product of some other problem that will disappear over time through modernization or democratization. Some people assume that minority nationalism will fade as the economy improves, or as democracy is consolidated, or as communications and media become globalized. On this view, if Asian states have the strength to hold out against minority demagogues and ethnic entrepreneurs, then the problem will gradually solve itself. This is precisely the expectation that Westerners have gradually relinquished, since minority nationalisms have in fact strengthened rather than weakened as Western states have become more democratic, prosperous, and globalized.

The expectation that minority nationalism will fade explains not only the resistance to the 'Indian model' of multination federalism but also the popularity of the 'Singapore model' of unitary nation-building. For example, some of those who oppose adopting federalism in Sri Lanka have suggested that Sri Lanka could instead follow Singapore's model (Krishna, 1999, pp.46-7). Insofar as one thinks that the Singapore model is successful (and clearly it is so in terms of peace and prosperity), this success is predicated on the fact that all three major groups are predominantly formed through immigration. None of them claims Singapore as its historic homeland, and none claims historic rights of self-government. The typical problem of minority nationalism simply does not arise. Tamils in Singapore do not make the same kinds of claims as Tamils in Jaffna or Tamil Nadu. So too with the Malays and Chinese: they were all primarily brought to Singapore by the former imperial powers.

Put another way, it would be inaccurate to say that Singapore has found an alternative way of dealing with the problem of a national minority that has mobilized along nationalist lines to defend its homeland against encroachment by a larger state into which it was involuntarily incorporated. Singapore never faced that particular problem. As a result, to suppose that Singapore provides a model for dealing with minority nationalism is, in effect, to suppose that the distinctive demands associated with minority nationalism will disappear. For example, to hope that Tamils in the Jaffna peninsula of Sri Lanka would accept the same status as Tamils in Singapore is to suppose that the former would abandon all the political aspirations and nationalist identities that have been built up around the ideas and myths of a historic Tamil homeland and of a historic Tamil kingdom. It is to suppose that Tamils in Sri Lanka would give up on the ideas that have inspired their political mobilization for over 50 years. This is the sort of hope that has long been given up by most people in the West.

In comparing East and West, we see a curious set of contrasts. In Asia, many intellectuals and politicians are deeply pessimistic about the prospect that substate national groups can exercise territorial autonomy in accordance with liberal-democratic norms, yet are surprisingly optimistic about the possibility that substate nationalism will simply disappear. By contrast, Western public opinion is optimistic about the capacity of substate national groups to govern within liberal-democratic constraints, but pessimistic about the likelihood that substate nationalism will disappear as a result of processes of modernization, democratization, or globalization.

These differing forms of optimism and pessimism account for some of the differences between the West and East; but there is one other important factor. The trend towards greater accommodation of diversity can be blocked by considerations of security. Whether in the East or West, states will not voluntarily accord greater powers or resources to groups that are perceived as disloyal, and therefore a threat to the security of the state. In particular, states will not accommodate groups that are seen as likely to collaborate with foreign enemies. This is rarely an issue in the West. For example, if Quebec gains increased powers, or even independence, no one in the rest of Canada worries that Quebec will start collaborating with Iraq or the Taliban or China to overthrow the Canadian state. Québécois nationalists may want to secede, but an independent Quebec would be an ally, not an enemy, and would cooperate with Canada in NATO and other Western defence and security arrangements. In most parts of the world, however, minority groups are often seen as a 'fifth column', likely to be working for an enemy. In some cases, the concern is that the minority has a 'kin-state' nearby – the minority is related to a neighbouring state by ethnicity or religion – so that the neighbouring state claims the right to intervene to protect 'its' minority. In other cases, the concern is that leaders of the minority group will act as pawns of former imperial powers, or of regional or international superpowers, or of foreign capitalists, who will foment minority unrest as a way of weakening the central state and maintaining hegemony over it. Under these conditions, we are likely to see the 'securitization' of ethnic relations (Waever, 1995). Relations between states and minorities are seen as a matter, not of normal democratic politics, but of state security in which the government must limit the normal democratic process in order to protect the state. Under conditions of securitization, minority self-organization may be legally limited (e.g., minority political parties banned), minority leaders may be subject to police surveillance, the raising of particular demands may be illegal (e.g., laws against promoting secession), and so on.[13] Even if minority demands can be voiced, they will be flatly rejected by the larger society and the state. After all, how can groups that are disloyal have any legitimate claims against the state? So securitization of ethnic relations erodes both the democratic space to voice minority demands and the likelihood that those demands will be accepted.

This is the situation we find in some parts of Asia. In several cases, this fear arises from the belief that the minority's main loyalty is to a (potentially hostile) neighbouring kin-state with whom it may collaborate. We see this in India regarding the Kashmiri minority (and the Muslim minority more generally); in Sri Lanka regarding the Tamil minority; in Afghanistan regarding the Uzbek minority; in Cambodia regarding the Vietnamese minority; in Pakistan and Bangladesh regarding the Hindu minority; in Bangladesh regarding the Biharis; in Thailand regarding the ethnic Malays; and in Vietnam regarding the Chinese minority. In several of these cases, there have even been policies to encourage or force the allegedly disloyal minority to 'return' to their 'home' country.

A related problem arises when a particular national group is found in two or more countries, divided by modern international boundaries, who may have dreams of forming (or regaining) a common state. The classic case in the Middle East is the Kurds, divided between Iran, Iraq, Turkey, and Syria, who have longed to create an independent Kurdistan. A comparable situation in Asia concerns the Baluchis, spread across Afghanistan, Iran, and Pakistan, who have sometimes expressed the desire for an independent state. The Pashtuns (Pathans) who are divided by the Afghan/Pakistan border have also periodically expressed a desire to be unified in a single state.

In both of these contexts, the state fears that the minority will collaborate with its kin across the border, whether it be a neighbouring kin-state or just a neighbouring kin-group. But there are other ways in which minorities can be suspected of collaborating with hostile external powers. In some cases, these external powers are former imperial powers (as with the South Moluccans in Indonesia who are seen as collaborators with the Dutch; or the Montagnards in Vietnam who are seen as collaborators with the French and Americans). In other cases, minorities are seen as collaborating with international movements that threaten the state. In the past, this often involved the fear that minorities were part of an international Communist conspiracy set upon overthrowing capitalist countries.[14] More recently, there is a fear that minorities are part of an international movement of radical Islamists to overthrow secular states. For example, Muslim minorities in Aceh and Mindanao are said to have links with international networks of Islamic militants. In other cases, the concern is that minorities are serving as agents of foreign capital, fomenting rebellion to gain preferential access to natural resources: this is sometimes said to apply to West Papua.

In all these cases, minorities are seen (rightly or wrongly) as allies or collaborators with external powers that threaten the state (Ho, 2000; Ganguly, 1997, p.266, pp.269-70; ICES, 1995, pp.17-25; Anderson, 2004; Krishna, 1999, chapter

3; Shastri, 1997, p.155; Dharmadase, 1992, p.141, p.230, pp.295-6; Nissan, 1996, p.34; MRG, 1997, p.579). To an outside observer, these minority groups might appear weak and marginalized, with little power or resources to challenge the state; but from the state's perspective, these minorities are the local agents for larger regional or international powers or networks that are very strong and pose a credible threat to the state. More generally, the history of imperialism, collaboration, and regional instability have encouraged three now widely accepted assumptions in many Asian countries: (a) many minorities are disloyal, not just in the sense that they lack loyalty to the state (that is equally true of secessionists in Quebec or Scotland), but in the stronger sense that they have collaborated or will collaborate with current or potential enemies; therefore, (b) a strong and stable state requires weak and disempowered minorities. Ethnic relations are seen as a zero-sum game: anything that benefits the minority is seen as a threat to the majority; and therefore (c) the treatment of minorities is above all a question of national security.

In the West, by contrast, minority nationalist politics have been almost entirely 'de-securitized'. Substate national groups are not seen as potential collaborators with neighbouring enemies, partly because countries in the West do not have neighbouring enemies. Also, national minorities in the West generally do not have a neighbouring kin-state, although the Catholics in Northern Ireland and the Turks in Cyprus are obvious exceptions. Nor are substate national groups in the West suspected of collaborating with international movements of Communism or radical Islam. On the contrary, members of national minorities are fully-integrated into the same basic liberal-democratic consensus as the dominant group. Indeed, surveys show that members of national minorities are typically indistinguishable from members of the dominant group in terms of their commitment to the values of a secular liberal-democratic constitution. In the absence of any grounds for securitization, the politics of substate nationalism in the West is just that – normal day-to-day politics. Relations between the state and national minorities have been taken out of the 'security' box, and put in the 'democratic politics' box. Under these circumstances, political mobilization for minority rights is safe, and the result is the trend towards accommodation of diversity.

This de-securitization of ethnic politics in the West even applies to the issue of secession. Even though secessionist political parties wish to break up the state, citizens in the West assume that secessionists must be treated under the same democratic rules as everyone else, with the same democratic rights to mobilize, advocate, and run for office. The reason for this remarkable tolerance of secessionist mobilization, I believe, is precisely the assumption that even if substate national groups do secede, they will become our allies, not our enemies (and also govern their seceding state in accordance with human rights and liberal-democratic values).[15]

In sum, there are at least three major obstacles to multination federalism in Asia: (a) scepticism about the likelihood that substate autonomies will be liberal-democratic; (b) the belief that ethnic mobilization, including substate nationalism, will eventually disappear as a result of modernization and development; and (c) the fear that minorities will collaborate with enemies of the state.[16] As a result, multination federalism in Asia is typically resisted across the political spectrum, by liberals, communitarians, and statists alike, and the prospects for multination federalism seem bleak, except as the outcome of violent struggle or international pressure.

## 4. Indigenous Peoples in Asia

What about the other two groups: namely, indigenous peoples and metics. How does their treatment in Asia compare with the West? Some Asian governments claim that the category of 'indigenous peoples' does not apply to minorities in Asia. For example, the People's Republic of China has argued at the United Nations that the concept of 'indigenous peoples' only applies in the context of overseas European colonization. Hence all peoples living in Asian countries prior to the era of European colonization are equally 'indigenous', whether they are majority or minority. It makes no sense, on this view, to say that some minorities in China or India are 'indigenous' while the majority is not (Kingsbury, 1995 and 1999; Colchester, 1998). This attempt to restrict the scope of 'indigenous peoples' to the context of European colonization rests on the so-called 'saltwater thesis'. The term 'indigenous peoples' is connected to that of colonialism: indigenous peoples have had their lands conquered and settled by a colonizing society, and forcibly incorporated into a larger state dominated by this colonizing society. A glance at history would suggest that this sort of colonialism has occurred in many different forms throughout the world, but the saltwater thesis claims that the only 'real' form of colonialism involves colonizers coming from overseas, that is, from Europe. The conquest and settling of Ainu lands by Japan cannot be called 'colonialism' on this view, since the conquering settlers did not come from overseas, and so the Ainu cannot be called 'indigenous'.

Restricting the categories of colonialism and indigenous peoples to cases of overseas conquest is out of step with the usual usage of these terms. For example, it is almost universally accepted that the Sami in Scandinavia are an indigenous people, and there are good reasons for this. After all, the way in which their lands were claimed and settled was very similar to the way that the lands of the Inuit in Canada were claimed and settled, with the same disastrous results. It is not clear why the injustice of colonizing the lands of another culture changes when the colonizing settlers come by land (backed by an army), rather than by sea (backed by a navy).

If we focus on this common experience of colonizing settlement, then we can find various groups in Asia – from the Ainu of Japan, to the Dayak of Indonesia and the Chittagong Hill Tribes of Bangladesh – which would qualify as indigenous peoples. The way in which their lands have been colonized is similar to that of the Sami in Scandinavia or the Inuit in Canada, and was rationalized on similar grounds.[17] And their claims today are also similar, including the protection of traditional lands, language rights and political representation. Hence it is not surprising that many of these hill tribes are adopting the international language of 'indigenous peoples'

(Colchester, 1998, p.4; Gellner, 2001, pp.187-8).

As in the West, the dividing line between indigenous peoples and other national minorities is not clear. One distinguishing feature is the extent to which a group has played a role in the process of state formation. In the European context, the reason why the Sami are considered indigenous while the Catalans are not is that the latter were contenders but losers in the process of forming the state of Spain, whereas the Sami were isolated from the process of forming the state of Sweden. Using this criteria, we can say that what distinguishes the indigenous Dayaks or Ainu from other national minorities in Asia – such as the Kashmiris and Sikhs in India, or the Tamils in Sri Lanka – is that the latter have been active contenders in modern state-formation. Had the balance of power differed slightly, they could easily have consolidated themselves as independent states; but they lost, and now face many of the same issues as substate national groups in Europe.

We can debate whether the term 'indigenous people' is the best one to mark this distinction. In one sense, the Catalans are just as 'indigenous' to Europe as the Sami, and the Tamils are just as indigenous to Asia as the Dayaks. But there surely is an important distinction between the Catalans and the Sami which needs to be marked, and I think a similar distinction is required between the Tamils and the Dayaks. For better or worse, the term 'indigenous peoples' has been used in international law to draw this distinction. Perhaps a better term could be devised, but whatever the terminology, the basic distinction between indigenous peoples and substate national groups seems as applicable in Asia as in Europe. And indeed some countries in Asia are accepting the validity of the term, especially the Philippines and Nepal. And while some other Asian countries continue to resist the term 'indigenous peoples', they recognize the need to create a distinct category for such groups, whether it is 'aboriginal tribes' (Taiwan), 'aborigines' (Malaysia), 'hill tribes' (Thailand), 'isolated peoples' (Indonesia), 'natives' (Borneo) or 'scheduled tribes' (India).

In any event it would be a mistake to focus exclusively on the differences between indigenous peoples and substate national groups while neglecting their similarities. Both tend to resist majority nation-building, and are committed to maintaining their traditional institutions, operating in their own language and culture, so that they can reproduce themselves as separate peoples within the larger state. Because of their historic isolation or fragile ecology, indigenous peoples may be more immediately threatened by nation-building than national minorities, and hence more urgently in need of minority rights protection. But the same principle that underpins their claims may also apply to the claims of substate national groups, and vice-versa (Kingsbury, 1999; Anaya, 1996).

Whatever the terminology, the crucial question is how these groups are treated. In the West, as we have seen, there has been a trend towards greater self-government and land-rights for indigenous peoples. The situation in Asia is more complicated.[18] There are comparable moves in some countries, or perhaps more accurately, in some parts of some countries. For example, there are relatively progressive laws in some parts of India, including collective land ownership and affirmative action. India has accepted the need for quasi-federal forms of territorial autonomy for smaller indigenous peoples or hill tribes for whom full statehood may not be appropriate, particularly in the northeast. There are other promising developments regarding land rights, but much less progress in self-government, in Nepal, Taiwan, and New Caledonia, although the weak rule of law often means that settlers/businesses can simply ignore indigenous title (Colchester, 1998, p.20).

Despite pockets of improvement, the situation remains grim in most Asian countries. Indigenous peoples in several countries continue to suffer from state policies to swamp their lands with settlers, including Indonesia, Bangladesh, Malaysia, Nepal, and Vietnam. Their land rights often receive minimal or no legal protection, as in Malaysia, Indonesia, Bangladesh, and Laos, and there is no attempt to restore land that was wrongfully taken from them historically. In several countries their lands have simply been unilaterally declared as national forests or national parks by the state, which then passes laws forbidding indigenous peoples to continue their traditional practices on 'state land'. Indigenous peoples are also subject to assimilationist policies in several countries, including Thailand, Indonesia (e.g., 'Operasi Koteka' to 'Indonesianize' indigenous peoples in West Papua), and Malaysia (where indigenous peoples are pressured to convert to Islam).

What explains this resistance to the recognition of indigenous rights to land and self-government? Some of the reasons are the same as for national minorities. For example, in some cases, there are security issues. Indigenous peoples often live in border areas, and governments worry that they will be used as pawns by neighbouring states or armed movements.[19] These sorts of security concerns regarding indigenous peoples were relevant in the past in the West, but rarely arise today.[20] There is also the widespread assumption that indigenous peoples, like national minorities, can be assimilated, and indeed would benefit from being assimilated. In the West, the long history of assimilationist policies towards indigenous peoples is now seen as having failed in practice, and as illiberal in principle. In several Asian countries, these policies are still seen as noble in intention, since they bring civilization to 'backward' peoples, and as likely to succeed in practice.[21]

Another factor that partly explains the resistance to indigenous rights in Asia is the belief that they impede economic development, which is the most urgent priority of developing states. The need for economic development was commonly invoked historically in the West as well to dispossess indigenous peoples of their lands and resources. But it may be particularly relevant to Asia today, since there are indeed many cases where the homelands of indigenous peoples include substantial resources that could help alleviate poverty in the larger society. Protecting the rights of indigenous peoples may make it more difficult to meet the basic needs of the majority. This is a powerful factor in countries with high levels of poverty.

However, it is not clear that indigenous rights are an obstacle to economic development. Any group with abundant natural resources surely has an obligation to share them with the poor. But is this a justification for settlement policies, or for denying indigenous peoples self-government? Not necessarily. For one thing, settlement or development policies that violate the rights of indigenous peoples often do not benefit the poor. When elites justify settlement policies in indigenous lands on the ground that these policies aid the heartland poor, this is often a dishonest rationalization for their own enrichment; the elites make sure that they acquire title to the most valuable land or mineral resources for themselves. Even when well-intentioned, these forms of settlement are often unsustainable. For example, turning rainforest into farms just does not work: land clearance leads to soil damage, erosion, and pollution, with soil exhaustion after one or two harvests, which leads to abandonment of the land and further deforestation (Colchester, 1998).

Settlement plans are often flawed in one or more of these ways: they serve the rich rather than the poor; and/or they lead to environmental destruction rather than sustainable development. This is an empirical question, which needs to be examined case-by-case. There may indeed be cases where an indigenous community's land-claims cover an unfair share of resources, and if so, it is legitimate for the state to insist that the community progressively economize on the use of resources. However, even here, there are just and unjust ways of gaining access to indigenous resources. Rather than the involuntary appropriation of their lands, the state could instead impose some form of a resource tax (Penz, 1993, p.121). It would be up to the indigenous peoples themselves to decide how to manage their resources to pay for this tax. Some communities may decide to sell some of their land, or lease it, or develop some of their mineral wealth, or invite outside people to develop the wealth for them. The point is that indigenous peoples must be actively involved in the process (e.g., through co-management), and the extraction of resources should seek to minimize cultural harm, for example, through limitations on settlement (Kymlicka, 2001, chapter 6).

In short, there may indeed be valid arguments for states to insist that indigenous peoples share some of the natural resources on their traditional territories, but these are not justifications for either settlement policies or for denying indigenous peoples self-government. Unfortunately, many Asian countries have assumed that the former justifies the latter. Under those circumstances, the prospects for greater recognition of indigenous rights remains bleak, except again as the outcome of violent struggle or international pressure.

## 5. Metics in Asia

Finally, let me conclude with a brief examination of the case of metics in Asia. One prominent example is the Koreans in Japan, who were stripped of citizenship after World War II, since they did not fit into the conception of 'nationhood' being promoted by the Japanese state. Like the Turks in Germany, it was initially hoped that the Koreans would return to Korea, but it was quickly realized that they are in Japan for good, and that Japan is the only home the children and grandchildren know. Like the Turks, the Koreans have fought for citizenship, which at first was only offered as a privilege, not a right, and only to those who had renounced their ethnic heritage and assimilated (e.g., by adopting Japanese names). Like the Turks, many Koreans have refused to naturalize on these terms, which they see as a continuation rather than repudiation of the earlier attitude that anyone who is identifiably Korean cannot be a Japanese citizen (Onuma, 1992; Hicks, 1997). Another example is the 'Upcountry Tamils' in Sri Lanka, brought by the British to work on plantations in the nineteenth century, who were stripped of their citizenship shortly after Sri Lankan independence. Similarly, the citizenship rules originally adopted in Indonesia and Malaysia excluded many long-settled Chinese residents, including many who were born in the country.[22]

In all of these cases, as with the Western examples I discussed earlier, exclusionary citizenship laws were originally adopted in the hope that metics would return 'home'. However, as in the West, it has become clear that these expectations were misguided, and citizenship rules have subsequently been liberalized to enable (some members of) the metic group to gain (or regain) citizenship. However, there are other cases where states continue to resist any liberalization of citizenship laws. For example, the Rohingya Muslims in Burma remain stigmatized as a metic group. The ethnic Chinese in Brunei are denied access to citizenship. The citizenship status of the ethnic Vietnamese in Cambodia remains contested. One reason why these cases have proven more difficult to resolve is, once again, the existence of security fears: the metics are seen as a potential fifth-column for a neighbouring power. Also, some metic groups, particularly the ethnic Chinese, are seen as unjustly wealthy, perhaps because of a privileged position in colonial times, and hence the denial of political rights is seen as compensating for their disproportionate economic power. By contrast, metics in the West are almost always less well-off than the majority society, so that the denial of political rights is seen as compounding their disadvantage and creating the danger of a racial underclass. Where these perceptions of security or unjust privilege exist, the trend towards liberalization of citizenship for metics is less likely to take place in the absence of international pressure.[23]

## 6. Conclusion

This chapter has identified some points of similarity and difference in the treatment of minorities in Asia and the West. I have focused particularly on three categories of groups: national minorities, indigenous peoples, and metics. In each case, I have identified a few Asian countries where developments are broadly similar to Western trajectory of minority rights, and many others where the trajectory is different.

There are many ethnocultural groups in Asia which do not fit easily into these three categories. For example, the Western models I have discussed do not cover the sort of group that Gurr calls 'communal contenders'. These groups have a share of state power, cherish their own separate cultural institutions, but do not seek territorial autonomy or independent statehood. They include the Hazars, Pashtuns, Tajiks and Uzbeks in Afghanistan, the Mohajirs, Pushtuns and Sindhis of Pakistan, and the Chinese and Indians in Malaysia. Unlike national minorities and indigenous peoples, they do not see themselves as distinct 'nations' with rights to self-government; unlike immigrants, they do not expect to integrate into the dominant nation; and unlike metics or racial caste groups, they share state power instead of being excluded from it.[24]

However, I hope enough has been said to make clear some of the major obstacles to the adoption of Western models of minority rights in the region. It seems unlikely that Western models will be adopted more broadly in Asia in the foreseeable future, unless significant international pressure is applied to do so. As noted earlier, this is not inconceivable. There are proposals to strengthen the international enforcement of minority and indigenous rights. However, I doubt that the international community today has either the power or the desire to impose meaningful minority rights standards on countries around the world. Nor would such pressure necessarily achieve its desired end. Legal and political reforms will only be enduring if they are accompanied by changes in people's attitudes about state-minority relations. The international community could attempt to impose political settlements on particular Asian countries, but these imposed institutions will not work if they lack legitimacy in the eyes of citizens, or if citizens lack the desire and trust needed to sustain them.

Therefore, the long-term prospects for minority rights depend on changing people's attitudes. To my mind, two sets of attitudes are central to the trajectory of minority rights. The first concerns the expectation that minority nationalism and indigenous mobilization will fade away with economic development, education, or greater intercultural contact. So long as this expectation persists, governments will be tempted to avoid addressing minority claims in the hope that they will go away in time. Many people in the West used to have this expectation, but it has gradually been abandoned, since there is no evidence to support it. On the contrary, national minorities and indigenous peoples in the West have become more politically mobilized as they have become more educated and prosperous. Minorities are also becoming more numerous demographically, not less. Recognition of these facts has pushed Western governments to finally take minority claims seriously.

By contrast, this expectation is still present amongst many key actors in Asia. However, I suspect that this will change, sooner or later. As in the West, minorities in East Asia are growing faster than dominant groups (MRG, 1997, p.591). Moreover, they are increasingly influenced by the same rights-consciousness that has inspired many Western minority groups to contest earlier forms of ethnic and racial hierarchy. They are also increasingly connected to international networks that support minority groups. Under these circumstances, expectations of the assimilation or political quiescence of minority groups become increasingly naive. If and when these expectations are abandoned, we may see greater similarity to the Western trajectory of minority rights.

The second core set of beliefs concerns the 'securitization' of ethnic politics that arises from the fear that minorities will collaborate with neighbouring enemies or hostile external powers. This is a more complicated issue, and probably can only be fully resolved by constructing effective regional and international structures of geopolitical security. It is difficult to ensure justice for minorities in a country when it is surrounded by unstable or predatory neighbours. Countries that feel threatened by neighbours are unlikely to have the sense of security needed to share power with their own minorities. Therefore, convergence on Western models is unlikely until political spaces in Asia have been de-securitized. On this issue, I am less optimistic. It is difficult to see how south and east Asia could become desecuritized in the foreseeable future. Recent events have, if anything, re-securitized politics in the region.

If this analysis is correct, we are likely to see a period of considerable uncertainty regarding ethnic relations in the region. Older models of assimilation or exclusion will be increasingly contested by minorities who are growing in numbers and in their rights-consciousness, and who have international support networks. Yet the geopolitical security conditions are not conducive to the adoption of policies that will satisfy these emerging minority aspirations. The result of these conflicting tendencies is difficult to predict.

## Notes

1    For a more detailed discussion of these trends (and the exceptions to them), see Kymlicka, 2001.
2    The Basque Country is the main exception, although the ETA campaign of violence began in the 1960s and 1970s as a response to the highly-centralized Fascist regime, and is unlikely to have emerged had Spain been a democratic multination federation.
3    However, many Asian countries have a 'surprisingly good' record on tolerating linguistic diversity, including India, PNG, Vanuatu, and the Federated States of Micronesia (Brown, 1997, pp.563-4).
4    Other partial exceptions include Russia and Nigeria, and, since 1986, the Federated States of Micronesia.
5    Consider promises of autonomy made regarding Baluchistan in Pakistan, Arakan and Kachinland in Burma, South Moluccas in Indonesia, East Turkestan in China.
6    This shift was due in part to the trauma of partition in 1947, which 'engendered an obsessive concern for warding off further fragmentation and disintegration, which extended to viewing the political expression of ethnolinguistic regional identities with suspicion and unease' (Mukarji and Arora, 1992, p.5).
7    I discuss the reasons why subunits dominated by national minorities typically need some form of asymmetric status within multination federations, and the difficulty in getting public acceptance of it, in Kymlicka, 2001, chapter 5.
8    For a list of these movements (citing 24 movements in 12 states), see R. Khan 1997c, p.264. For detailed studies of two movements, see Singh, 1997 and Waheed, 1998. Cf. Patil, 1998, pp.154-7.
9    In his study of the formation of new states in the North East, K. Saigal argues that this purely reactive approach has left the impression of weakness: 'In no case was the impression given that the Central Government was acting from a position of strength and giving concessions because it formed a part of its ideological commitment' (Saigal, 1992, p.229). Instead, the central government treated movements for new states as threats and

as adversaries, so that the ultimate acceptance of their demands was seen as capitulation, rather than as the implementation of a coherent principle of federal democracy or justice. It would be interesting to compare this process in India with the creation of the new territory of Nunavut in Canada.

10   There remains a serious split between those leaders who see the accommodation of ethnolinguistic groups as merely a matter of strategy (i.e., a necessary evil), and those who see it as a matter of principle (i.e., a way of promoting democratization and of respecting diversity). Hardgrave (1993, pp.57-9) argues that 'the democratic logic behind the call for linguistic states – the notion that state administration and judicial processes should be conducted in the language of the local majority – was compelling'. I defend this link between politics in the vernacular and democracy in Kymlicka, 2001. However, this 'democratic logic' in favour of accommodating national minorities has not always prevailed, either in India or the West.

11   Examples of these fears includes Harrison's (1960, p.338) claim that with the reorganization of the states, 'The odds are almost wholly against the survival of freedom...the issue is, in fact, whether any Indian state can survive at all'; S.R. Mohan Das's (1975, p.175) claim that 'the linguistic states as set up have contributed towards the balkanization of the country quite sharply'; and L.P. Vidyarthi's (1976, p.130) claim that the creation of linguistic states 'has further generated hatred, conflict and mutual suspicion among the various ethno-linguistic groups'.

12   As happened in the late 1980s in the Philippines, and as is happening at the moment with Sri Lanka, and may happen in Indonesia and Burma/Myanmar, all in response to inconclusive armed struggles.

13   For laws banning various forms of minority nationalist claims see Shastri, 1997, pp.151-3 (banning advocacy of secession in Sri Lanka); Ganguly, 1997, p.257, p.264 (prohibiting discussion of 'sensitive issues' in Malaysia).

14   Several minorities in Indonesia were suppressed on the grounds that they collaborated with China in the 1965 Communist coup. In some cases, assumptions about ethnic kinship and ideological kinship reinforce each other: for example, Chinese minorities in several Asian countries have been assumed to have both ethnic and ideological reasons for collaborating with China.

15   For a discussion of the reasons why secessionist mobilization is tolerated in the West, see Kymlicka, 2004.

16   Another factor in some countries is the perception that minorities have historically been privileged by colonial powers at the expense of the dominant group. Perceptions of historic injustice are then invoked to reject demands for minority rights. In the West, by contrast, considerations of historic injustice almost always operate to strengthen the claims of minorities. For more on how perceptions of historic injustice affect state-minority relations, see Kymlicka, 2004.

17   For the parallels between the treatment of the Ainu and North American indigenous peoples, see Siddle, 1997.

18   For an overview of indigenous peoples in Asia, see Colchester, 1998; Barnes, 1995.

19   In Thailand, for example, there has been the fear that tribal minorities would ally themselves with ethnic nationalist movements in Burma and Laos.

20   Indigenous peoples were often used as pawns in the struggle between European colonial powers in the Americas, as the English, French and Spanish recruited their own indigenous allies.

21   Anti-colonial nationalist leaders who objected to the European discourse of

'advanced' and 'backward' cultures have often been happy to invoke the same discourse when discussing their own indigenous peoples.

22  For a comparison between Malaysian Chinese and Turks in Germany, see Gurr and Harff, 1994, pp.106-14.
23  International pressure of the sort applied in the Cambodian context to gain citizenship for the Vietnamese minority.
24  The most relevant model would be the sort of 'consociationalism' adopted historically to ensure peace between Catholics and Protestants in the Netherlands and Belgium, and adopted most recently as part of the peace agreement in Northern Ireland (Lipjhart, 1996).

# References

Ahmed, Aftab (1993), 'Ethnicity and Insurgency in the Chittagong Hill Tracts Region', *Journal of Commonwealth and Comparative Politics*, vol.31, pp.32-66.

Ahmed, Samina (1997), 'Centralization, Authoritarianism and the Mismanagement of Ethnic Relations in Pakistan', in Brown and Ganguly, 1997, pp.83-128.

Anaya, S. James (1996), *Indigenous Peoples in International Law*, Oxford University Press, New York.

Anderson, Ben (2004), 'The Future of Indonesia', in Michel Seymour (ed.), *The Fate of the Nation-State*, McGill-Queen's University Press, Montreal.

Arora, Balveer and Nirmal Mukarji (1992), 'Introduction: The Basic Issues', and 'Conclusion: Restructuring Federal Democracy', in Mukarji and Arora, 1992, pp.1-23, pp.265-78.

Bachler, Gunther (ed.) (1997), *Federalism against Ethnicity*, Verlag Ruegger, Zurich.

Banerjee, Ashis (1992), 'Federalism and Nationalism' in Mukarji and Arora, 1992, pp.41-63.

Barnes, R.H. *et al.* (eds.) (1995), *Indigenous Peoples of Asia*, Association of Asian Studies, Ann Arbor.

Bell, Daniel A. (2002), 'Is Democracy the 'Least Bad' System for Minority Groups?' in Susan Henders (ed.), *Democratization and Identity: Regimes and Ethnicity in East and Southeast Asia*, Lexington, New York.

Bell, Gary (2001), 'Minority Rights in Indonesia: Will Constitutional Recognition lead to Disintegration and Discrimination?' *Singapore Journal of International and Comparative Law*, vol.5, pp.784-806.

Bhattacharya, Mohit (1992), 'The Mind of the Founding Fathers', in Mukarji and Arora, 1992, pp.87-104.

Brown, Michael (1997), 'The Impact of Government Policies on Ethnic Relations', in Brown and Ganguly, 1997, pp.511-75.

Brown, Michael and Sumit Ganguly (eds.) (1997), *Government Policies and Ethnic Relations in Asia and the Pacific*, MIT Press, Cambridge.

Colchester, Marcus *et al.* (1998), *Forests and Indigenous Peoples of Asia*, Report 98/4, Minority Rights Group, London.

Connor, Walker (1999), 'National Self-Determination and Tomorrow's Political Map', in

Alan Cairns *et al.* (eds.), *Citizenship, Diversity and Pluralism*, McGill-Queen's University Press, Montreal, pp.163-76.

Dabla, Bashir Ahmad (1998), 'Ethnic Plurality and Problems of Nation-Building in South Asia: A Study of the Kashmiri Problem', in Vijapur, 1998, pp.224-35.

Das, S.R. Mohan (1975), 'Discrimination in India' in Veenhoven, vol.2.

Davis, Michael (1999), 'The Case for Chinese Federalism', *Journal of Democracy*, vol.10, pp.124-37.

Dharmadase, K.N.O. (1992), Language, Religion and Ethnic Assertiveness: The Growth of Sinhalese Nationalism in Sri Lanka, University of Michigan Press, Ann Arbor.

Edrisinha, Rohan (2001), 'Meeting Tamil Aspirations within a United Lanka: Constitutional Options', Centre for Policy Alternatives, Colombo.

Ganguly, Sumit (1997), 'Ethnic Policies and Political Quiescence in Malaysia and Singapore', in Brown and Ganguly, 1997, pp.233-72.

Gellner, David (2001), 'From Group Rights to Individual Rights and Back: Nepalese struggles over culture and equality', in Jane Cowan *et al.* (eds.), *Culture and Rights: Anthropological Perspectives*, Cambridge University Press, Cambridge, pp.177-200.

Guha, Ramachandra (1994), 'Fighting for the Forest: State Forestry and Social Change in Tribal India', in *The Rights of Subordinated Peoples*, Oxford University Press, New Delhi.

Gurr, Ted (1993), *Minorities at Risk: A Global View of Ethnopolitical Conflict*, Institute of Peace Press, Washington.

Gurr, Ted and Barbara Harff (1994), *Ethnic Conflicts in World Politics*, Westiew, Boulder.

Hardgrave, Robert (1993), 'India: The Dilemmas of Diversity', *Journal of Democracy*, vol.4.

Harrison, Selig (1960), *India: The Most Dangerous Decade*, Princeton University Press, Princeton.

He, Baogang (1998), 'Can Kymlicka's Liberal Theory of Minority Rights be Applied in East Asia?', in Paul van der Velde and Alex McKay (eds.), *New Developments in Asian Studies*, Kegal Paul International, London, pp.20-44.

He, Baogang (2004), 'Confucianism versus Liberalism over Minority Rights: A Critical Response to Will Kymlicka', *Chinese Journal of Philosophy*, vol.31, pp.103-23.

Hicks, George (1997), *Japan's Hidden Apartheid: The Korean Minority and the Japanese*, Ashgate, Aldershot.

Ho, Chin Ung (2000), *The Chinese of South-East Asia*, Minority Rights Group, London.

ICES (International Centre for Ethnic Studies) (1995), *Minorities in Cambodia*, Report 95/2, Minority Rights Group, London.

Khan, Arshi (1997), 'The Importance of Article 356', in Khan, 1997b, pp.103-31.

Khan, Rasheeduddin (1997a) 'India, the Federal State and the Kashmir Problem', in Bachler, 1997, pp.269-89.

Khan, Rasheeduddin (ed.) (1997b), *Rethinking Indian Federalism*, Inter-University Centre for Humanities and Social Sciences, Shimla.

Khan, Rasheeduddin (1997c) 'Uttar Pradesh and Federal Balance in India', in Khan, 1997b, pp.253-65.

Kingsbury, Benedict (1995), '"Indigenous Peoples" as an International Legal Concept', in Barnes, 1995, pp.13-34.

Kingsbury, Benedict (1999), 'The Applicability of the International Legal Concept of `Indigenous Peoples' in Asia', in Joanne Bauer and Daniel Bell (eds.), *The East Asian Challenge for Human Rights*, Cambridge University Press, Cambridge, pp.336-77.

Kohli, Atul (1997), 'The Bell Curve of Ethnic Politics: The Rise and Decline of Self-Determination Movements in India', in Wolfgang Danspeckgruber (ed.), *Self-Determination and Self-Administration: A Sourcebook*, Lynne Reiner, Boulder, pp.321-5.

Krishna, Sankaran (1999), *Postcolonial Insecurities: India, Sri Lanka and the Question of Nationhood*, University of Minnesota Press, Minneapolis.

Krishna, Sumi (1992), 'Language Situation', in Mukarji and Arora, 1992, pp.64-86.

Kymlicka, Will (2001), *Politics in the Vernacular*, Oxford University Press, Oxford.

Kymlicka, Will (2004), 'Justice and Security in the Accommodation of Minority Nationalism', in Alain Dieckhoff (ed.), *The Politics of Belonging: Nationalism, Liberalism and Pluralism*, Lexington, New York, pp.127-54.

Liddle, William (1997), 'Coercion, Co-optation and the Management of Ethnic Relations in Indonesia', in Brown and Ganguly, 1997, pp.273-320.

Lijphart, Arend (1996), 'The Puzzle of Indian Democracy: A Consociational Interpretation', *American Political Science Review*, vol.90, pp.258-68.

MRG (Minority Rights Group) (1997), *World Directory of Minorities*, Minority Rights Group International, London.

Mukarji, Nirmal and Balveer Arora (eds.) (1992), *Federalism in India: Origins and Development*, Vikas Publishing, Delhi.

Nandy, Ashis (1992), 'Federalism, the Ideology of the State and Cultural Pluralism', in Mukarji and Arora, 1992, pp.27-40.

Nissan, Elizabeth (1996), *Sri Lanka: a Bitter Harvest*, MRG, London.

Onuma, Yasuaki (1992), 'Interplay Between Human Rights Activities and Legal Standards of Human Rights: A Case Study of the Korean Minority in Japan', *Cornell International Law Journal*, vol.25, pp.515-40.

Patil, S.H, (1998), 'State Formation in Federal India', in Vijapur, 1998, pp.148-59.

Penz, Peter (1992), 'Development Refugees and Distributive Justice: Indigenous Peoples, Land and the Developmentalist State', *Public Affairs Quarterly*, vol.6, pp.105-31.

Penz, Peter (1993), 'Colonization of Tribal Lands in Bangladesh and Indonesia', in Michael Howard (ed.), *Asia's Environmental Crisis*, Westview Press, Boulder, pp.37-72.

Saigal, K. (1992), 'Federal Democracy and Pluralism in the North East', in Mukarji and Arora, 1992.

Schwartzberg, Joseph (1985), 'Factors in the Linguistic Reorganization of Indian States', in Paul Wallace (ed.), *Region and Nation in India*, American Institute of Indian Studies, Delhi, pp.155-82.

Shastri, Amita (1997), 'Government Policy and the Ethnic Crisis in Sri Lanka', in Brown and Ganguly, 1997, pp.129-63.

Siddle, Richard (1996), *Race, Resistance and the Ainu of Japan*, Routledge, London.

Silverstein, Josef (1997), 'Fifty Years of Failure of Burma', in Brown and Ganguly, 1997, pp.167-96,

Singh, Ajay Kumar (1997), 'Jharkhand Movement: Assertion of Socio-Cultural Identity and the Demand for a Separate State', in Khan, 1997b, pp.241-52.

Sisk, Tim (1996), *Power Sharing and International Mediation in Ethnic Conflicts*, US Institute of Peace Press, Washington.

Smith, Alan (1997), 'Ethnic Conflict and Federalism: The Case of Burma', in Bachler, 1997, pp.231-59.

Snyder, Jack (2000), *From Voting to Violence: Democratization and Nationalist Conflict*, Norton, New York.

Srinivasavaradan, T.C.A. (1992), 'Pluralistic Problems in the Federal System', in Mukarji and Arora, 1992, 127-57.

Thier, Alexander (1999), 'Afghanistan: Minority Rights and Autonomy in a Multi-ethnic Failed State', *Stanford Journal of International Law*, vol.35, pp.351-88.

Veenhoven, W. (ed.) (1975-76), *Case Studies on Human Rights and Fundamental Freedoms*, 3 volumes, Martin Nijhoff, The Hague.

Vidyarthi, L.P. (1976), 'Inter-group Conflict and Tension in Contemporary India', in Veenhoven, vol.3.

Vijapur, Abdulrahim (ed.) (1998), *Dimensions of Federal Nation Building*, Manak, Delhi.

Waever, Ole (1995), 'Securitization and Desecuritization', in Ronnie Lipschutz (ed.), *On Security*, Columbia University Press, New York, pp.46-86.

Waheed, Abdul (1998), 'Movement for Uttarkhand State: The Resurgence of Pahari Identity in Uttar Pradesh', in Vijapur, 1998, pp.249-58.

Walzer, Michael (1983), *Spheres of Justice*, Basic Books, New York.

Weiner, Michael (ed.) (1997), *Japan's Minorities: The Illusion of Homogeneity*, Routledge, London.

Weiner, Myron (1998), *Sons of the Soil*, 2nd edition, Oxford University Press, Oxford.

Wimmer, Andreas and Conrad Schetter (2002), *State Formation First: Recommendations for Reconstruction and Peace-Making in Afghanistan*, Discussion Paper #45, Center for Development Research, University of Bonn, Bonn.

Yan Jaiqi (1996), 'China's National Minorities and Federalism', *Dissent*, vol.43 (Summer), pp.139-44.

# Chapter 10

# Montaigne's Cannibals and Multiculturalism

## Cecilia Wee

Increasing ethnic and cultural heterogeneity in countries in the West – the result of increased recent immigration – has led to an interest in multiculturalism as a likely model for societal arrangements in the future. In a multicultural state, different cultures are allowed to flourish and no attempt is made to assimilate the individuals in these cultures into a 'mainstream' culture (usually the culture of the majority). Such a policy has the merit of recognizing that individual lives are lived within diverse ethnic and cultural frameworks. However, multiculturalism is not without its questions and dangers. For example, should group-differentiated rights be accorded to the various minority traditions? Or should one intervene in the long-standing practices of minority traditions (for example, compulsory arranged marriages, female circumcision)?

As a sixteenth-century French philosopher, Michel de Montaigne never commented directly on issues arising in the context of the multicultural state.[1] However, in his *Essais*, Montaigne displayed a deep and culturally sensitive interest in the practices of remote traditions such as the Aztecs and the cannibals of Brazil, as well as a clear recognition that it is customary frameworks that 'give form' to human lives. It is thus worthwhile to investigate whether his views may be brought to bear on those issues that arise in respect of having divergent traditions coexist in a multicultural context.

Montaigne has often been portrayed as a moral relativist, who sees all moral appraisals as relative to standards in a particular community or tradition, such that there is no 'objective' or 'universal' standpoint by which the standards of various traditions can be appraised. This chapter begins by arguing that this portrayal is mistaken, and that Montaigne does in fact think that one can objectively evaluate the standards and practices of various traditions. It then outlines Montaigne's criteria for such evaluation, and suggests that these criteria may usefully be brought to bear with respect to various issues that arise in the context of today's multicultural states.

**Montaigne: Moral Relativist or 'Unconscious' Universalist?**

There is much in Montaigne that suggests that he embraces moral relativism. Montaigne frequently emphasizes that one's conception of the good life is firmly rooted in custom (*coustume*), that is, in the practices and habits of the tradition one is born into:

> I should be prone to excuse our people for having no other pattern and rule of perfection than their own manners and customs; for it is a common vice, not of the vulgar but of almost all men, to fix their aim and limit by the ways to which they were born (1:49, p.215).[2]

Moral judgments which one deems to be 'born of nature' are in fact born of one's particular tradition:

> The laws of conscience, which we say are born of nature, are born of custom. Each man, holding in inward veneration the opinions and behavior approved and accepted around him, cannot break loose from them without remorse, or apply himself to them without self-satisfaction (1:23, p.83).

Much of what Montaigne says indicates that he thinks reason cannot provide a universal standpoint by which to judge the standards and practices of various traditions.

> I think that there falls into man's imagination no fantasy so wild that it does not match the example of some public practice, and for which, consequently, our reason does not find a stay and a foundation (1: 23, p.111).

Here reason, far from transcending traditional custom, appears instead to be its slave. As Todorov (1983) puts it, 'instead of encompassing all customs to distinguish the good from the bad, [the] function [of reason] is to find plausible justifications for the most varied customs'.

Montaigne also points out that our so-called 'rational' judgments are in fact derived from custom – 'what is off the hinges of custom, people believe to be off the hinges of reason' (1:23, p.83). Moreover, even if there are judgments made through custom-transcending reason, it appears that one will be unable to distinguish them from custom-derived judgments because of the 'tyranny' of custom:

> For in truth habit is a violent and treacherous schoolmistress. She establishes in us, little by little, stealthily, the foothold of her authority; but having by this mild and humble beginning settled and planted it with the help of time, she soon uncovers to us a furious and tyrannical face against which we no longer have the liberty of even raising our eyes (1:23, p.77).

One never has any assurance that so-called 'rational' assessments of moral practices are not in fact custom-derived.

Given Montaigne's acceptance of the tyranny of custom over reason, it seems one cannot rely upon reason to provide a universal standpoint from which one can objectively evaluate the practices of different traditions – whether one's own or another's. This, in conjunction with his frequent claims that one's conception of the good life depends upon the practices of the tradition one inhabits, offers significant grounds for the claim that Montaigne is a moral relativist.

That he is a relativist also receives support from the non-judging and benign attitude he apparently evinces towards the practices of those in other traditions and cultures:

> Here they live on human flesh; there it is an act of piety to kill one's father at a certain age; elsewhere the fathers ordain, while the children are still in their mothers' wombs, which ones they want to have brought up and kept, and which abandoned and killed. Elsewhere old husbands lend their wives to the young for their use; and elsewhere still, they are had in common, without sin (1:23, p.82).

In delineating here the differing practices of those in different traditions, Montaigne seems to suggest that the moral evaluation of an act always depends on the norms accepted by a particular tradition. Thus, while one tradition strongly condemns anyone who kills his father, another deems that it could be an act of piety to do so. Appreciation of the vast diversity of differing traditions and norms leads one to realize that one cannot and should not judge the behaviour of those inhabiting other traditions by one's own norms.

However, recent commentators express unease about the claim that Montaigne is a moral relativist. They point out that a close analysis of Montaigne's writings reveals that he does in fact pass his own moral judgments on the behaviour of those in other cultures and traditions. For instance, in 'Of Cannibals', he describes the Brazilians' practice of hacking to death their enemies, and roasting and eating them as one of 'barbarous horror' (1:31, p.155), while approving of their valor. In 'Of coaches', he praises the Aztecs for 'their devoutness, observance of the laws, goodness, liberality, loyalty and frankness' (3:6, p.694).

Todorov suggests that such judgments reveal a conflict of theory and practice in Montaigne. While he avows moral relativism and advocates a non-judgmental approach to the practices of other traditions, he is in reality 'a universalist without knowing it' – someone who unconsciously judges other cultures according to his own ideals (derived from Greek civilization). Todorov criticizes Montaigne thus:

> The relativist does not judge others. The conscious universalist can condemn them, but he does so in the name of an explicit ethic, which can then be automatically questioned. The unconscious universalist [that is, Montaigne] cannot be attacked, since he pretends to be a relativist; but this does not prevent him from judging others... (Todorov, 1983, p.125).

I shall argue that Montaigne is neither a moral relativist nor an unconscious universalist. It is quite clear from a reading of the *Essais* that Montaigne exhibits in general an attitude of benign acceptance towards the practices of other traditions; but this general stance can be reconciled with the fact that he *consciously* evaluates morally the practices of other traditions. His position in this respect may provide useful pointers for relating to other traditions within the context of a multicultural state.

**The Role of Reason in Montaigne's *Essais***

As mentioned, various passages in Montaigne's *Essais* suggest that reason cannot transcend custom and hence cannot provide an objective evaluation of the norms and practices of different traditions. However, a careful reading of these passages reveals that they do not necessarily commit him to such a stance.

Montaigne does hold that reason may be used to justify any existing practice under the sun. Yet even Descartes, for whom the moral life is centrally located in doing whatever reason tells us with a firm will, accepted that reason could be so abused.[3] Similarly, that Montaigne held that reason may be (mis-)applied to justify any existing practice does not preclude his accepting that reason, properly used, can provide an objective moral evaluation of the practices of different traditions.

While Montaigne claims custom is a tyrannical schoolmistress, he also suggests that although it is very difficult to escape its grip, it is not *impossible* to do so:

> the principal effect of the power of custom is to…ensnare us in such a way that it is *hardly* (*a peine*) within our power to get ourselves back out of its grip and return into ourselves to reflect and reason about its ordinances (1:23, p.83).

Montaigne writes that we can *hardly* escape the influence of custom in order to 'return into ourselves' to rationally reflect on customary practices, suggesting that while this procedure is difficult to achieve, it is not impossible. That reason *can* be used to evaluate custom is supported by this crucial passage in 'Of custom':

> Whoever wants to get rid of this violent prejudice of custom will find many things accepted with undoubting resolution, which have no support but in the hoary beard and the wrinkles of the usage that goes with them; but when this mask is torn off, and he refers things to truth and reason, he will feel his judgment as it were all upset, and nevertheless restored to a much surer status (1:23, pp.84-5).

Montaigne allows that custom leads to the unquestioning acceptance of many practices, but holds nevertheless that one *can* refer these practices to truth and reason for evaluation. While such referral may result in initial dislocation for one's judgment, one's judgment will eventually be restored to a much surer status (being founded on reason rather than unquestioning habit).[4]

In sum, key passages often quoted in support of Montaigne as moral relativist do not, upon closer examination, commit him to this position. Montaigne indicates that one *can* refer norms and practices to 'truth and reason' for evaluation.[5] Thus, it is unsurprising that he offers moral evaluations of the practices of the French, Brazilians, and Aztecs in his writings.

How precisely does reason work in order to provide an objective and universal standpoint for the evaluation of practices? Montaigne does not, of course, have anything close to a systematically articulated theory on this matter. Nevertheless, one is able to discern, on the basis of Montaigne's own moral judgments of various practices, his view of the role(s) played by reason in evaluating the practices of different traditions.

In 'Of Cannibals', Montaigne decries the practice of killing an enemy and then cooking and eating him as one of 'barbarous horror'. However, he goes on to add:

> I am not sorry that we notice the barbarous horror of such acts, but I am heartily sorry that, judging their faults rightly, we should be so blind to our own. I think there is more barbarity in eating a man alive than in eating him dead; and in tearing by tortures and the rack a body still full of feeling, in roasting a man bit by bit...than in roasting and eating him after he is dead (1:31, p.155).

Montaigne states here that he (and other Frenchmen) judges rightly that it is a 'fault' in the Brazilians that they have the barbaric practice of killing and eating their enemies (an act, Montaigne makes clear, that is done purely out of revenge). However, the failure of the French is in not applying the same yardstick to their own practices. In fact, their practice of torturing living persons is even more barbaric than the Brazilians'.

It is evident that Montaigne is using a universal standard here to judge of the practices of different traditions. In 'Of Cruelty', Montaigne describes cruelty as 'the extreme of all vices'. In both 'Of Cannibals' and 'Of Cruelty', he judges the French torture of live victims as far more cruel than Brazilian roasting and eating dead flesh. Hence the French are at greater fault than the Brazilians: insofar as the Brazilians ought not to have their practice, it is even more urgent that the French eliminate theirs.

What precisely are the universal standards which Montaigne appeals to judge of practices across different traditions, and how are such standards supported by reason? In the passage above, Montaigne apparently evaluates the respective practices of the Brazilians and French according to whether a particular *trait* or *quality* – in this case, cruelty – is manifested in the conduct of these practices. In other passages, Montaigne condemns the French for treachery, dissimulation, and tyranny, and notes approvingly that Brazilian (cannibal) society is free from these traits.[6]

One may surmise that Montaigne holds that there are certain evils which are universal for humans across all traditions. Cruelty, treachery, and tyranny are judged to be evils by all humans. In 'Of Cannibals', he writes tellingly that 'there never was any opinion so disordered (*desreglee*) as to justify (*excusast*) treachery, disloyalty, tyranny, and cruelty, which are our ordinary vices' (1:31, pp.155-6, my emphasis). For Montaigne, there is a limit to what reason can justify: no matter how 'disordered' or unruly one's use of reason is, it can never be so unruly as to provide a (convincing) justification of treachery, disloyalty, tyranny, and cruelty.[7]

Montaigne's position here needs to be disambiguated carefully. It is quite plausible to see Montaigne as claiming in the passage above that there is no tradition in which one's use of reason is so disordered as to justify that cruelty, treachery, and such are *intrinsic* goods (that is, final goods that one ought to aim at). Considered in themselves, these are such that no person in any tradition could offer a convincing rational justification that they are ends in themselves. Reason is thus never disordered enough to provide a 'stay and a foundation' for them as intrinsic goods.

Such a reading of the passage is plausible enough. However, most traditions do not justify cruel, treacherous, or such vicious practices on the grounds of their intrinsic value. Such traditions as attempt to rationally justify such practices usually do so by arguing that they are *instruments* to some further good. Is Montaigne also claiming in the passage above that reason can never justify any cruel, treacherous, or such vicious practice whatsoever, even those that are instruments for promoting a greater good? Such a reading would indeed be hard to defend. For example, Montaigne is clearly willing to accept (political) treachery, insofar as such treachery is a necessary evil to achieve the larger public good. Indeed, he sees the occasional use of treachery (and even cruelty) as a *sine qua non* of working to promote the public good:

> The more vigorous and less fearful citizens [must] sacrifice their honor and conscience for the good of their country...The public welfare requires than a man betray and lie and massacre...(3:1, p.600).

For Montaigne, cruelty, treachery, and such are evils, but there are circumstances in which practices that manifest them may be rationally justified and (if not quite approved) would at least be morally permitted.

Nevertheless, Montaigne makes clear that reason would also limit the extent to which we can instrumentally justify such practices. For example, Montaigne criticizes the French practice of torture, not just on the grounds that cruelty is an intrinsic evil, but because this cruel practice is *inconsistent* with promoting what the French tradition considers a good. He writes:

> Even in justice, all that goes beyond plain death seems to me pure cruelty, and especially for us who [as Christians] ought to have some concern about sending souls away in a good state; which cannot happen when we have agitated them and made them desperate by unbearable tortures (2:11, p.314).

The Christian tradition of sixteenth-century France sees it as a good that a human who is dying makes his peace with God and the world, but the practice of torturing a man before killing him would not allow him to do so. One can thus call into question the instrumental justifiability of a practice if it is inconsistent with promoting a good important to the tradition in question.

Montaigne also stresses the need to be careful in determining and assessing the precise instrumental justifications offered for the perpetuation of practices that are evil (considered in themselves), and to reject such practices as lacking sound rational justification. For example, Montaigne points out that monarchs regularly require their subjects give up their livelihoods and lives to further the conduct of wars. For Montaigne, warfare is a 'human disease' (1:31, p.156) – something that cannot be considered a good in itself. He urges that one should be careful to establish that wars are indeed for good causes before taking part in them. Often, those who fight in these wars may have no inkling of what they are fighting for; Montaigne disapproves of the ignorance and blind obedience to the prince of the soldier who, when asked why he is fighting, states that he himself 'has no passion and quarrel in this' (3:4, p.637). A careful enquiry into the cause for which the war is being fought often reveals it to be a frivolous cause or even no cause at all – 'a daydream without body or subject [which] dominates and agitates [the soul]' (3:4, p.637) – in which case one should resist taking part in it.

Montaigne also urges caution in accepting the reasons which are publicly put forward for such wars (and other matters of public interest). Such reasons may often turn out to be spurious, and the result of dissimulation. He points out that 'fine statements' by public figures are often covers for 'ambition and avarice' (1:39, p.174), and one should not accept them blindly. Reason may indeed be mis-used to provide an (instrumental) 'stay and foundation' for particular practices, but we can (and should) use reason to determine whether the justifications for practices which involve cruelty, treachery and such are acceptable.

All this is not to deny that Montaigne does accept that there are situations in which, say, treachery, dissimulation, and even cruelty are necessary evils for the larger public good, and so permissible. Even here, however, Schaefer (1990) has argued convincingly that Montaigne thinks some political structures breed more evils such as treachery and correspondingly require more of the same in order to promote the public good than others. Montaigne writes that he prefers a structure in which what he owns is his by 'right and authority' rather than by 'reward and grace'. Schaefer shows that Montaigne thinks that a political structure that allows the individual maximum freedom to pursue her own private interests is less likely to breed and hence require less treachery than, for example, a monarchy. In a monarchy, where wealth and power are obtained either as a reward from or as a result of grace by the monarch, there is likely to be more treachery by those competing for the monarch's favours or influence with the monarch. Given the pervasiveness of treachery, one would need to exercise treachery to ensure one's political survival, let alone to realize the (disinterested) goal of promoting the public good. Montaigne did not perhaps hold that a liberal democracy is always the best form of political organization for all societies at all stages of development – but he clearly did think of it as the ideal form of political organization, insofar as it needs less perpetuation of evils such as treachery to sustain it.

## Montaigne's Restricted Universalism

If the interpretation of Montaigne I have sketched is correct, then Montaigne is not, *pace* Todorov, an 'unconscious universalist'. He is instead quite a conscious one, someone who holds that one *can* rationally judge and morally evaluate the practices and norms of various traditions. Montaigne thinks that certain qualities – cruelty, treachery, and such – would never be accepted as intrinsic goods by anyone in any tradition unless he or she is 'disordered'. (This of course does not mean that there are no cruel, treacherous, or such vicious persons in these traditions – only that none of them could *rationally* justify their cruelty, treachery, and so on as intrinsic goods.) In that case, those practices which manifest such qualities would receive initial disapprobation, unless and until they can be shown to be genuine instruments for achieving some significant good within the tradition.

Montaigne is then not a moral relativist who holds that there are no means of evaluating the practices within a tradition that is independent of the tradition itself; but this may create a puzzle. There are numerous passages in which Montaigne clearly evinces the kind of benign and non-judging acceptance that is regarded as the hallmark of the relativist. He often emphasizes that practices may be very different in different traditions, in such a way as to leave one no doubt that he does not think one should criticize the practices of other traditions. He reminds French wives not to judge cannibal wives by their moral standards (1:31, p.158), and intimates that the French should not criticize the Swiss, Italian, and Germans because their practices are different, for each nation has many customs and usages that may seem 'savage and miraculous' to other nations but actually are not (3:13, pp.827-8). How is this pervasive and benign acceptance of difference to be reconciled with his universalist stance?

The two are quite compatible. For Montaigne, other traditions may hold things to be goods that one's own tradition does not, and may institute specific practices that differ markedly from those in one's own tradition. As long as these practices do not involve cruelty, treachery, and such (or, more weakly, do involve them but have sufficient rational justification), Montaigne would say in respect of these practices – *to each his own*. Montaigne often includes under such practices those pertaining to familial and marital arrangements. He notes that such arrangements differ widely across traditions and thinks that none of these arrangements in themselves is any worse than any other, or particularly cruel, treacherous, and so on. He therefore holds that in this arena we should simply respect each other's differences.

To Montaigne, then, any moral agent operates with two differing sets of moral standards. We judge of agents in other traditions according to whether their behaviour manifests cruelty, treachery, and such, without acceptable instrumental justification, and condemn them when their behaviour does not fulfill this criterion. In the case of agents in our own tradition, we judge of their behaviour according to the above criterion as well; but we also judge them according to whether their behaviour conforms to the *specific* standards found in our own tradition. For example, Montaigne criticizes those in the (Catholic) French tradition who would prevent a man's making his soul before he dies (because the latter is a good in this tradition). He would not condemn a Brazilian for such a failure, because obviously the cannibal tradition does not regard this as a good. Thus, in addition to certain universal standards which we would employ to judge of all humans, we have tradition-specific moral standards by which we would judge of those in our own tradition.

Montaigne's universalism is thus a restricted universalism – it leaves considerable space for those in different traditions to carry out their different practices. I now explore how Montaigne's views can be usefully deployed in respect of communal issues within a multicultural context.

## Montaigne and Multiculturalism

Montaigne's position provides an attractive basis for dealing with issues that arise within the multicultural context. This is because it generally respects that there are different forms of life, and allows considerable room for different traditions to pursue their particular practices (and so preserve their cultural identity). Moreover, it allows this *without* accepting that 'anything goes', that one can never make any judgments about the practices of another tradition.

On Montaigne's view, the different traditions should be allowed to pursue their specific practices, insofar as these practices can be established not to involve cruelty, treachery, and such, or if there is acceptable instrumental justification for practices which *do* involve them. What impact on multicultural states might accepting such position with respect to the practices of different traditions have?

One area in which accepting this Montaignian position might make a difference concerns the granting of group-differentiated rights. While group-differentiated rights and legislation are already a feature of Western countries, such as the United States and Canada, accepting Montaigne's position might result in a recommendation that such countries go further in promoting them than they currently do.

As Kymlicka points out, the group-differentiated rights granted in the United States and Canada were granted to early settlers or to native peoples. Later waves of immigrants are not granted such rights. Montaigne, however, constantly emphasized that it is custom which 'gives form to our life' (3:13, p.827) and recommended acceptance and respect of those practices of other traditions that do not manifest treachery, cruelty, and such. Accepting Montaigne's position involves accepting that all practices which do not manifest these qualities should be allowed to flourish, even if they are different from one's own. Thus, at least in principle, group-differentiated rights could be granted to all traditions, whether they are those of recent immigrants or earlier settlers.

This does not deny that caution is needed in the actual implementation of such rights. Montaigne himself was well-known for his political conservatism, urging extreme caution when bringing about changes in policy and legislation that might be disruptive of stability.[8] We too could recognize the need to exercise care in the wider implementation of group-differentiated rights. This is particularly so as the wider granting of such rights may result in considerable changes in social structure. For example, let us assume along with Montaigne that the different familial and marital arrangements are none of them particularly cruel or treacherous, and hence should all be respected. If one extrapolates this to apply to the multicultural state, this might well require the state to allow, say, a Muslim man to practice restricted polygamy and *talaq* divorce, while requiring men belonging to Christian traditions to be monogamous. Adjusting personal law (laws that pertain to marriage, divorce, inheritance, and so on) so that persons in different traditions are treated differently is going quite far, and certainly further than Western countries have done with respect to recent immigrants.

One criticism of such wide group-differentiated rights is that it violates a central principle of justice – namely, that all individuals are equal before the law. This issue is too broad to be tackled satisfactorily in a short paper. However, a quick Montaignian reply to this point would be that enforcing a law that requires monogamy is in fact discriminating against those in non-monogamous cultures, in effect requiring them to submit to the practices of the dominant tradition. This amounts to imposing one's tradition-specific moral standards on someone in another tradition, and goes against the Montaignian position that one should respect tradition-specific standards that do not violate universal ones.

More pragmatic objections would include that differences in the laws applicable to persons in different traditions could create jealousy and communal tension. Again, allowing too much room for different traditions to preserve their norms and cultural identity may run the risk of fragmenting the state, as the primary allegiance of the citizen is to his community or tradition, and not to the state.

In reply to this, it may be acknowledged that the actual implementation of such differential laws depends very much on the specifics of the state in question, and that such introduction would have to be gradual and require political skill and timing. With respect to the point that differences in law might generate communal tension, it might be argued that such granting of group-differentiated rights could play a role in *defusing* such tension. Such tension is usually at its greatest when the state demands that the minority traditions give up their practices and even their language, and adopt the practices and language of the dominant tradition. It is in such cases that the dissatisfactions of the oppressed minorities express themselves in tense communal relations.

A similar reply can be made to the point that, in giving different traditions too much room to pursue their own practices, the state runs the risk of fragmentation – namely, that it may be that not giving traditions enough room to pursue their own practices puts the state at greatest risk of fragmentation. Moreover, while there is an admitted risk that the individual's allegiance will first be to the tradition and not to the state, this can to some extent be mitigated by the pursuit of policies that would encourage citizens to see themselves as stakeholders in the state, as belonging to and having interest in the well-being of the state.

In sum, accepting Montaigne's position might commit one to accepting that fairly extensive group-differentiated rights should be granted to minority traditions, since all practices which do not violate non-tradition-specific (that is, universal) standards should (in principle) be countenanced. But how does one deal with practices in such traditions which *do* violate such standards? Following Montaigne, practices which are cruel, treacherous, and so on without sound instrumental justification should receive disapprobation. Given such disapprobation, does it follow that intervention in the existing practices of the minority traditions would be appropriate?

The answer to this cannot be adequately dealt with here.[9] Assuming that these existing practices do not have adequate instrumental justification, the question of when those external to the tradition (including the state, NGOs, or individuals in other traditions) may appropriately intervene in such practices has been much discussed. Similarly, the modes of intervention (for example, persuasion, legislation, or force) that are appropriate to adopt have also been the subject of some debate. In the case of practices that are indeed extreme in their cruelty, treachery, and so on, some form of intervention is clearly justified; but in cases of mild forms of these vices (which are, as Montaigne points out, among our 'ordinary vices'), this is perhaps less clear. One might need to weigh the drawbacks of the practice against, for example, the extent to which it 'gives form' to the individual's life and invests her life with meaning. Again, there are issues (particularly in respect of intervention by the state) concerning intrusion into the private sphere. This would have to be another project.

A broader question that may arise concerning my attempt to apply Montaigne's views to the multicultural context is this. Montaigne holds that practices involving cruelty, treachery, and so on without adequate justification should be respected, but those which do involve unjustified cruelty, treachery, and so on should be condemned. But it might be objected that such criteria are vague and unhelpful: under what conditions would a practice be deemed to be cruel or treacherous?

An answer to this requires a much more detailed examination into Montaigne's views than there is space for. I would like to focus, in the last segment of this chapter, on one of Montaigne's key criteria – viz., cruelty – and examine how this criterion might be applied to particular practices. This criterion seems especially worthy of examination in the context of a multicultural state: in many instances where there has been an outcry by those in one tradition against the practice of another, this has often (I suspect) been based on the visceral response that the practice is somehow 'cruel'. (For instance, female circumcision and compulsory arranged marriages might be seen as cruel to women.) So what are the circumstances in which Montaigne would deem an act to be cruel?

Unlike Locke, Montaigne accepts that an·act can be cruel even if the person perpetrating it does not *intend* to inflict pain/distress (far less feel, as Locke intimates, a 'seeming kind of pleasure' in doing it). In his *Essais*, Montaigne spends a lot of time examining the various examples of cruelty in quite graphic detail. Significantly, he hardly makes reference to the mental state of the perpetrators in these accounts. Again, he includes among the milder forms of cruelty the lopping off of a chicken's head, where such a deed is evidently done for the purposes of dinner (rather than from any intent to inflict distress). For Montaigne, then, a deed or practice is assessed as cruel (or not) independent of considerations involving the intent of the perpetrator. This being so, Montaigne would accept that a practice may be condemned as cruel, even if the perpetrators do not *intentionally* inflict pain/distress on its victims.

What then makes a particular deed or practice cruel? Montaigne instances among the more extreme cases of cruelty the gladiatorial sports of Rome, and the various forms of Inquisition torture, but includes as milder forms of cruelty the fore-mentioned lopping off of a chicken's head or simple forms of death (by guillotine or strangulation). While Montaigne's instances of cruelty usually involve damage to the body, it is clear that he thinks the cruelty in the deed is proportionate to the amount of *mental* distress inflicted upon the victim. The simple forms of death are less cruel because they involve less mental distress in the victim than does the prolonged agony of human torture. Again, the Brazilian roasting of their dead enemies is far less cruel than French torture of living persons, because far less mental distress is involved. As Montaigne points out, once the enemy has been strangled, the roasting and eating of his flesh is unlikely to bother him.

For Montaigne, then, cruelty is proportionate to the mental distress inflicted on the victim. Significantly, he also accepts that this proportion of mental distress does not necessarily correspond to the physical damage done to the body, or even the physical pain felt. In 'Of Custom', he cites Aristotle's example of the son found beating the father:

> The man whom they found beating his father replied that it was the custom of his house: that his father had beaten his grandfather thus, his grandfather his great-grandfather; and pointing to his son: 'And this one will beat me when he has come to my present age'. And the father whom his son was dragging and bumping along the street ordered him to stop at a certain door, for he had dragged his own father only that far; this was the limit of the hereditary rough treatment that the sons traditionally practiced upon the fathers in their family (1:23, p.83).

The father does not seem unduly distressed or bothered by his son's treatment of himself, even though he has been beaten and dragged (painfully, one presumes) along the street. For Montaigne, his equanimity derives from the fact that this is a long-standing practice in the family. Clearly, this practice does not cause the father as much mental distress as it would have in, say, the Chinese tradition, where filial respect is emphasized, and being beaten by one's son would involve great shame and a sense of failure. Thus, what would have been a very cruel thing to do to a Chinese father is not as cruel in the context of this family's tradition.

This being so, one should be careful to assess the cruelty of a practice according to the degree of mental distress it would engender in a person in *that specific tradition*. For example, a tradition reared to the notion of marrying for love might find the practice of compulsory arranged marriages where the parties have little choice cruel and stifling. However, it does not follow that those in a tradition in which this is a long-standing practice would feel the same sort of mental distress. The latter might accept it as a fact of life or even as the way things *ought* to be done. Thus, Montaigne would hold that establishing a practice as cruel involves that it should give rise to great mental distress to persons *within* the tradition that carries out the practice.

It is also possible, however, that the longstanding practice of compulsory arranged marriages has been a longstanding source of misery and distress to the individuals in the tradition. Or again, it may be that, as traditions evolve, what had been a practice that caused little mental distress may come to cause a great deal (for example, as daughters and sons come to be educated in schools in the West and interact with classmates from Western traditions, they might come to feel grave mental distress at this practice). In such cases, Montaigne would hold that, if there is no sound justification for that practice, it must be condemned as cruel.

We have examined above Montaigne's criteria for picking out a particular practice as cruel. The assumption thus far has been that the practices in question have no good instrumental justification. It might be argued that the community or tradition's leaders will always find instrumental justification for their practices, and so resist condemnation (and possible intervention). Montaigne's response would be that one should be careful to never take such justification at face value, but use reason to evaluate whether such justification is adequate – one will most often find that it is not.

## Conclusion

A brief sketch has been offered of the ways in which one could deploy Montaigne's views on other cultures and traditions in a multicultural state. The position arrived at might depart somewhat from the current position adopted by Western countries, but might nevertheless be viable. The Montaigne-based position outlined above gives due recognition to the importance of custom in giving meaning to a person's life, but at the same time ensures that cruel and treacherous customs (no matter which tradition they come from) should not be countenanced except under the very strongest of rational justifications.

## Notes

1   April Carter has suggested that Montaigne's views concerning other traditions might be usefully related to his own experiences in sixteenth-century France, particularly in respect of the 'wars' (cultural and otherwise) between Catholics and Huguenot Protestants.
2   Citations from the *Essais* give book and essay numbers, followed by page numbers in the translation by Frame, 1957.
3   As Descartes points out in the *Discourse on Method*, the 'diversity of opinions' come about not because some of us are more rational than others, but because 'we direct our thoughts along different paths and do not attend to the same things'. He stresses that it is not enough to be possessed of reason – one must also 'apply it well' (Cottingham *et al.*, 1984, p.3).
4   Discussions of Montaigne's view of reason can be found in Locher, 1995; Duval, 1983; Frame, 1995; La Charite, 1995. Montaigne's *Apology for Raymond Sebond* is often thought to express scepticism about reason. However, as commentators often point out, the *Apology* is a complex and obscure work whose claims pose a profound hermeneutical challenge. It has been suggested that there are grounds for thinking that the scepticism expressed there pertains to knowledge rather than reason.
5   It might be objected that these passages show that one can submit the practices and norms of one's *own* tradition to reason for evaluation. It does not follow that reason provides a universal standpoint for judging across all traditions. For example, one might use reason to eliminate inconsistencies in one's traditional practices and to bring

reason in line with the tradition's identified ends, but in such cases reason is not obviously tradition-transcending. These passages are not amenable to a reading which sees reason as performing such a subordinate role, wherein reason would still operate within the influence of custom. These passages exhort one to get out of the grip of custom, and 'return into ourselves' to reflect and reason, suggesting that one needs to break free of all influence by custom. Reason is thus to play a tradition-transcending role in assessing the practices of the tradition.

6    He also praises the Brazilians for their bravery in battle, liberality, and loyalty. One may correspondingly infer that those practices manifesting such virtues would receive approbation. I will focus on those traits which receive condemnation, leaving Montaigne's treatment of those which receive approbation to another occasion.

7    As it is rather tedious to list continually all four qualities in my subsequent discussion, I shall from now on use 'cruelty and treachery' as a shorthand for Montaigne's list of qualities. I highlight 'cruelty' and 'treachery' as these two qualities receive relatively prominent discussion in my paper. Note also that I do not claim that the qualities which may be regarded universally as vices are *limited* to the four qualities listed by Montaigne. There may well be other qualities that could be added to the list.

8    See, for example, 'Of Custom': 'Whoever meddles with choosing and changing usurps the authority to judge, and he must be very sure that he sees the weakness of what he is casting out and the goodness of what he is bringing in' (1:23, p.88).

9    I would like to thank Steven Lukes, Kok-Chor Tan, James Tiles, and particularly Barry Hindess for their useful comments on the relationship between moral disapprobation of a practice and intervention in that practice.

# References

Berven, Dikka (ed.) (1995), *Montaigne: A Collection of Essays*, Garland Publishing Press, New York.

Cottingham, John *et al.* (trans.) (1984), *The Complete Writings of Descartes*, vol.I, Cambridge University Press, Cambridge.

Duval, Robert (1983), 'Lessons of the New World: Design and Meaning in Montaigne's "Des Cannibales" and "Des Coches"', *Yale French Studies*, vol.64, pp.95-112.

Frame, Donald M. (1995), 'Montaigne's Dialogue with his Faculties', in Berven, 1995, vol.4, pp.161-74.

Frame, Donald M. (trans.) (1957), *The Complete Works of Montaigne*, Hamish Hamilton, London.

La Charite, Raymond C. (1995), 'The Relationship of Judgment and Experience in the Essais of Montaigne', in Berven, 1995, vol. 4, pp.29-8.

Locher, Caroline (1995), 'Primary and Secondary Themes in Montaigne's "Des Cannibales"', in Berven, 1995, vol.2, pp.155-62.

Schaefer, David Lewis (1990), *The Political Philosophy of Montaigne*, Cornell University Press, Ithaca.

Todorov, Tzvetan (1983), 'L'Etre et L'Autre: Montaigne', *Yale French Studies*, vol.64, pp.113-45.

# Chapter 11

# Citizenship and Cultural Equality[1]

## Baogang He

Saul Bellow is famously quoted as saying something like, 'When the Zulus produce a Tolstoy we will read him'. This is taken as a quintessential statement of European arrogance, not just because Bellow is allegedly being de facto insensitive to the value of Zulu culture, but frequently also because it is seen to reflect a denial in principle of human equality (Taylor, 1994, p.42).

The notion of cultural equality has assumed increasing importance in the normative discourse of international relations. Since the end of World War II, the international community has repudiated decisively the older tradition of a racial or ethnic hierarchy, and come to endorse the idea of human and ethnic equality. Indeed, with the rise of East Asian economic power in the 1980s, policy-makers and academia placed particular emphasis on the notion of cultural equality. Nevertheless, the events of 11 September 2001 seem to have stalled this trend, undermining the value of cultural equality and perhaps rendering it impossible because of a supposed civilizational conflict between Western and Islamic cultures.

A number of theorists have focused on the idea of cultural equality. Notable in this respect are Edward Said's idea of equality of civilizations, Will Kymlicka's concern with the cultural equality of minorities, Charles Taylor's emphasis on the equal value of cultures, and Iris Marion Young's demand for the equal value of different cultures to be publicly affirmed. Recently, however, Brian Barry has mounted a substantial critique of this body of work with its support for multiculturalism and the equal value of cultures. As reflected in the title of his book, *Culture and Equality*, Barry seeks to separate culture from equality, and indeed repudiates the notion of 'cultural equality' (2001, p.266). This chapter offers a critical response to Barry's argument.

In contrast to Barry's approach, this chapter aims to defend the concept of cultural equality by critically engaging with the idea and dealing constructively with attendant problems and limitations. It begins by assessing arguments in support of cultural equality and discussing its multiple meanings and value. It then canvasses some of the arguments against cultural equality, highlights the complex theoretical difficulties and problems that arise if the question of cultural equality is taken seriously, and suggests strategies for dealing with these problems.

Clearly, as Robert B. Walker (1990) points out, there is a great deal of confusion over the concept of 'culture' itself. For the purposes of this chapter, culture includes religion, civilization, language, cultural practice, custom, and philosophical interpretation and excludes practices such as those associated with organized crime (for example, the mafia and drugs trade). Cultures are understood as open, multifaceted, and dynamic systems that possess essentially overlapping memberships that are interactive and internally negotiated. They are sites of contestation and heterogeneity, of hybridization and cross-fertilization, whose boundaries are inevitably indeterminate (Tully, 1995, p.30). Importantly, the cultural collective can be understood as an inter-subjective realm populated by creative and critical individuals who define, defend, and deconstruct their cultures. In this context, 'culture' should be understood as an open system in which individuals can struggle against the tendency for 'organic culture' to regulate and control community, while 'collective' should be interpreted as a realm of inter-subjective internal and external relationships.

It is also important to distinguish two conceptions of equality. One is a universal conception of equality, which stresses the equal treatment, right, opportunity, and entitlement of all human beings. The other is a differential approach, which emphasizes cultural differences. Most writings on cultural or minority rights adopt this latter differential approach, seeing it as unjust for a disadvantaged group to be forced to compete with a dominant group on unequal terms. As Kymlicka (1989, p.162) puts it, 'the members of minority cultural communities may face particular kinds of disadvantages whose rectification requires and justifies the provision of minority rights'. A clear exception to this position is that of Brian Barry, who rejects the differential notion of equality in favor of an egalitarian approach to group rights.

This chapter deviates from the differential notion of equality espoused by thinkers such as Kymlicka and adopts instead a global perspective of cultural equality. This is because the politics of international relations tends to associate the notion of cultural equality primarily with the equal respect and treatment of other cultures. So by taking a differential notion of cultural equality at the global level we may neglect the important question of an equal respect for cultures across nation-states.

By stressing the importance of cultural equality, this chapter also attempts to bypass the relativist critique. Crucially, the idea of *cultural* equality highlights the importance of cultures and their differences. At the same time, cultural *equality* assumes cultural interaction and holds a universal cross-cultural perspective that sees equality as the basis for the communication, production, and distribution of culture both internally and externally. Thus the idea of cultural equality avoids the position of cultural relativism, which is forced to endorse a type of equality that holds all cultural practices equal and is unable to distinguish between their relative values. What is being canvassed here is not relativism but a willingness to allow the possibility for all cultures to be given an equal hearing, not that all cultural practices are equally valuable. This avoids the dilemma faced by cultural relativists who are forced into a solipsistic stance that precludes open dialogue between cultures and renders consensus impossible.

**Arguments for Cultural Equality**

*Linking Culture and Citizenship*

Citizenship and culture have traditionally been regarded as mutually exclusive, especially by classical liberals; yet, we can detect more than a hint of hypocrisy. For instance, in colonial India, classical liberalism took indigenous culture seriously so much so that it formed the view that inhabitants of this culture were rendered incapable of autonomous action and thereby unsuited to citizenship (Hindess, 2001). Meanwhile, back at home culture and citizenship were seen as separate. In the case of the French Revolution, which was premised on the view that all humans are equal, it declared equality for all irrespective of race, ethnicity, and culture. We see that there is no space here for 'cultural equality' and culture appears to be largely irrelevant to the liberal conception of equality, in which a secular civic state should be ethnically and culturally neutral. In other words, the French civic tradition favors the universal over the particular, civic over ethnic and cultural values.[2]

In practice, however, there is inequality in the nation-state system where minority cultural groups are treated differently and majority culture tends to assume a privileged position as the paradigm of national identity and nationhood. Nic Craith Mairead (2002) argues, for instance, that in Britain English has been institutionalized as the national language, a symbol of national coherence, while Welsh and Irish have long been regarded as a 'commodity', so that government subsidy for their rejuvenation is seen as some sort of paternalistic favor. In other words, a supposed 'neutral' state has favored, financed, and privileged a majority language (English), thereby putting minority cultures in a weak position. The problem now is how to level the playing field according to the principle of cultural equality and to link citizenship with culture. Mairead suggests that the idea of citizenship should seriously embrace that of cultural equality regarding it as integral to citizenship.

*Deepening the Idea of Equality*

There is a progressive current to the idea of equality which has traversed the spectrum from the political equality of rights and suffrage in democratic systems, through economic equality (embraced through socialist principles) and social equality which stresses equal access to jobs and social services, to the notion of cultural equality. The idea of citizenship has been associated with the struggle for political, economic, and social equality. According to T. H. Marshall (1963), the idea of 'full citizenship' for all is linked to the welfare state's attack on poverty. However, citizenship is no longer exclusively concerned with the struggle for political, economic, and social equality, but has become a major site of conflict over cultural identity and demands for the recognition of cultural rights and equal cultural status.

Cultural right is the claim made by a cultural group for cultural empowerment, namely the equal capacity to participate effectively, creatively, and successfully in one's society. Cultural claims to language and religion are typically extra-state or supra-national rights.

The idea of cultural equality extends the claims of cultural right, demanding equal status for different cultures. Adherents to the idea of cultural equality may well think multiculturalism insufficient because it recognizes cultural diversity but not cultural equality. While multiculturalism aims to 'resolve' minority culture problems by granting minority rights, it does not attempt to do anything with the taken for granted privileged position of the majority culture. Thus to be fully effective as a tool of cultural equality, multiculturalism needs to be based upon the principle of equal respect.

*Culture as a Primary Good*

According to John Rawls there are things that we need regardless of our natural talents and our aims. These he calls 'primary goods' and his list includes liberty, opportunity, income, wealth, and the bases of self respect. Fundamental to his theory of justice is the premise that parties to the original position will rationally seek to maximize their share of these primary goods, which are to be distributed equally unless an unequal distribution benefits the least favored (Rawls, 1971).

The issue here is what Rawls means by the 'bases of self respect'. More particularly, can Rawls's idea of self respect be extended to include the equal recognition of cultures? Tully (1995, p.189) argues the affirmative: that in making self respect one of the primary goods, Rawls is committed to the public recognition and affirmation of all cultures. By contrast, Barry (2001, p.268) argues that Rawls does not describe self respect as one of those 'primary goods' whose distribution is the concern of social justice. Rawls only mentions 'the social bases of self respect' that refer to equal civil and political rights. It is questionable whether Rawls has anything meaningful to say on this issue. Instead it may be more constructive to look at the work of other social justice theorists, such as Michael Walzer, Will Kymlicka, and Bhiku Parekh, who all emphasize culture as a primary good in institutional design.

For instance, while Walzer's list of social or basic goods includes offices, wealth, honor, education, health, membership, and safety, he also sees cultural membership as a fundamental value because it defines the shared understanding of social goods within a given culture (Walzer, 1983). The problem, as Kymlicka points out, is in identifying which community is in fact the bearer of cultural membership. Here Walzer faces a challenging boundary problem: how can two different historical communities within one nation-state work out the shared meanings of all citizens?

Kymlicka (1989, p.162) also argues for the primary good of cultural membership: 'The individuals who are an unquestionable part of the liberal moral ontology are viewed as individual members of a particular cultural community, for whom cultural membership is an important good'. In his view the intrinsic value of cultural diversity lies in the context of choice that the cultural structure provides; individual choice is dependent on the presence of a societal culture, defined by language and history (Kymlicka, 1995, p.8). Jeremy Waldron (1995, p.106) disagrees with Kymlicka's assessment: 'from the fact that each genuine option must have a cultural meaning, it does not follow that there must be one cultural framework in which each available option is assigned a meaning'. On the other hand, Bhiku Parekh (1994, p.13; 1998, p.206) leans towards Kymlicka's position with regard to equal respect for different cultures: 'The liberal is in theory committed to equal respect for persons. Since human beings are culturally embedded, respect for them entails respect for their cultures and ways of life'.

*Global Citizenship and Cultural Equality*

The theory of global citizenship is premised on the notion that all peoples – insiders and outsiders – are equal, as are all funding agencies and recipients. In practice, however, there are always structural inequalities that prevent the equal distribution of goods and resources. As Alexius Jemadu (2004) argues, transnational networks remain challenged to overcome the structural inequalities in the relationship between the Indonesian NGOs and their international partners. Transnational activists may use resources and funding in undemocratic ways and this should be seen as an internal contradiction of global citizenship.

Such structural inequalities pose a challenge to transnational activists who are committed to the notion of global citizenship and who value democracy. How does one deal with structural inequality? One way is to push the idea of world citizenship in the direction of democratic citizenship. That is, if one understands democracy as primarily concerned with equality, then global citizenship must address the issue of cultural equality. Global cultural citizenship transcends national borders and is concerned with cultural equality between different civilizations and cultures. To be effective, the agenda directed to the democratization of global culture must take cultural equality seriously.

Global citizenship is premised on the notion of a floating or transcendent cultural identity that is not situated in or related to any specific form of national identity. Yet it does not deny the importance or value of national and local cultures nor does it undermine the desire of individuals to belong to a specific place. Indeed, those who support the right to self-determination also tend to see the need, in certain circumstances, for global and local cultures to align themselves against certain forms of national culture. Global citizens and transnational activists will always encounter different cultures and be faced with the question of whether to treat the cultures of strangers and refugees as equal or inferior.

Moreover, as the processes of cultural and economic globalization march on, commercial culture has come increasingly to prevail over and so undermine traditional cultures, albeit without the use of force, giving rise to what Benjamin Barber (1995) refers to as the 'McWorld' phenomenon. This tendency for global commercial culture to threaten the survival of small cultures adds further impetus to the project of realizing cultural equality.

**What is Cultural Equality?**

Equality has many meanings:

1.    All people are equal, because they share humanity in common;
2.    All people should be equal, and should be treated as equal beings;
3.    All people are entitled to equal opportunity (Williams, 1971);
4.    All people should be equally subject to the law;
5.    Law should be impartially administered;
6.    All the advantages of society should be thrown into one common stock (Stephen, 1993, p.124).

Similarly, we can trace multiple meanings of cultural equality. It should be stressed, however, that cultural equality does not refer to the equal value of cultural artifacts such as oil paintings and novels. As Taylor (1994, pp.66-7) states clearly, 'There is no reason to believe that, for instance, the different art forms of a given culture should all be of equal, or even of considerable, value; and every culture can go through phases of decadence'. If we unpack the idea of cultural equality we can isolate various conceptual components.

Who defines culture? What constitutes culture? Where are the boundaries of cultures? Who has the right to interpret culture? Who can be construed as a cultural actor? While one cannot definitively settle these questions, a normative commitment to the equality principle seems to provide the most constructive starting point. For instance, going back to Rawls, he suggests that parties in the original position under the veil of ignorance are likely to choose equality as the principle to protect their lives and advance their cultures. And, according to Taylor (1994, p.66), equal respect for all cultures should be 'a starting hypothesis with which we ought to approach the study of any other culture'.

*Equal Weight in Institutional Design*

Equal respect for cultures should be taken into account in institutional design, although its incorporation may take different forms where circumstances dictate. For example, the Singapore government has been able to institutionalize the traditional festivals of Chinese, Malay, and Indians as national public holidays. In China, Vietnam, and Laos, however, where there are more than 56 ethnic groups, it is not possible for their governments to recognize *all* the traditional festivals of ethnic minorities through *national* public holidays. In these cases, therefore a differential public holiday system has to be designed.

*Equal Access to Cultural Communication, Production, and Distribution*

The distribution of or access to certain cultural goods should be arranged more equitably. For example, in an international gathering, people from different cultural backgrounds should have equal access to a range of different foods that derive from their traditions. There should also be an equal right to use one's own language in multicultural communication. While international organizations such as the UN and the EU use multi-languages in their official communications, this is not a universally accepted practice. For instance, in France, speaking languages other than French is sometimes seen as culturally divisive, politically threatening, or detrimental to French nationalism. Such attitudes surely contradict the idea of cultural equality.

*Equal Status of Cultural Practices*

Some people in Europe protest against the consumption of dog meat in Korea, Taiwan, and Hong Kong; but why should Europeans not respect the East Asian cultural custom of eating dog meat, particularly during winter? Similarly, should it be legitimate for Europe to impose its own views of capital punishment on some states in the United States and Asia? It could be argued that different cultures, which practice different customs, should be entitled to enjoy equal status and be equally accommodated in institutional arrangements and social policy. Respecting cultural difference is one way of implementing the principle of cultural equality.

Moreover, cultural order and mutual dialogue must be established on the basis of equality. For example, any discussion of the relationship between Confucianism and liberalism should be based on the assumption that the two traditions exist on an equal footing because all civilizations have the right to respect and cultural equality. Such an assumption is obviously implied in the universal discourse of human rights, where all human beings regardless of their cultural background deserve the right to equal respect and consideration. Thus a necessary step towards cultural equality in this case would be to separate Confucianism from its association with authoritarianism – which has given it an inferior status to liberalism – and to see it purely as a theoretical framework that offers an alternative way of thinking to liberalism.

*Equal Right to the Interpretation of Culture*

A serious problem associated with global cultural production is that weak cultures are forced to gain recognition from more powerful cultures. Indeed the final arbiters of culture, at least with respect to the global social sciences, seem to be located in the hallowed halls of Harvard, Cambridge, Oxford, Princeton, and other renowned Western universities. Yet the idea of cultural equality seems to suggest that academic arbiters should be more representative and located more equitably within different cultural communities. In this respect, it is suggested that along with traditional Western interpretations, such as rational choice theory and institutionalism, non-Western theoretical frameworks, such as Confucianism and Islam, should be deployed to help fully explain the cultural phenomena of East and West. The current practice which privileges Western approaches serves to deny the principle of cultural equality.

Nevertheless, caution should be exercised in designating the equal right to cultural interpretation. It could be argued that to posit a necessary relationship between Islam and terrorism is to be biased. The fact is terrorism seems to occur not only in and through Muslim culture but also in Western and Confucian cultures, and this needs to be recognized.[3] However, any such recognition cannot be used to legitimize terrorism. It cannot be argued, for instance, that because 'your culture has terrorism, the practice of terrorism in my culture can be tolerated!' Clearly all forms of terrorism must be condemned, no matter what the justification.

*Equal Esteem*

The idea of cultural equality rejects traditional categories of high versus low cultures thereby challenging cultural and racial superiority. If one accepts the view that the Anglo-Saxon race is destined to 'spread itself over the earth' or that it is the mission of 'the American people as [God's] chosen nation to finally lead in the regeneration of the world', there seems little room for cultural equality and plenty of scope for racial inequality (Chace, 2002, p.34). While Amy Gutmann (1994, p.5) raises a difficult question of whether a liberal democratic society should respect cultures that hold themselves ethnically or racially superior to others, there are in reality few if any non-democratic cultures that hold superior positions in the face of Western domination. Rather, the urgent question is to deal with the taken for granted superiority of the West and Western democratic traditions.

By pursuing the idea of cultural equality, different understandings of what it might entail will inevitably emerge, which will in turn offer very different and sometimes contradictory perspectives. It also suggests that criteria for assessing institutional requirements that can accommodate cultural equality will need to change.

It is also true that one sort of equality always implies and involves another kind of inequality; but this argument does not render cultural equality meaningless. Instead, we should consider the *context* in which the principle of cultural equality can be defended and what sort of cultural inequality is acceptable. In other words, it is important to have a clear sociological understanding of the context and content of cultural equality. Any defense or rejection of the idea of cultural equality must be made in the concrete context in which the specific content of cultural equality has particular meanings. This is the major problem with Barry's argument against cultural equality: it fails to contextualize the concrete content of cultural equality. Instead, his approach is to examine critically the ideas of cultural equality put forward by Taylor and Young (Barry, 2001, pp.264-71). Consequently, he overlooks the context and content of cultural equality itself.

**The Value of Cultural Equality**

Most important, the idea of cultural equality provides a normative basis from which transnational activism can deal with the structural inequalities outlined. It does so by challenging a form of political power in which cultural superiority plays a part in the domination of the weak by the strong. In particular, it challenges the master concept of liberty in international trade and within the cultural sphere. According to the idea of cultural equality, liberals should listen and think about non-liberal questions arising from non-liberal societies and even make a concession to non-liberal practices that can be shown to have normative validity.

Parekh (2000, p.14) argues that liberalism 'represents a particular cultural perspective and cannot provide a broad and impartial enough framework to conceptualize other cultures or their relations with it'. Indeed we can say that liberalism is neither salient nor predominant in the Middle East and in East Asia. This raises the question of whether liberals can in fact ultimately impose their liberal mode of thinking on others or whether they must recognize the legitimacy of alternative modes of normative thought. For example, drug policies reflect different historical and cultural traditions. Thus, while Holland adopts a more liberal and lenient approach towards drug issues, Malaysia, Singapore, and China take a much tougher line. It is difficult to say that the Dutch liberal approach is superior to the non-liberal policies of Malaysia, Singapore, and China.

The right to bear arms and the right for gay couples to adopt children suggest a life style that depends on the particularity of cultural conditions and history; but the pressure for such rights hardly exists in poor societies that are more concerned with survival and to put bread on the table. In these societies the pursuit of such liberties would be regarded as a luxury that has little to do with the daily necessities of food, medicine, and clean water. The right to bear arms and the right for gay couples that might be seen to have primacy in certain Western cultures, are simply insufficient to meet the needs of the poor in the third world.

Given its claims to openness, tolerance, and plurality, liberalism promises genuine dialogues between different cultures; but, by viewing equality as secondary to liberty, liberalism can come to regard as inferior other cultures that seek equality first. So while the voice from the 'South' may be heard it is not generally taken seriously in the area of transnational activities such as international conferences and publications. Occasionally, organizers of global or international conferences will include people from the third world or the South as token 'representatives' but seldom are they taken seriously as equal participants. An example illustrates the point. Professor Paul M. Evans, from the Institute of Asian Research, University of British Colombia, Canada, has produced a study of the various kinds of 'engagement' that occur in international politics. It provides 39 definitions that include the categories of comprehensive, constrained, cooperative, deep, deeper, realistic, selective, and conditional engagement. However, there is no mention of *equal* engagement.[4] The justification for this neglect is that an authoritarian regime like China does not respect equality and is thus not entitled to be treated equally. 'It is equally unjust to treat unequals equally as it is to treat equals unequally' (Crick, 1992, p.13).

**Arguments against Cultural Equality**

One common strategy in rejecting equality is to stress the incoherence and inconsistency of such a demand. J. R. Lucas (1971, pp.138-9) argued in 1965 that '...this demand [for equality] is incoherent, because what is demanded is both internally inconsistent and incompatible with other more precious ideals'.

Similarly, Barry (2001, p.265) points out the inconsistencies in Taylor's approach to equal concern for cultures, suggesting 'he still tries to whistle a tune about the equal value of cultures while at the same time continuing to sing the old song about incommensurability'. The idea of incommensurability implies that there is no impartial or universal standpoint from which the claims of all particular cultures can be rationally assessed, while the idea of the equal value of cultures, according to Peter Jones (1998, p.44), 'requires us to bring a common standard of values to all cultures'.[5] As a result, Barry (2001, pp.264-5) argues strongly that the idea of cultural equality is logically incompatible with the idea that cultures are incommensurable. While Barry's critique of Taylor is convincing, his argument is not convincing in the eyes of those who hold the idea of cultural equality but do not endorse the idea of incommensurability.

Another argument against cultural equality is that inequality is a natural phenomenon. Most cultures are patriarchal and even pluralist societies contain elitist and unequal elements (Okin, 1999, p.17). Moreover, as Thomas Nagel (1991, p.131) asserts, 'a complex culture magnifies their inequality and diversity by permitting a wide range of achievement and the flourishing of different talents'. In other words, culture has been used as an instrument for gaining and maintaining power.

> Power cannot be equally divided and distributed over the whole population. It is necessarily concentrated in few hands...Besides an inequality of power, there is an inequality of prestige, which will arise in any society...It will stem from men's natural inequality of ability resulting in their being able, some to a greater, others to a lesser, extent to be successful in achieving their ideals (Lucas, 1971, p.147).

The above argument surely questions the feasibility of cultural equality. It holds that the idea of cultural equality contains the hoary old chestnut of utopianism. Thus Barry (2001, pp.229-71) argues that the demand for equal recognition of all cultures is not only psychologically unattainable but also logically impossible. One who holds the ideal of cultural equality is doomed to, borrowing Lucas' phrase (1971, p.150), 'a life not only of grumbling and everlasting envy, but of endless and inevitable disappointment'.

However, this argument is not fully corrosive of the principle of cultural equality and will not deter those who cherish a hope for its realization. In their view the cultural practice of inequality can and must be changed, and human psychology reshaped to enable cultural equality to occur. For proponents of cultural equality the battle is one over human feelings. The key issue for them is to criticize any tendencies towards cultural bias, arrogance, prejudice, and superiority. In Taylor's words (1994, pp.66-7), 'withholding the presumption [of equal respect for cultures] might be seen as the fruit merely of prejudice or of ill will. It might even be tantamount to a denial of equal status'. However, for those who reject the idea of cultural equality, it represents only stupidity, confusion, and illogical reasoning. According to Stephen (1993, p.124), cultural equality is nothing more than 'a vague expression of envy on the part of those who have not against those who have', or 'a vague aspiration towards a state of society in which there should be fewer contrasts than there are at present between one man's lot and another's'.

There are those who fear that the equalization of different cultures will result in the loss of elite culture and a subsequent vulgarization. Nevertheless, an assertion of equal respect for cultures can be combined with an unequal evaluation of cultural products through making, as Mill did, a distinction between higher and lower pleasures, or between high and low evaluations of cultural product.

## Problems Associated with Cultural Equality

### *Inherent Paradoxes*

Stephen (1993, p.163) said that the recognition of substantial equality is 'usually a step towards the development of inherent inequalities'. If cultural equality is taken to be an integral part of world citizenship, one confronts a series of paradoxes. For example, demands for equality between different cultures and civilizations constitute *external* forms of cultural equality. However, the external equality of cultures does not necessarily ensure *internal* cultural equality. Rather it entails the possibility of justifying unequal arrangements within a culture or civilization. Theoretically, one could therefore hold the thesis that each culture has an equal right to interpret what constitutes equality while others can entertain the antithesis that an equal right to interpret what is equality will lead to a justification of inequality.

There is another paradox. One may hold the thesis that each culture should enjoy an equal right to use its language in global communication and that each language should be regarded as equally valuable. Yet there are many who maintain that it is necessary for English to be the global language. According to Rosenau (1997, pp.88-9), for instance, the cultural institution of English should be regarded as a universal functional control system which offers a key to individual liberation within all cultures, despite the fact that it gives rise to reactive linguistic nationalism. Indeed, it can be conceded that even though global English language results in unequal status for other languages, it does make cultural dialogue and daily communication possible and is particularly important in transnational activities that involve different peoples who speak different languages.

Clearly, multi-linguistic practice is also difficult to develop for economic reasons. Suppose, for instance, the Chinese, Malay, and Indian cultural communities in Singapore demand their cultural languages as official ones, then communication between them would require interpretation; but how would these cultural communities share the cost of interpretation? An apparent and easy solution is to stick to a common official language, as Singapore has done. There, as a colonial legacy, the official language is English and this seems fair to all ethnic groups despite the resentment felt by the older generation of the Chinese majority. By contrast, where multi-ethnic countries, such as India and Sri Lanka, have abandoned English as an official language in the wake of their independence, cultural inequality and tension between different ethnic groups has arisen.

Interestingly, Malaysia attempted to introduce English as a teaching language for science and mathematics in 2002. While this may seem an equitable language arrangement it presents a problem for the Malaysian Chinese cultural community, implying a reduction of teaching hours for Chinese language in Chinese schools.

## The Structure/Agency Problem

How far can the idea of cultural equality be institutionalized and enforced? Who is an agent with the capacity to enforce cultural rights and equality? How can an unequal international structure promote and realize cultural equality across civilizations? Typically, nation-states employ the institutions of citizenship to create cultural homogenization within civil society and thus deny the cultural rights of minority groups. In this way they tend to promote national cultures at the cost of minority cultures.

If the state promotes and protects the minority rights of one culture, this cultural community has in return a duty and obligation to respect other cultures and the principle of equality itself. But a central problem associated with realizing cultural equality is the difficulty of defining exactly what constitutes 'cultural obligation' without which rights are often passive and empty.

In addition, there is the problem of convergence. This is the problem of whether or not individuals under the to-be-designed institutions for cultural equality will ultimately support them. Obviously, under institutional arrangements designed to realize cultural equality, some would fare better than others. How can these individuals accommodate each other so that convergence on the project of cultural equality is possible?

## Some Methodological Problems

Methodological differences underpin the variety of opinions and assessments of cultural equality. This challenging problem for the realization of cultural equality and its institutional arrangements is common to all discussions of equality. As Nagel (1991, p.3) pointed out, 'The unsolved problem is the familiar one of reconciling the standpoint of the collectivity with the standpoint of the individual'. In other words, individualist and collectivists or communitarians hold different perspectives on what counts as culture, and how and through whom it develops.

An individualist tends to see culture as an open and dynamic way of life predicated upon the ideas and actions of individuals. In contrast, a communitarian views culture as closed and exclusive, stresses cultural rights and citizenship, and focuses on the means by which individuals access *their* own culture and common space. Communitarians assert that culture, including language, cannot be reduced to individuals. The problem here is determining who counts as the representative of so called collective culture.

While individualists assert that the wellspring of culture is the individual, communitarians hold that cultural community shapes the identity of individuals within it, providing their sense of self. Moreover, they argue it is through the common perspectives and attitudes of cultural community that social norms and standards are established and internalized, thereby accounting for homogeneous behaviour within specific communities.

## Strategies to Deal with the Problems of Cultural Equality

We can identify a number of strategies to deal with the paradoxes of cultural equality. The challenging question is how to avoid utopianism and persistently to search for realistic strategies for cultural equality.

### Negotiations over Cultural Difference and Equality

Rather than rejecting the idea of cultural equality, one can acknowledge that, although we cannot resolve or eradicate the tension or contradictions, we can reduce the tension and negotiate between the universal and the particular, the absolute and the relative. We can negotiate over cultural difference and equality to develop some sort of minimal overlapping consensus. Such a negotiation strategy offers hope as a useful mechanism towards achieving greater cultural equality.[6] Each culture, recognizing its incompleteness, limits, and weaknesses, will engage in dialogue with others, learn from them, and so an overlapping consensus will develop. As Andrew Linklater argues, what is needed 'is a transnational public sphere in which different and overlapping moral communities can all have an input into the decision-making which affects them' (Hutchings and Dannreuther, 1999, p.3).

### Distinguishing between Human Beings and Culture

A global citizen will never compromise the equality between human beings and will always treat others as ends rather than means; but such equal respect does not compromise our capacity to criticize some traditional practices in other cultures. Human rights are now widely respected in different parts of the world and by different cultural societies. This provides us with a minimal standard whereby we can engage in cultural critique. While a global ethics respects different cultures it does not retreat into them and become ossified.

### Cultural Equality is Limited by Human Rights

Let us consider some of the politics associated with the realization of cultural equality. For instance, the idea of 'cultural equality' can be used to promote the status of 'Asian values' against human rights. It also entertains the idea that Islamic culture should enjoy equal status in the struggle against new forms of neo-liberal 'imperialism'. Demanding equality between Western and Islamic civilizations can downplay human rights for they are seen as products of Western culture.

To counter this possibility, one can insist that all cultures are accorded equal value only if they respect or honor human rights, which specify that governments should protect their own people and should not kill innocent people. Accordingly it is illegitimate for any one culture to justify torture and killing on the basis of cultural difference. While I disagree with Barry's (2001, p.127) arguments against equal respect for culture, I do endorse his point that 'Equal respect for people cannot therefore entail respect for their cultures when these cultures systematically give priority to, say, the interests of men over the interests of women'.

The principle of human rights must constitute the first order of culture, and define the basic rules with which all cultures must comply. Today we see more and more nation-states endorsing international human rights regimes; but there remain differences in the interpretation of human rights and different understandings of how strongly human rights should be applied. John Rawls (2001, pp.79-80) deals well with this issue by insisting that membership in the Society of Peoples requires respect for a list of human rights including the right to life, liberty, and security of the person; security of ethnic groups from mass murder and genocide; rights against slavery and torture; freedom of movement; the right to marry and start a family; the right to own property; the right to freedom of conscience. These rights are universally applicable to liberal peoples and decent hierarchical peoples. At the same time, Rawls omits the freedom of speech and opinion, the freedom of assembly, the freedom to participate in governance and the right of equal access to public services, the right to the free choice of employment and to non-discrimination in employment, and the right to education.

*Self-Criticism as a Precondition for Cultural Equality*

For two cultures to recognize and respect each other, each must be prepared to engage in mutual criticism. Just as genuine friendship involves open and frank criticism and advice, mutual criticism between cultures is a crucial element of cultural equality and a fruitful way to develop mutually successful relationships. Importantly, each culture must be prepared to subject itself to both external and internal criticism in order to help overcome cultural bias and prejudice and thus improve its cultural practice. In short, each culture must maintain a stance of critical self-reflection and criticism, without which its claims to equal status lack legitimacy.

*Cosmopolitan Virtue*

It is not beyond the realms of possibility to envisage that, in an increasingly interdependent world, the structures of each culture will come more and more to overlap and enmesh, thereby giving rise to hybrid cultures that might display a preoccupation with cosmopolitan thought and behavior. In this way an intercultural perspective could serve to endorse and support multicultural citizenship because individuals are able to hold membership of multiple cultures and thus have access to shared culture and space.

Rather than polarizing the two extremes of Jihad and McWorld, one might explore the possibility of some sort of coexistence between the two that furthers an intercultural ethics which encourages mutual tolerance rather than mutual threat. This idea is usually greeted with derision and skepticism because Jihad tends to be seen merely as a fundamentalist, militaristic movement that supports terrorism. Yet, there are multiple meanings of Jihad. According to Dr. Patricia Martinez (2003), University of Malaya, Jihad should be understood as the struggle with one's own heart and the attempt to bring oneself into accord with the will of God. The means appropriate to this struggle are prayer, study, and various forms of inner-worldly asceticism. A more nuanced and perhaps sympathetic understanding of Jihad is crucial to realizing any sort of coexistence with McWorld. Islamic fundamentalism may be partially explained by the resentment caused by a sense of cultural inferiority vis-à-vis the West's economic and political domination. Were the Muslim world to experience a sense of cultural equality the resentment against Western culture would likely be reduced.

What is suggested here is that cosmopolitan virtue is a necessary condition for realizing cultural equality. In the current climate the major barrier to achieving cultural equality is that attempts to preserve certain cultures against the threats of Western domination are all tied up in a vicious cycle between terrorism and the war against it. Yet surely violence and terrorism are not the civilized way to defend the existence of a culture. Equally a war against terrorism is most likely to prove unproductive and ineffective in restraining terrorism and even likely in the long run to provoke more of it.

*Developing Psychologically Complex Feelings of Ambivalence*

Because there are contradictory impulses associated with notions of cultural equality, psychologically complex feelings of ambivalence are likely to occur. One might value cultural equality yet at the same time remain sensitive to internal inequality and the multiplicity of issues involved. Thus there is a need to develop skills to manage the complexity and contradictions associated with realizing cultural equality. Indeed, it is vital for a global citizen to see 'contradictions' as the driving force that enables the dialectical development of world citizenship. It could even be said that the successful furtherance of a politics of transnational activism depends on the development of a cross-cultural psychology that is able to deal with the inevitable problems that will arise from intercultural conflicts.

**Concluding Remarks**

Habermas once distinguished between culture and *political* culture. While the former does not need to be shared by all citizens, the latter is marked by mutual respect for rights. Constitutional democracy dedicates itself to this distinction by granting members of minority cultures 'equal rights of co-existence' (Habermas, 1994). In the case of cultural equality, it is necessary to make similar distinctions between the state and the individual, the public and private spheres. Clearly the state has a major role to play in maintaining neutrality and ensuring maximal cultural equality. In contrast, individuals can make different choices and enjoy their private views of culture, even to the point of asserting their own cultural superiority, providing it remains in the private sphere. However, any such public assertions or acts certainly cannot be tolerated.

Drawing on the public/private distinction, Barry (2001, p.229) provides a crucial argument against the claim that cultures should be presumed or affirmed to be equal in value. Such a claim, he suggests, shifts matters that should be left to individual judgment into the realm of public control. In his view the state has no right to interfere in matters of individual judgment. Barry's position leaves issues of cultural equality within the purview of individual choice and rejects any role for the state. Such an option is unacceptable. To achieve substantial cultural equality, one must wage a 'war' against all cultural prejudice and bias at the level of both state and individual. For this to occur, cultural equality must be a public matter.

For Barry, cultural equality is ultimately a matter of individual choice, which seems a weak basis for its realization. Yet does that mean we are doomed to suffer cultural inequality with all its attendant problems? Surely it is more rational to prefer cultural equality to cultural inequality. If so, one can be forgiven for attempting to develop strategies to overcome the apparent barriers to realizing cultural equality. Perhaps this is the pressing task for a global or intercultural citizen who values cultural equality: to aspire to build a culturally equal society where the principle of cultural equality becomes a powerful force for change.

Inequality may have held sway throughout history while the idea of political equality is in its infancy. Although political equality is yet to be fully realized, the notion of cultural equality as a late comer in the battle for equality cannot be ignored. Indeed, it is hoped that the idea of cultural equality serves to disrupt the normative discourse of international relations at least for long enough to ensure it receives serious consideration.

## Notes

1   The author would like to thank Barry Hindess, Will Kymlicka, April Carter, C. L. Ten, Sor-hoon Tan, David Held, and Robert Walker for their suggestions and comments, and Christine Standish and Eric Zhang for their help. The chapter benefits from delightful conversations with Steven Lukes, Nic Craith Mairead, Geoffrey Stokes, Wang Gungwu, and Benjamin Wong.

2   By contrast, German citizenship was defined in terms of blood and ethnic origin. Both French and German citizenships are expressions of the contradiction of modern citizenship.

3   Such an argument was presented at the Workshop on 'After Bali: the Threat of Terrorism in Southeast Asia', organized by the Institute of Defense and Strategic Studies, Nanyang Technological University, Singapore, 27-28 January 2003.

4   His talk given at the East Asian Institute, National University of Singapore, 2001.

5   George Grower (2002, pp.2-3, pp.49-54) distinguishes incomparable, immeasurable, and unrankable; while it is difficult to compare, measure and rank the total properties of cultures, it is possible to compare, measure and rank certain features of cultures.

6   Jacques Derrida (2001) has advocated the negotiation strategy as a way of handling the internal contradiction of cosmopolitanism.

# References

Barber, Benjamin (1995), *Jihad vs. McWorld*, Random House, New York.

Barry, Brian (2001), *Culture and Equality*, Harvard University Press, Cambridge.

Bedau, Hugo A. (ed.) (1971), *Justice and Equality*, Prentice-Hall, New Jersey.

Chace, James (2002), 'Tomorrow the World', a book review of Warren Zimmermann, *First Great Triumph: How Five Americans Made Their Country a World Power New York Book Review*, 21 November, pp.33-6.

Crick, Bernard (1992), *In Defense of Politics*, 4th edition, Weidenfeld, Nicolson, London.

Derrida, Jacques (2001), *On Cosmopolitanism and Forgiveness*, Routledge, London.

Grower, George (2002), *Liberalism and Value Pluralism*, Continuum, London.

Gutmann, Amy (ed.) (1994), *Multiculturalism*, Princeton University Press, Princeton.

Habermas, Jurgen (1994), in Gutmann, 1994, pp.107-48.

Hindess, Barry (2001), 'Not at Home in the Empire', *Social Identities*, vol.7, pp.363-77.

Hutchings, Kimberly and Dannreuther, Roland (eds.) (1999), *Cosmopolitan Citizenship* MacMillan, Basingstoke.

Jemadu, Alexius (2004), 'Transnational Activism and the Pursuit of Democratization in Indonesia: National, Regional and Global Networks', in Nicola Piper and Anders Uhlin (eds.), *Transnational Activism in Asia: Problems of Power and Democracy*, Routledge, London, pp.149-67.

Jones, Peter (1998), 'Political Theory and Cultural Diversity', *Critical Review of International Social and Political Philosophy*, vol.1, pp.28-62.

Kymlicka, Will (1989), *Liberalism, Community and Culture*, Clarendon, Oxford.

Kymlicka, Will (1995), *Multicultural Citizenship: A Liberal Theory of Minority Rights*, Clarendon, Oxford.

Lucas, J. R. (1971), 'Against Equality', in Bedau, 1971, pp.138-51 (originally published in *Philosophy*, vol.40, pp.296-307).

Mairead, Nic Craith (2002), 'Can Citizenship Accommodate Cultural Difference? A View from Europe', paper presented at Cultural Citizenship Conference, 5-8 December, Deakin University, Australia.

Marshall, T. H. (1963), 'Citizenship and Social Class', in *Sociology at the Crossroads, and other Essays*, Heinemann, London.

Martinez, Patricia (2003), 'Deconstructing Jihad', paper presented at the Workshop on 'After Bali: the Threat of Terrorism in Southeast Asia', organized by Institute of Defense and Strategic Studies, Nanyang Technological University, Singapore, 27-28 January.

Nagel, Thomas (1991), *Equality and Partiality*, Oxford University Press, Oxford.

Okin, Susan Moller *et al.* (1999), *Is Multiculturalism Bad for Women?* J. Cohen, M. Howard and M. C. Nussbaum (eds.), Princeton University Press, Princeton.

Parekh, Bhikhu (1994), 'Superior People: The Narrowness of Liberalism from Mill to Rawls', *Times Literature Supplement*, 25 February.

Parekh, Bhikhu (1998), 'Cultural Diversity and Liberal Democracy', in Gurpreet Mahajan (ed.), *Democracy, Difference and Social Justice*, Oxford University Press, Delhi.

Parekh, Bhikhu (2000), *Rethinking Multiculturalism: Cultural Diversity and Political Theory*, Macmillan, Basingstoke.

Rawls, John (1971), *A Theory of Justice*, Oxford University Press, Oxford.

Rawls, John (2001), *The Law of Peoples*, Cambridge: Harvard University Press.

Rosenau, James N. (1997), *Along the Domestic-Foreign Frontier*, Cambridge University Press, Cambridge.

Stephen, James Fitzjames (1993), *Liberty, Equality and Fraternity*, Stuart D. Warner (ed.), Liberty Fund, Indianapolis.

Taylor, Charles (1994), 'The Politics of Recognition', in Gutmann, 1994, pp.25-73.

Tully, James (1995), *Strange Multiplicity: Constitutionalism in an Age of Diversity*, Cambridge University Press, Cambridge.

Waldron, Jeremy (1995), 'Minority rights and the Cosmopolitan Alternative', in Will Kymlicka (ed.), *The Rights of Minority Cultures*, Oxford University Press, Oxford, pp.93-122.

Walker, Robert B. (1990), 'The Concept of Culture in the Theory of International Relations', in Jongsuk Chay (ed.), *Culture and International Relations*, Praeger, New York, pp.3-17.

Walzer, Michael (1983), *Spheres of Justice: A Defense of Pluralism and Equality*, Blackwell, Oxford.

Williams, Bernard (1971), 'The Idea of Equality', in Bedau, 1971, pp.116-37.

# Chapter 12

# On the Confucian Idea of Citizenship[1]

## A.T. Nuyen

I want to address the question of whether we can construct a model of citizenship within the Confucian framework. The success of such a project will go a long way towards dispelling the common belief that Confucianism at best has nothing to contribute to the idea of citizenship, and at worst is antithetical to such an idea. This common belief is understandable given the fact that the idea of citizenship emerged only recently together with, or perhaps as a part of, what is called 'modernity', whereas Confucianism is thought by many as having only a historical value. Furthermore, recent theoretical developments of the idea of citizenship are shaped by contemporary political, demographic, and economic factors, factors that were not in play in the times in which Confucianism developed. This being the case, the construction the Confucian idea of citizenship (or the idea of Confucian citizenship – I use the two constructions interchangeably) must begin with the negative task of removing scepticism towards it. This will be attempted in the first section. As for the positive task of building a model of citizenship within the Confucian framework, I can only make some tentative suggestions in the second section, which aims to show what might be the key features of Confucian citizenship, and how it compares with contemporary Western understanding of citizenship.

## Possibility of Confucian Citizenship

As if to reinforce the scepticism towards the notion that we can develop an idea of citizenship within the Confucian framework, commentators are quick to point out that the Chinese words for 'citizen' and 'citizenship' are modern constructions and could not be found in classical Confucian writings. The three common constructions are *shimin*, *guomin*, and *gongmin*. The first of these, *shimin* (people of the city) is too literal and not commonly used as an equivalent for the English 'citizen'. Of the other, more commonly used, words, *guomin* (people of the state) emphasizes the legal and political dimension of citizenship and refers to persons within the jurisdiction of a legally recognized country. The term corresponds to the idea of citizenship as understood by, for example Oommen (1997), who constructs the idea of citizenship on a legal and political basis. By contrast, the term *gongmin* (public people) emphasizes the cultural and communal aspects of citizenship and refers to persons belonging to a certain nation (bearing in mind what Habermas (1994, p.22) has reminded us about the term 'nation', namely, its being derived from the latin *natio*, which in ancient Rome referred to 'peoples and tribes who were not yet organized into political associations'. *Gongmin*, then, is close to Miller's (1995) idea of citizenship as nationality. These terms, it might be said, are meant to refer to the modern, Western, notion of citizenship, not to anything discussed, let alone valued, by Confucians. Wittgensteinians, for whom the limits of one's language determine the limits of one's world, might say that the Confucian world has no room for the idea of citizenship. Against this, it can be argued that Confucians did use *forms of words* that are close enough to the modern idea of citizenship. For instance, in characterizing one of the five relationships, Mencius speaks of a subject in relation to his or her sovereign. Arguably, this idea of a subject is close enough to the idea of a citizen as a person belonging to a state (*guomin*), as in 'British subject'. Mencius would have little difficulty in understanding the term 'British citizen' as referring to a 'British subject' who stands in a certain legal and political relation to the British Monarch. In any case, it is not my intention to argue that the modern notion of citizenship *was* part of the Confucian thought in Confucian times, in which case the lack of a specific term would be a problem. Rather, my claim is that Confucian thought can be a basis for developing a modern idea of citizenship, that it has the resources to fill in the conceptual space marked out by the modern term *guomin* or *gongmin.*

What, then, does the term *guomin* or *gongmin* denote? For the Chinese term to be equivalent to 'citizen' in the contemporary debate, it must denote an idea that incorporates the key elements of the modern idea of citizenship. Unfortunately, what these key elements are depends to a large extent on the underlying political theory. While the dominant underlying theory is liberal-democratic in nature, many alternative conceptions have been developed in recent years (see for example, Faulks, 2000). However, various conceptions of citizenship do share certain elements in common. Arguably, these include the idea of a citizen as an individual distinct from the state, or the nation, to which he or she belongs, the idea of equality among such individuals, the idea of certain rights attached to them, and the idea of democratic institutions which safeguard those rights. The notion of Confucian citizenship will not make sense if Confucian thought is incompatible with such ideas. To say the same thing differently, if we are to argue that it is possible to construct an idea of citizenship within the Confucian framework, it has to be shown that Confucianism is compatible with, if not committed to, the ideas of individuality, equality, citizen rights, and democracy. Many critics have argued that Confucianism fails on all of these counts. Some have argued that Confucianism emphasizes the community over the individual, promotes elitism at the expense of equality, advocates community obligations over individual rights and community welfare over individual autonomy, and is anti-democratic. A defense of Confucianism against these charges is a necessary step towards establishing the idea of Confucian citizenship.

The first argument we need to counter is the following: The idea of citizenship presupposes the idea of citizens as separate individuals; Since

Confucianism does not see human beings as separate individuals, it is incompatible with the idea of citizenship. Recent pronouncements of many commentators can be seen as supporting the crucial premise in the argument, namely, Confucianism does not see human beings as separate individuals. For instance, Julia Ching (1998, p.72) declares that 'the Chinese view of the human being tends to see the person in the context of a social network *rather than* as an individual'. Chenyang Li (1999, p.95) contends that in 'the Confucian view, [the] self is not an independent agent who happens to be in certain social relationships' but rather 'is constituted of, and situated in social relationships', and goes on to assert, emphatically: 'This is very different from the traditional Western view'. Insofar as the 'traditional Western view' of the human self as a separate independent individual is presupposed in the idea of citizenship, we have here, apparently, support for the above argument. Maoist exhortations to the effect that each person must serve as a 'cog in the (social) machine' only serve to entrench the view that there is no room for the idea of citizenship in Confucianism, even though Maoism has little to do with Confucianism. However, it can be shown that views similar to those expressed by Ching and Li above do not support the claim that there is no such thing as a separate independent individual or a being with an individual identity in Confucianism.

To understand views such as those expressed by Ching and Li, we need to distinguish between individualism and individuality. Roughly, individualism is the view that the individual is the primary unit of all metaphysical and axiomatic constructions. Societies and social values are constructed from individuals and individual values. Individuality, again roughly, refers to the characteristics that uniquely identify each person as an individual, separate from other individuals and from any group he or she may be a part of. Individualism implies individuality but not conversely. The question now is whether the idea of citizenship presupposes individualism or just individuality. I will try to say something about this in the next section. Suffice it to mention here that not all conceptions of citizenship presuppose individualism even though, it would appear, the idea of individuality has to be presupposed in any conception thereof. Arguably, in contrasting the Confucian view of the self with the 'traditional Western view', Li at least is speaking of individualism, hence not arguing that there are no separate identifiable individuals in Confucian metaphysics. This appears to be the case with Ching as well, given the context of discussion, although admittedly it is less clear in her statement above. These commentators notwithstanding (the Maoist notion that there are only 'cogs in the machine', not individuals, is of course just a slogan that has nothing to do with Confucianism), it is abundantly clear that Confucian teachings are geared towards separate identifiable individuals, thus presupposing individuality. It does see the self as an individual, or an entity distinct from others in the society, albeit an individual constituted by social relationships, having his or her most important values shaped by such relationships. In all the Confucian classics, the stress is always on the development of the individual, on the process of individual learning, and on becoming a distinct gentleman (*junzi*). The teachings in the Confucian classics make use of exemplary individuals with distinct and unique characteristics, individuals who are the driving force of the moral society, not anonymous and dispensable cogs of a social machine. It is true that, as pointed out by many commentators, individuality is not seen as something formed in isolation from the community, or the society, but this only means that an individual's interests are more likely to be shaped by his or her social relationships, not that there is no such thing as individuality (nor that individual interests are discouraged or must be ultimately sacrificed for the sake of community interests). If I am right, then the Confucian metaphysics of the self as an individual standing in a network of social relationships does not make it incompatible with the idea of citizenship.

Turning now to the idea of equality among individuals, once again there are critics who claim that Confucianism promotes elitism and meritocracy at the expense of equality, and so cannot embrace the idea of citizenship insofar as the latter presupposes the ideal of equality and aims to promote equality in practice. Often cited is the distinction that Confucians speak of between the masses (*min*), the superior men, or gentlemen (*junzi*) and the sages (*shengren*), or more generally between ordinary people (*min*) and superior people (*junzi*). The complaint is that the Confucian society is hierarchical where the *junzi* occupy the higher rungs and are accorded a disproportionate share of rights and privileges. Even sympathetic commentators such as Hall and Ames (1987, p.156) contend that the 'distinction between the masses (*min*) and the elites (*jen* and *chün tzu*) is rather more severe than might be comfortable for the contemporary Anglo-European proponent of liberal democracy'. It is no wonder, some critics might say, that the Chinese term for equality, namely *pingdeng*, did not appear in the *Analects* or the *Mencius*.

Since I have elsewhere challenged the claim that Confucianism is against the idea of equality (Nuyen, 2001), I will only make a few remarks here. First, as in the case of the Chinese equivalents for 'citizen' and 'citizenship', while the term *pingdeng* was not used in the Chinese classics, equivalent terms such as 'sameness' were used throughout. For instance, 'Mencius said, 'How should I be different from others? Yao and Shun were the same as other men'' (*Mencius* 4B32); and 'The sage and I are the same in kind' (*Mencius* 6A7).[2] This 'sameness' is also found at various places in the *Analects*, such as *Analects* 17.2 ('By nature close together [or alike, or the same], through practice set apart'). For Irene Bloom (1998, p.96), the inclusion in the UNESCO 'Statement on Race' of *Analects* 17.2 is wholly appropriate because it aptly expresses 'a modern sense of human equality and relatedness'. Bloom goes on to say that the spirit expressed in *Analects* 17.2 is 'distinctly egalitarian'. We need not go as far as Bloom, not so much because she may have overstated the case, but because what is needed for the idea of citizenship in general is not egalitarianism but equality. On the latter, the passages cited here are certainly evidence to support the view that Confucianism advocates at least equality of human worth. However, critics might insist that what is important for citizenship is not just equality at the basic level of human worth, but equality at higher levels of rights and social rewards, and that Confucianism is found wanting at these levels. For instance, Kwok (1998, p.90) claims that the Chinese recognized only the 'right of the prince, right of the patriarch, right of the ruler (*jun quan, fu quan, zhi quan*) – and such rights as those of the people, son and self-rule (*min quan, zi quan, zizhi quan*) are not encountered in past historical ages'.

Two things can be said in reply. First, while the term *quan* is used to translate 'right', its literal meaning is 'power', and Kwok could well be right if we take *quan* in a sense closer to the literal meaning of the term. But in the sense of power, it can hardly be expected that there is equality in any society, as long as there is differentiation of functions. Not only that princes and rulers have certain powers that others do not, a police officer has the power of arrest that others do not; a security officer at the airport has the power of search that others do not, and so on, right down to those on the lowest rungs of the social order. The question is whether there is in Confucianism any equality in the process of acquiring powers. On this, we can say that Confucians explicitly endorse equality of opportunities, particularly educational opportunity. We have seen that both Confucius and Mencius believed that we could all learn to be gentlemen and ultimately sages, to be like Yao and Shun. Confucius himself said that 'there should be no class distinction' in education (*Analects* 7.7), and never refused to teach anyone, no matter how poor. Beyond that, Confucianism also advocates the equality of job opportunity. In the case of jobs in the public sector, this was effected in the open, and by all accounts, fair administration of the civil service examination system.

Secondly, it is true that the hierarchical structure of the Confucian society assigns unequal powers and rewards. However, it does not follow that there is no commitment to the idea of equality. I have argued that equality should be understood along the Aristotelian lines, namely as having a horizontal aspect, where 'equals' should be treated equally, and a 'vertical' aspect, where 'unequals' should be treated unequally. To treat unequals equally is to violate the principle of equality in its vertical aspect. Thus, it can be argued that the unequal treatments of different people in the Confucian society merely reflect the fact that they are unequals. If so then what appears to be meritocracy and elitism could well be a commitment to equality. Perhaps Confucians are too honest in their admission that no matter how equal people are at the start – having equal worth and equal potentiality, and even given equal opportunity – they will end up being different for various reasons, not least of which is the difference in personal commitments and exertion. *Analects* 17.2 is worth quoting again: 'By nature close together, through practice set apart'.

We turn now to Confucianism and democracy. It is not entirely clear that the idea of citizenship can make sense only within the framework of democratic institutions. On the assumption that it does, critics argue that Confucianism is incompatible with the idea of citizenship insofar as it is anti-democratic. For instance, according to Samuel Huntington (1991, p.24), 'Confucian democracy' is a contradiction in terms because Confucianism emphasizes 'the group over the individual, authority over liberty…responsibilities over rights'. Once again, I have elsewhere argued against such notion (Nuyen, 2000), and I will only offer some brief remarks here. To begin with, the fact that history does not yield any example of a democratic Confucian society is not an argument that such a society is not possible. The key question is whether Huntington is right in suggesting that the idea of citizenship presupposes the priority of the individual over the group, liberty over authority and rights over responsibility. As I will argue below, on a certain conception of citizenship, Huntington may be right. However, as I will also show, there are rival conceptions of citizenship that privilege the interests of the group over those of an individual, advocate respect for authority and the importance of responsibilities. Given these conceptions, what Confucianism stands for does not render it incompatible with the idea of citizenship. Still, it is possible for Huntington to insist that the trouble with Confucianism is precisely the privileging of the group, of authority and responsibilities *at the expense of* the individual, of liberty and of rights. In other words, the individual and his or her liberty and rights are dispensable in a Confucian society, and that is why 'Confucian democracy' is a contradiction in terms. But this stronger claim can be rejected.

I have already remarked on the relationship between the individual and the group. If I am right, there is no suggestion in Confucian teachings that the individual, or his or her individuality, is dispensable in the service of group interests. The emphasis on group interests derives from the individual's own moral thinking, not something imposed on the individual without any moral basis. The same thing can be said for respect for authority and acceptance of responsibilities. Undeterred, critics such as Huntington may cite ideas such as filial piety and the Three-Bonds doctrine as evidence for the anti-democratic nature of Confucianism. Two quick responses are warranted. First, the Three-Bonds doctrine appeared only in the works of Han Fei Zi, a legalist. According to Tu Wei-ming (1998, p.122), the doctrine was used by the Han legalists as a means of social control. The nearest thing to it in canonical Confucian writings is the Mencian doctrine of the five relationships (*Mencius* 3A4) which does not advocate strict obedience to the sovereign. There is also evidence to show that Mencius believed that the people had the right to rebel against a ruler who has violated the 'mandate of Heaven' (Nuyen, 2000). Second, the notion of filial piety can be interpreted in such a way as to suggest neither blind nor absolute obedience (Nuyen, 2003). More positively, as in the case of the idea of citizenship, of which many different conceptions are possible, there can be certain conceptions of democracy that do not rule out the idea of a Confucian democracy. But even if we adhere to the account of democracy in terms of a government 'of the people, for the people and by the people', I have suggested that the Confucian notion of *minben* (people as root) shows that Confucianism has the resources to develop such a notion. In a recent work, Sorhoon Tan (2003) has shown that Confucianism can be given a Deweyan reading, which would make sense of the notion of Confucian democracy.

I have argued against the claim that Confucianism is inconsistent with the idea of citizenship by showing that the arguments to the effect that Confucianism is against the key presuppositions of citizenship, such as individuality, equality, liberty, and rights, can be dismissed. However, dismissing such arguments merely establishes the possibility of Confucian citizenship. While it is important to establish this possibility, given the common negative impressions of Confucianism, we need to ask further questions such as: What would the idea of Confucian citizenship look like? What would be its main characteristics? How does it compare with other conceptions of citizenship in the contemporary debate? I try to approach these questions in the next section.

## Some Features of Confucian Citizenship

The most influential conception of citizenship is probably one that grows out of the liberal democratic tradition. Indeed, the claim that Confucianism is incompatible with the idea of citizenship is typically held by those who subscribe to the liberal democratic conception of citizenship. However, recently there have been many strong challenges to this conception, leading to many alternatives. To answer the questions raised above, a quick survey of the contemporary debate on the idea of citizenship is in order.

Whether world history will come to an end with the adoption of liberal democracy as Francis Fukuyama (1992) has claimed, it is true that the modern idea of citizenship was born of the liberal tradition, the foundation of which was laid by liberal thinkers of the sixteenth and seventeenth centuries. The practice of citizenship as it is understood today in the West came a little later, with the French Revolution, which marked the transition from subjecthood to citizenship. With Hobbes, even though individuals were still regarded as subjects of a sovereign who could exercise the power of life and death over them, they were thought by Hobbes to be the primary political units, replacing collective entities such as an estate. Furthermore, as political units, they were thought to be equal and to be subject only to the authority of the state. Most importantly, the choice to live under the authority of the state, the Leviathan, was a rational choice, made by individuals who considered it preferable to life in the state of nature. Locke then constructed the notion of an individual as a political unit with certain rights, in particular the rights to life, liberty, and property, thus consolidating the idea of political membership in exchange for the security that Hobbes spoke of. After Locke, Bentham, Mill, and other liberal thinkers solidified the liberal foundation on which grew the modern theory and practice of citizenship. The nature of modern citizenship, of course, has been shaped by political forces, the main one being the growth of international organizations such as the UN that establish state boundaries and delineate sites of political authority. Such forces have sharpened the sense of identity of a state as a legal and political entity, as distinct from a nation, the identity of which is largely historical and cultural. The two identities have now merged in the notion of a nation-state, which defines the identity of the individuals over whom the nation-state has authority. The same political forces also highlight the question of security for a nation-state and give rise to the idea of the citizens' responsibilities to the nation-state.

Central to that liberal conception of citizenship are the ideas of individuality, equality, and individual autonomy. Individuals, as equals, voluntarily and rationally choose to be members or citizens of a nation-state, so that their individual interests can be best served. Obligations and responsibilities are taken on only insofar as they foster those interests. Liberal thinkers such as Mill have drawn a sharp distinction between the private and the public domains. They typically insist that the nation-state, particularly as state, should not impinge on the private domain. They typically see citizenship as the means to ensure a proper relationship between the private individual and the public community, namely, a relationship that guarantees individual autonomy and protects it from state intrusions. Thus, liberals typically see citizenship in terms of a set of rights designed to allow a person to develop fully his or her individuality, without interference from the state and from other individuals. Modern liberals, or those that Faulks (2000) refers to as the neo-liberals, take the idea of citizenship to be linked to the idea of democracy, at least the idea of liberal democracy. Certain basic citizenship rights are a precondition of democracy while the democratic system is necessary for the practice of citizenship. Commentators such as Fukuyama would endorse the liberal-democratic model of citizenship as the ultimate one. Other neo-liberals, such as Hayek, see democracy as linked to market capitalism. For them, individual rights inherent in citizenship are civil democratic rights to participate in the market, not political or social rights, such as the right to equal representation, or the right to a minimal income. Faulks (2000, pp.64-65) calls the rights that neo-liberals identify with citizenship (and democracy) 'market rights', which include 'the right to accumulate and spend wealth as one sees fit, to assert self-interest in the market place, and to choose between a wide range of service providers'.

I have argued in the previous section, the basic presuppositions of the idea of citizenship within the liberal-democratic framework can all be found in Confucianism; but this does not mean that the Confucian idea of citizenship will look like the liberal-democratic idea as outlined above. Confucianism possesses many characteristics that distinguish it from liberal democracy, and the Confucian idea of citizenship would be different from the liberal-democratic idea, as much as a Confucian society is different from a society favoured by the 'neo-liberals'. Many liberals, such as Fukuyama, are convinced that liberalism, or liberal democracy ought to be, and for some already is, the standard socio-political mode of human existence. However, this has been rejected by many commentators. Martin Hollis (1999, p.36) reminds us that 'liberalism is for the liberals' as much as 'cannibalism is for the cannibals'. For Faulks, the main problem with the liberal conception of citizenship is that it contains an internal contradiction: it is meant to be both inclusive and exclusive. The idea of equality requires citizenship to be universal, hence inclusive, while the idea of citizen rights is exclusive. Within a nation-state, universality requires conformity, hence the exclusion, or at least the suppression, of minority rights: 'The state, through its efforts to create unity and symmetry between citizens, necessarily denies and suppresses difference' (Faulks, 2000, p.49). Immigration, globalization, and other factors have resulted in a modern nation-state having within its boundaries many different minority groups. Minorities are not just cultural and racial. They are also religious, social, gender-based, and economic. Liberalism, with its emphasis on individual rights and its acceptance of the nation-state as the context of citizenship, is unable to resolve the conflict that arises because of minorities. Also, the liberals' emphasis on individual rights and their suspicion of the community have resulted in a practice of citizenship that, at best, does not address the social biases against minorities, and at worse, deepens them. Faulks (2000, p.58) contends that 'inequalities associated with the class system, patriarchy and racism are deeply rooted in society and are crucial to understanding why the formal rights of citizenship are not effective for some groups'. We can add to this the fact that market capitalism endorsed by liberals has resulted in an economic underclass who are often unable to exercise their political rights.

Critics of the liberal conception of citizenship argue that we must move away from the emphasis on individual rights and the idea that citizenship is essentially a means of promoting them; but in moving away, some theorists have reached the other extreme. Thus, we have communitarians who argue that what is crucial to citizenship is the idea of community obligations, or responsibilities, not individual rights. If there are any rights, they are determined by the political community. However, the emphasis on community-based responsibilities and rights does nothing to address the problems faced by minorities, who still face the risk of being excluded from deliberations concerning what is in the interest of the community. Somewhere between a vision focused on the individual and one focused on the community is one focused on groups in a community. For instance, Young (1990) argues for a 'politics of difference' and a corresponding notion of citizenship that protects the interests of oppressed and disadvantaged groups. Along the same lines, Kymlicka (1995) argues for 'multicultural citizenship' as a means to enable citizens to retain their different cultural identities. A variation on Kymlicka's theme is Aihwa Ong's (1999) 'flexible citizenship' which allows expatriates in a state to participate in the citizenship of that state while retaining their cultural identities in being citizens of their home states, a notion designed to cope with the effects of mass migration and economic globalization. All these suggestions deal with the problems of minorities, or heterogeneity generally, by inserting group rights in-between individual rights and community-based rights. However, Faulks contends that they all raise serious problems. One problem is, how are groups to be defined and 'what is to prevent a proliferation of new groups demanding rights and thereby fragmenting the polity still further?' (Faulks, 2000, p.92). Another is that there could well be oppression and mistreatment of members within a group, an issued discussed by Alan Montefiore and Cecilia Wee in chapters 8 and 10.

The shift of focus from the individual to something beyond the individual, be it a group in a society or the society itself, is for Faulks a move in the right direction. However, Faulks thinks that it is a mistake to abandon the standpoint of the individual and believes that in one way or another the idea of individual rights is crucial for a theory of citizenship. What has to be abandoned is the liberal understanding of the individual and hence of individual rights, and what has to be done is to find a replacement for it. He proposes what he calls a 'postmodern' conception of citizenship based on an understanding of the individual not as an atomistic being standing over against the community, but as an individual whose individuality is shaped by the community. In this understanding, the rights of an individual and his or her responsibilities to the community are mutually dependent. Faulks (2000, p.17) wants to retain the liberal insight that the idea of citizenship is the idea that the community should not obliterate the individual, but wants to add to it the Aristotelian notion that to be fully human, a person, an individual, has to be a part of a community and to take part 'in the running of the community's affairs'. An individual person is not just a rational animal as the liberals contend, but a political animal. To be a citizen, an individual has to cultivate certain civic virtues, or to acquire civility. This view finds support in Rouner's (2000) contention that civility is linked to political community. A citizen must necessarily have a public face. Faulks (2000, p.1) concurs with Oldfield (1998, p.159) that 'the concept of the "private citizen" is an oxymoron'. As I understand it, what is 'postmodern' about Faulks' view is that true citizenship deconstructs the private-public duality that liberals subscribe to.

Whether or not we go along with Faulks' 'postmodernisation' of the idea of citizenship, it has to be said that he might be right in his rejection of the liberals' metaphysics of personhood or individuality. Cartesian metaphysics, which underlies the liberal view, has been seriously challenged not just by neo-Aristotelianism but also by the existentialist contention that to be is to be in the world, or thrown into a world as Heidegger puts it, and by the Wittgensteinian account of a person as a language user and of language as communal activity. The idea of a private citizen is just as oxymoronic as the idea of a private language. From whatever angle, it seems that there is no person, no individual, without a world, or a community. Not just any world, but a world of one's own making. To be an individual person is to participate in the making of one's own world, one's own community. Herein lies the essence of what it is to be a citizen. With this in mind, we have a basis for constructing a theory of citizenship that avoids the liberal contradiction and the above-mentioned problems of minorities. In this conception of citizenship, rights and responsibilities are the citizen's tools with which he or she builds the community which in turn defines his or her individuality. Different minorities, different cultural, racial, ethnic, and other groups share in the common task of building an all-inclusive community that allows for differences rather than obliterating them. Given what is said about Confucianism in the previous section, it is clear that Confucianism sits most comfortably with this conception of citizenship.

As we have seen, Confucianism does not conceive of a strict private-public duality and does not see an individual person as an atomistic autonomous being standing over and against his or her community. An individual person is necessarily a social being standing in a complex network of social relations, although this does not mean that there are no separate individuals with identifying individuality. What it does mean is that the Confucian notion of citizenship is inconsistent with the idea of the individual as the ultimate basis of social and axiological values, the view roughly identified as individualism above. We have seen that the Confucians did not entertain any notion of rights pertaining to an individual qua individual, or any notion of individual rights not grounded in any social context. The same goes for responsibilities. Furthermore, in the social context, rights and responsibilities are mutually dependent.

The Confucian understanding of the individual and of rights and responsibilities entails that Confucianism cannot accommodate the idea of citizenship as primarily the protection of individual rights against the community of which he or she by necessity but reluctantly is a part. However, such understanding makes Confucianism most hospitable to a conception of citizenship that emphasizes the social dimension of the citizen, such as Faulks'. For Faulks, 'citizenship is always a reciprocal and, therefore, social idea' (Faulks, 2000, p.4). In terms of practice, Confucianism is certainly hostile to what Tilly (1995) calls the practice of 'thin' citizenship in which the citizen's main concern is the protection of his or her rights, in which the state's function is merely to maintain a legal apparatus for such protection, and in which a citizen's responsibilities are minimal and subordinate to the concern about rights. 'Thin' citizenship presupposes the public-private duality, and pertains only to the public dimension of the individual person, who is independent of the community. It is, of course, what the liberals endorse; but there is a rival practice in which the notion of citizenship is a 'deep' (Clarke, 1996) or 'thick' one (Faulks, 2000). In the practice of 'deep' or 'thick' citizenship, the citizen plays an active part in the 'shared and communal activity' (Clarke, 1996, p.4), where 'rights and responsibilities are mutually supportive', and are seen not in legal but in 'moral' terms (Faulks, 2000, p.11). The individual is at once a citizen, whose relationship with the community is one of interdependence. Clearly, Confucianism, with its understanding of the individual person as a social being whose rights and responsibilities are governed by the moral concept of *li*, would be perfectly at home in the practice of 'deep' or 'thick' citizenship.

Going hand in hand with the Confucian understanding of the person is the Confucian account of the cognitive process. Confucianism does not see a duality between purely rational deliberations and affective states that are totally non-cognitive. Liberal thinkers typically consign emotions to the private sphere and require the display of rationality as appropriate for the public sphere. In Confucianism however, just as a person is both public and private, his or her cognitive process is both rational and affective. Just as there is no public-private duality, there is no duality of the rational, or mind, and the affective, or heart. Rather, what there is, is a heart-mind (*xin*) with which a person makes decisions within a network of relationships. This is why Confucianism cannot conceive of a person as someone capable of cold and purely rational calculations designed to promote personal interests, and hence cannot conceive of a citizen as such a person. There is no such thing as a purely rational mind that can make calculations detached from how one feels about others. The Confucian heart-mind is not the liberal mind and cannot understand the liberal idea of citizenship. However, the notion of heart-mind seems perfectly suited to a conception of citizenship that locates the citizen, as a person, at the node that connects the public and the private, the political and the personal, rights and responsibilities. Whereas the liberal mind thins out the individual person, the heart-mind thickens and is thus perfectly suited to the practice of thick, or deep, citizenship.

We have seen that Confucianism advocates an inclusive notion of the individual person. In addition to this crucial conceptual advantage, three other elements of Confucianism can be seen as valuable in addressing the problems of modern citizenship. One problem is that poverty effectively rules out the practice of citizenship. For most of those below the poverty line, citizen rights are there only in name. Critics of the liberal conception of citizenship claim that it leaves this problem unsolved. Supporters of a 'thick' notion argue for a notion of 'citizen's income' that enables everyone to be a meaningful citizen. It can now be shown that the Confucian notion of *minben* (people as roots), in addition to having the potential to contribute to the idea of Confucian democracy as mentioned above, incorporates the idea of ensuring each and every individual a decent livelihood, and as such makes the idea of a Confucian citizen much more meaningful. Thus, to govern according to *minben* is to govern for the people (*min*), for their well-being, their prosperity and their security, tending to them as one would tend to the roots (*ben*) of a tree. There is some mention of this idea in the writings of Confucius (for example, *Analects* 13.9), but clear expressions of it are found elsewhere. For instance, Mencius speaks of *minben* as the protection of the people, protecting them against poverty and insecurity. As pointed out by Kung-chuan Hsiao (1979, p.150), throughout 'the seven books of the *Mencius*, Mencius focuses his concern on enriching the people's livelihood, decreasing taxes and imposts, bringing wars to an end, and correcting boundaries'. Rulers are exhorted to ensure that people's livelihood is such that they have enough to look after their parents and children (*Mencius* 1A7-21). Only when livelihood is guaranteed can people be expected to behave morally, to have a 'constant heart' (*Mencius* 3A3). Clearly, this is consistent with the idea of a citizen's income sufficient to allow the people to have a 'constant heart' in participating in the community's affairs. Indeed, Mencius can be interpreted as positing a state's responsibility to provide a minimum standard of living for all, the correlate of which is the people's social right to a minimum income. While this is contrary to the liberals' advocacy of 'leaving it to the market', it is in line with what many theorists take to be a condition for thick citizenship.

The Confucian idea of citizenship can claim two other advantages. The first relates to the commitment to harmony (*he*) in Confucianism. While the implementation of *minben* is likely to remove the economic disadvantage for some groups in the society, the emphasis on harmony (*he*) will go a long way towards solving the problem of minorities that besets the liberal practice of citizenship. The Confucian cosmology sees the world as a harmonious blending of different and often opposing forces. The force that maintains harmony is the Way (*dao*). In human affairs too, there are different and often opposing forces, and efforts should be made to maintain harmony. One way of doing so is to maintain a balance between opposing forces, or not to lean too much in any direction. This is outlined in the Confucian classic *Doctrine of the Mean* (*Zhongyong*). However, an ordinary person who has no knowledge of *zhongyong* can still promote harmony by following the rites, or rituals (*li*), because harmonious actions have been distilled and retained in the rituals (*li*) of the society: 'Of the things brought about by the rites, harmony is the most valuable' (*Analects* 1.1). Unfortunately, the notion of harmony is too frequently misunderstood as conformity, as something that requires the obliteration of differences in favor of unity. In truth, it is precisely in harmony that differences are maintained. Orchestral harmony requires the blending of different sounds, but in such a way that each instrument can still be heard. A good cook will blend different ingredients, thus harmonizing different tastes and textures, but in such a way that the distinctiveness of a particular ingredient is preserved. A society that practices harmony will enable different groups to blend harmoniously but at the same time retain their differences. Thus, the Confucian notion of harmony has the potential to cope with the problem of minority groups in its advocacy of a harmonious society in which different groups can blend their efforts in contributing to the community's affairs while retaining their distinctive identities. The worry that Kymlicka has is that cultural minorities have to conform, but as

Faulks has pointed out, to accord special rights to certain groups is to risk fragmentation. The answer clearly is harmony, bearing in mind that harmony is not conformity but is rather a sublation of both individuality and conformity that allows for individual differences to manifest in community action.

Critics of liberal citizenship are also concerned that the liberals' acceptance of the nation-state as the context of citizenship will render the liberal practice incapable of dealing with the effects of globalization. Problems of security, pollution and conservation extend beyond nation-state boundaries, and will be exacerbated by the liberal practice of thin citizenship. The creation of the European Union is seen by many critics as a response in the right direction, but for many, such as Falk (1995), nothing short of the implementation of the idea of 'global citizenship' will suffice. Here too Confucianism has much to contribute with its advocacy of an outward expansion of the self to encompass the family, the community, the society, and finally the world at large. As stated in *The Great Learning*, the idea of learning is to 'rectify the mind' in order to 'cultivate the person', which in turn contributes to the next step, to regulate families, and the next step, to govern the country well, and eventually, to make the whole world virtuous. It might be said that the Confucian vision is a global one. Indeed, Confucian harmony is ultimately harmony with the world and with Heaven itself.

I have argued that Confucianism is committed to certain standards and values in such a way as to make the idea of Confucian citizenship intelligible. However, it is a notion very different from citizenship constructed within the liberal-democratic framework. For some critics, this is all the worse for it. However, the liberal conception of citizenship is not the only one, nor the most viable according to some commentators. As we move towards a thicker or deeper conception of citizenship, Confucianism becomes more and more relevant. I have shown that the Confucian conception of citizenship would be a thick or deep one. If I am right, Confucianism can contribute to a practice of citizenship that has the best chance of offering recognition for all and of dealing with global issues. Indeed, it might be said that Confucianism endorses a notion of membership of a world community that might be called 'Heavenly citizenship'.

## Notes

1    Materials in this chapter have also appeared in A.T. Nuyen, 2002.
2    Translations from *The Mencius* and *The Analects* have been adapted from various sources.

## References

Bloom, Irene (1998), 'Fundamental Intuitions and Consensus Statements: Mencian Confucianism and Human Rights', in de Bary and Tu, 1998, pp.94-116.
Ching, Julia (1998), 'Human Rights: A Valid Chinese Concept?' in de Bary and Tu, 1998, pp.67-82.

Clarke, Paul (1996), *Deep Citizenship*, Pluto Press, London.
de Bary, Wm. Theodore and Tu Weiming (eds.) (1998), *Confucianism and Human Rights*, Columbia University Press, New York.
Falk, Richard (1995), *On Human Governance*, Polity Press, Cambridge.
Faulks, Keith (2000), *Citizenship*, Routledge, London and New York.
Fukuyama, Francis (1992), *The End of History and the Last Man*, Free Press, New York.
Habermas, Jürgen (1994), 'Citizenship and National Identity', in Bart Van Steenbergen (ed.), *The Condition of Citizenship*, Sage, London, pp.20-35.
Hall, David and Roger T.Ames (1987), *Thinking Through Confucius*, State University of New York Press, Albany.
Hollis, Martin (1999), 'Is Universalism Ethnocentric?' in Christian Joppke and Steven Lukes (eds.), *Multicultural Questions*, Oxford University Press, Oxford, pp.27-43.
Hsiao, Kung-ch'uan (1979), *A History of Chinese Political Thought, vol.1: From the Beginnings to Sixth Century A.D.*, Frederick W. Mote (trans.), Princeton University Press, Princeton.
Huntington, Samuel (1991), 'Democracy's Third Wave', *Journal of Democracy*, vol.2, pp.15-26.
Kwok, Daniel W.Y. (1998), 'On The Rites and Rights of Being Human', in de Bary and Tu, 1998, pp.83-93.
Kymlicka, Will (1995), *Multicultural Citizenship*, Oxford University Press, Oxford.
Li, Chenyang (1999), *The Tao Encounters the West*, State University of New York Press, Albany.
Miller, David (1995), *On Nationality*, Oxford University Press, Oxford.
Nuyen, A.T. (2000), 'Confucianism, the Idea of *Min-pen*, and Democracy', *Copenhagen Journal of Asian Studies*, vol.14, pp.130-51.
Nuyen, A.T. (2001), 'Confucianism and the Idea of Equality', *Asian Philosophy*, vol.11, pp.61-71.
Nuyen, A.T. (2002), 'Confucianism and the Idea of Citizenship', *Asian Philosophy*, vol.12, pp.127-39 (available at http://www.tandf.co.uk/journals).
Nuyen, A.T. (2003), 'Filial Piety as Respect for Tradition', in Alan K.L. Chan and Sor-hoon Tan (eds.), *Filial Piety in Chinese Thought and History*, Open Court, La Salle, pp.203-14.
Oldfield, Adrian (1998), *Citizenship and Community: Civic Republicanism and the Modern World*, University of Minnesota Press, Minneapolis.
Ong, Aihwa (1999), *Flexible Citizenship: The Cultural Logics of Transnationality*, Duke University Press, Durham.
Oommen, T.K. (1997), *Citizenship, Nationality and Ethnicity*, Polity Press, Cambridge.
Rouner, Leroy (2000), *Civility*, Notre Dame University Press, Notre Dame.
Tan, Sor-hoon, *Confucian Democracy: A Deweyan Reconstruction of Confucianism*, State University of New York Press, Albany.
Tilly, Charles (1995), 'The Emergence of Citizenship in France and Elsewhere', *International Review of Social History*, vol.40, Supplementary no.3, pp.223-36.
Tu, Wei-ming (1998), 'Probing the "Three Bonds" and "Five Relationships" in Confucian Humanism', in Walter H. Slote and George A. DeVos (eds.), *Confucianism and the Family*, State University of New York Press, Albany, pp.121-36.
Young, Iris (1990), *Justice and the Politics of Difference*, Princeton University Press, New Jersey.

## Chapter 13

# Exemplary World Citizens as Civilized Local Communicators: Politics and Culture in the Global Aspirations of Confucianism

Sor-hoon Tan

The previous chapter proposing a Confucian idea of citizenship suggests that Confucianism is committed to a world community and could contribute to moving beyond citizenship confined to the nation-state. Such global aspiration is certainly evident in the works of some contemporary scholars of Confucianism. This chapter examines the interaction between politics and culture within such Confucian global aspirations to illustrate that being a world citizen does not mean being neutral towards or transcending cultures, but is instead rooted in culturally-informed local communications across political and cultural boundaries.

### Cultural Diversity and Cosmopolitan Citizenship

While ethnic and cultural differences have been perceived as attributes that should not matter in a liberal democracy wherein all citizens are equal, recent trends toward identity politics raise serious questions about if and how politics should take into account cultures, among other social differences that constitute group identity (Young, 1990; Taylor, 1995). Identity politics may be viewed as a form of resistance to the grand narratives of modernity, the universalism and essentialism attributed to the Enlightenment worldview that has dominated modernization; it is also in part a reaction against certain homogenizing tendencies of globalizing processes, and the insecurities resulting from the fraying of traditional social fabric, of family and communal ties, under the stress of late modernity.

The spectre of McWorld, global capitalism 'pressing nations into one homogeneous global theme park...tied together by communications, information, entertainment and commerce' (Barber, 1995, p.4), gives rise to defensive localizing forces within nation-states and ethnic conflicts on the international stage; it fuels a cosmopolitan revival proposing global democracy and cosmopolitan citizenship as antidote to the poison of advanced capitalism. The idea of a 'citizen of the world' dates back to ancient Greece, and Kant's defence of a 'universal community' with 'a cosmopolitan right' as necessary to 'perpetual peace' continue to influence contemporary thinkers.[1] Notwithstanding Kant's explicit rejection of colonial conquest, some hold Enlightenment universalism and essentialism responsible for a Western imperialism that sometimes resulted in colonial ethnocide.[2] To exorcize these Enlightenment ghosts, current defendants of cosmopolitanism need to take cultures seriously by resisting the temptation of any 'empire of uniformity' without surrendering to relativist paralysis in the face of ethnic and cultural conflicts.

Somewhat sympathetic to cosmopolitanism but critical of its Enlightenment baggage, Craig Calhoun (2003) argues that reconstructing an adequate concept of citizenship for the future will require both cosmopolitan ideals and social solidarity at least partially embedded in particular cultures. Instead of an attenuated cosmopolitanism that cannot ground mutual commitment and responsibility, that at its worst treats cultural diversity as a proliferation of consumer choices and at its best concerns itself only with transnational political institutions and rights, cosmopolitan citizenship needs a stronger account of social solidarity to complement its stronger account of representation. Though Calhoun often emphasizes the importance of public discourse in democratic politics, he acknowledges that, at both national and global level, 'it is important to recognize that relations across meaningful groups are not simply matters of rational-critical discourse but involve the creation of local hybrid cultures, accommodations, collaborations, and practical knowledge' (Calhoun, 2003, p.109).[3]

Cosmopolitan citizenship requires a global ethics that would be multicultural in its stand against the crass commercialism that threatens to wipe out cultural heritages and divisive uses of cultures that add venom and hatred to global conflicts. Such conflicts appear almost inevitable to Samuel Huntington and his followers; his 'clash of civilizations' may be considered a version of virulent 'identity politics' on a global scale.[4] If they are right, then the future is 'Jihad versus McWorld' rather than any cosmopolitan order based on universal international laws and rights. Meanwhile, some argue that it is time to recognize the Enlightenment worldview as only one of many possible cultural particularisms, and 'any form of culture claiming a metaphysically privileged status for one particular model of political organization now seems hopelessly parochial, and even an obstacle to international cooperation' (Bridges, 1994, p.7). This is music to the ears of those who claim that Western values, especially those of liberal democracy, are unsuitable for non-Western cultures.

While Western aid and models provided a great deal of the impetus for modernization in Asia immediately after World War II, certain Western influences, especially political ideas of liberal democracy and human rights, were soon questioned by some Asians. When politicians such as Singapore's Lee Kuan Yew (Fareed, 1994) emphasised the importance of cultural factors in East Asia's economic success and argued that cultural differences also mean that various aspects of Western thought and practice, even if they work in the West, do not suit Asian societies, such comments are often dismissed as self-serving. However, the view that modernization need not mean Westernization has fairly wide support not only in the East but also among some Western scholars who have been studying the East. If modernity is a Western project imposing the values of the West on the rest of the world, then it is best left unfinished. Culture is a major plank of Asian exceptionalism in the human rights and Asian values debate. Its Western advocates consider human rights the closest we have to a normative global ethics and some seek the basis for transnational citizenship in human rights.[5] Others worry that the claim of universality is actually Western ethnocentrism in disguise.[6] Even if Asian values (whatever they are) and existing conceptions of human rights are incompatible in some ways, their differences could be grounds for intercultural dialogue rather than signifying the 'clash of civilizations'. More reflective, 'unofficial' East Asian viewpoints are 'contributing to a genuine dialogue that goes to the heart of the debate: the meaning of "universality" and the areas of justifiable differences' (Bauer and Bell, 1999, p.4). There is increasing support for more inclusive constructions of 'intercivilizational' human rights (Onuma, 1999).[7]

One engages one's own and others' cultures in a multicultural setting by being willing to reason about cultural norms and practices, treating them as solutions to problems which at least as a matter of logical possibility have alternative solutions, and recognizing the political legitimacy of comparing different solutions and questioning criteria for comparisons (Waldron, 2000). However, demands for respect could also be uncompromising and non-negotiable, treating any question as an insult to one's culture, thereby ending dialogues prematurely and escalating conflicts. Asian countries are as multicultural as Western ones, if not more so. Playing the culture card in contesting global hegemony could have repercussions on the local multicultural situation. For example, some perceive Singapore's state-orchestrated Confucian revival's emphasis on 'Chinese culture' as threatening the delicate balance of local multicultural politics. In response, a 1991 Government 'White Paper for the Shared Values' clarifies specifically that Singapore's shared values, while implying Confucian values, are not Confucian – these values are not meant to be 'a subterfuge for imposing Chinese Confucian values on [non-Chinese] Singaporeans' (Kuo, 1992, p.2).

As Chantal Mouffe (1997, pp.387-8) remarks, 'what we commonly call 'cultural identity' is both the scene and the object of political struggles'. If we wish to avoid the violence latent in every construction of exclusive collective identity so that mutual recognition and respect become the focus of identity politics, within nation-states or on a global basis, we must resist the essentialist view of culture as discrete, static, impervious to external influences, homogenous, without internal dissent, and determining behaviour almost mechanically.[8] I understand culture as networks of interpretive created or inherited products by which a group understands itself and its world. Culture is learned and acquired in social life, its boundaries are often vague and its content contested. Though inter-generational transmission is necessary, culture is 'not a passive inheritance but an active process of creating meaning, not given but constantly redefined and reconstituted'; neither is culture mere 'life-style choices' or useful fiction (Parekh, 2000, p.153; Bauman, 1999, p.xiv). Both creativity and normative regulation exist and must remain in the composite idea of culture.[9]

Culture is not destiny; but the particular culture in which one is raised and lives provides the context for one's choices and actions (Kymlicka, 1995, pp.82-4).

Citizenship needs a cultural component so that being a citizen could be an integral part of who we are as well as how we choose and act. Liberals view citizenship as membership in a community constituted by enjoyment of basic rights, control over government, and equality in an inclusive polity; but citizenship must be more than a legal status.[10] It is difficult to create shared loyalty to a polity and common goals if we only think in terms of institutions that protects our individual rights and limits our obligations.[11] Certain cultures are more conducive to active citizenship than others. However, any attempt to inculcate culture from above carries high risk of oppression. Culture could bind people together across time and space, but this very power could also cause conflicts. The culture of citizenship in a multicultural world, in each multicultural nation-state, should be compatible with recognition and respect for different cultures; it should contribute to harmony rather than induce resentment. We tend to think of citizenship as a political solution to human conflicts, including those caused by cultural differences; but culture could also prevent or resolve conflicts, which are political problems. Confucianism contains some interesting clues of the cultural resources that might help resolve conflicts and nurture solidarity in the midst of differences.

**Exemplary World Citizen:**
**Confucian Humanism's Contribution to Global Community**

Tu Wei-ming (1989, p.6) claims that 'If the English speaking community were to choose one word to characterize the Chinese way of life for the last two thousand years, the word would be "Confucian."' He of course appreciates that Chinese culture does not reduce to Confucianism, and Confucianism is an integral part of other East Asian cultures of Japan, Korea, and Vietnam. Chinese culture itself defies definition. Given that the Chinese, in response to different environments in different parts of the world, have introduced so many variations and innovations of thought and practice into their ways of life, one could consider Chinese culture a convenient term for an indefinite variety of hybrid cultures loosely related to one another by 'family resemblances' rather than sharing any essence.[12] Though hybridity is a new concept in cultural studies, the phenomenon it picks out is arguably ancient. Chinese civilization did not begin with the expansion of a single cultural core, but emerged from a confederation of several developed cultural areas; nor was there ever any ethnic or racial homogeneity. The boundaries of Chinese culture are unclear and unstable, and the relationship between cultural centre and periphery has never been one of simple domination and submission; there is continuous tension and contest both within China itself and the larger 'cultural China'.[13]

Confucianism is unique in the long history of China in the way it makes Chinese culture its responsibility. Even when denied political power during the Warring States period (fifth to third century BCE), Confucianism still became 'a notable social force exerting control over the cultural system' (Tu, 1993, p.17). Contemporary scholars observe that Confucianism helped inspire the self-consciousness of the Chinese people as a distinct cultural entity.[14] The Confucian ideal of an exemplary person (*junzi* 君子) is one whose basic dispositions and cultural accomplishments are appropriately balanced (*wenzhi binbin* 文質彬彬, *Analects* 6.18). Confucius understood his own mission as one of continuing and developing the culture of King Wen (*Analects* 9.5). His admiration for the Zhou dynasty is not solely for its political achievement, which is valued as part of its cultural achievement (*Analects* 3.14). By Confucius' time, the political decline of Zhou was already well underway, but its culture would be more enduring. Sinologist Angus Graham once remarked that the Chinese has discovered the secret of the immortal social organism – that secret of immortality lies in its culture.

This endurance is not the persistence of the same unchanging way of life, but a matter of continuity (*Analects* 2.23); otherwise, one would have to agree with Julia Ching (2000) that 'Traditional Chinese culture, including Confucianism, is dead'.[15] Despite being frequently criticized for being conservative and causing China's stagnation, Confucianism does have a place for creativity and innovation (Tan, 2005). Moreover, the tradition has endured because of its amazing adaptability, despite occasional lapses into xenophobia and ethnocentrism.[16] Even though ethnocentric Confucians present Chinese culture as transforming other cultures and gaining their voluntary political submission by demonstrating its superior virtue, the reality is not so one-sided. Confucianism would not have spread so far and wide, nor would its influence have endured, if it had been impervious to reciprocal influence by other cultures. If the Chinese has influenced other cultures in East Asia and beyond, those cultures have transformed Confucianism for their own use and in turn influenced Chinese thought and cultural life – the mutual transformation of Confucianism and Buddhism between the Han and Song dynasties is the best example of such interactions (Tu, 1986; Tang, 1988).

Present efforts to reconstruct Confucianism, in what Tu Wei-ming calls the 'third epoch of Confucian humanism', have learnt much from other cultures, notably those of the democratic West; at the same time they contribute to the inquiries that cut across cultural boundaries (Tu, 1989, p.39). Among the most important contributions to this Confucian humanism are Tu's own works, which reject Joseph Levenson's verdict that the fate of Confucianism in modern China is that of a historical relic in a museum without walls. Tu explores the rich symbolic resources of the Confucian tradition and renders the core values of Confucianism comprehensible and meaningful for English-speaking audiences from different philosophical traditions, attempting to show 'how, beyond ethnic identity, Confucian humanism can meaningfully contribute to the cultivation of cultural competence, ethical intelligence and spiritual values of young people East and West' (Tu, 1998, p.XXVII). Thanks to scholars like Tu Wei-ming, Robert Neville (1994) is able to describe Confucianism as a 'world philosophy'.

Human rights and world citizenship have a place in Tu's Confucian humanism. At a 1995 lecture in Singapore, he declared that today's Confucians would, 'as citizens of the global community, maintain the universality of human rights...profess the desirability of democracy as providing to this day the most effective framework in which human rights are safeguarded' (Tu, 1995, p.5). Tu responded to multiculturalism, as 'an enduring feature of modernity', by urging the fostering of 'a fiduciary global community', the possibility of which depends on certain core values. Instead of imposing artificially constructed values on all communities, 'each community, large or small, must take the local commitment to articulate its own configuration of core values'. On both personal and communal levels, this search for core values should not lead to premature imposition of one's own values on others; instead, 'we invite an ever expanding circle of the human community to take part in our own establishment and enlargement. This may provide an opportunity to explore ways to help us define anew who we are and what we ought to become' (Tu, 1992, pp.343-4).

In Tu's Confucian humanism, the ideal human being is an exemplary world citizen, whose cultural accomplishments are comprehensible to other cultures and respectful of them and whose political commitments, if not exactly those of liberal democracies, bear a close resemblance to them. Confucian humanism is compatible with both liberal rights approach to citizenship as well as republican approach emphasizing participation and community; its preferred approach to citizenship, if pressed for one, would be to combine the two to address both liberty and community concerns. Tu has no trouble combining Confucian culture and liberal democratic politics because his Confucian humanism is one purged of what Tu calls 'politicized Confucianism', which is implicated in the authoritarian political culture of imperial China.

Tu (1993, p.28) rejects the 'politicization of Confucian moral symbols for the primary purpose of ideological control' as a betrayal of the Confucian intention to moralize politics and transform the legalist state bureaucracy and control mechanisms inherited from Qin dynasty. It is too convenient to blame everything authoritarian in China's past on Legalist subversion of Confucian good intentions. If Confucians were mistaken that a good ruler/official could achieve Confucian goals with legalist means, then grafting Confucian ideals onto liberal democratic systems may be equally problematic, unless Confucian ideals are democratized, or liberal democratic systems Confucianized. Tu emphasized the former almost exclusively; more attention needs to be paid to the latter. By Confucianizing liberal democracy, I refer not to institutional reforms even though these are necessary, but more broadly to cultural transformation that facilitates the kind of political processes we need in multicultural societies of the global age.

In his discussion of the core values required for a global fiduciary community, Tu (1992, p.343) mentions in passing the Indonesian government's attempt to build consensus on *Pancasila* (the Five Principles) and Singapore Government's attempt to define values for the entire country as examples raising the universal central issue, 'how can we commit ourselves to the core values specific to our community in an increasingly pluralistic cultural context'. The history of politicized Confucianism shows that the State's appropriation of cultural initiatives and cultural capital usually perverts the philosophical ideals embedded in a culture. Tu (de Bary and Tu, 1998, p.xvii) discusses this danger explicitly in questioning whether the Confucian revival in the People's Republic of China is 'merely an exercise in the co-opting of scholars by cultural commissars'. Top-down approaches to national culture risk substituting propaganda and indoctrination for the kind of cultural change required for global community. The state could play a positive role in cultural changes only if it limits itself to providing resources to individuals and civil society groups, and a broad regulatory framework including a flexible regime of individual and group rights, to protect the autonomy of dissenters from overzealousness on the part of those promoting cultures or cultural changes. The work of nurturing a global fiduciary community belongs first and foremost to each and every exemplary world citizen.

Confucians could cite ancient sources (*The Great Learning*) to support this approach of anchoring global aspiration, through local communities, in the moral life of individual persons.

> ...when the personal life is cultivated, the family will be regulated; when the family is regulated, the state will be in order; when the state is in order, there will be peace throughout the world (Chan, 1963, p.87).

Those who consider Confucianism parochial will point out that historically 'all under heaven' (*tianxi* 天下) did not include the whole world. From a hermeneutical stance, there is no reason to let the much more limited horizons of past readers limit our own interpretation of the text; but remembering past ethnocentric tendencies of Confucians (if not Confucianism) cautions us against too summarily equating what Confucius calls 'this culture' (*siwen* 斯文) with 'human culture'. Looking for 'universal humanistic teachings' in Confucianism may set up another hegemonic impulse, which will clash with similar Western impulses in a contest over the definition of 'human'. Rather, we should recognize that the meanings of Confucianism in a global age are *particular*, but in a way that aims to participate in intercultural dialogues to create an aspirational universal that each participant could claim as her own. Interpreting *The Great Learning* for today's global village, one's endeavour in cultivating oneself remains inadequate if one's horizons could not accommodate the entire world; professed commitment to humanity or the whole world remains abstract and empty if it finds no purchase in the daily life of personal cultivation and social interaction.

Addressing the challenges of globalization, Tu Wei-ming observes that the 'conceptual framework informed by the exclusive dichotomy of universalism and particularism' gives rise to a kind of 'schizophrenia'. Tu (1992, p.339) aligns himself with cosmopolites:

> If we insist upon an either-or choice between global consciousness and local commitment, we – self-styled cosmopolitan citizens of the world under the influence of Enlightenment mentality – are prone to condemn all alien forms of quests for roots as narrow-minded and dangerous particularisms. Curiously, at the same time, our own commitment to ethnicity, gender, mother tongue, fatherland, class, and faith often compels us to take radically exclusivist position despite our avowed cosmopolitanism.

Tu believes that the Confucian golden rule, and the related glossing of general virtue of humanity (*ren* 仁 ) in terms of 'wishing to establish oneself, one establishes others; wishing to enlarge oneself, one enlarges others', could transform the contradictions between global consciousness and local commitment into 'an intimate mutuality'.[17]

The Confucian resources Tu highlights are most useful not as a commitment to some humanist universals but in emphasizing the need to take differences seriously. If cosmopolitan commitment to rational humanity leads to an assumption that others would or should think like us, then we are substituting the other's thought and voice with our own. One culture's understanding of reason and humanity should not be imposed upon another. Empathy that respects differences only occurs in careful and attentive communication that does not assume that others think and feel as we do but nevertheless hope for a possible mutual understanding. If there are to be common human projects and ideals that could be shared across different cultures, they must be painstakingly formed through collaborative intercultural communication rather than taken for granted. A Confucian ethic of communicative virtues would improve intercultural communication and contribute to a pluralistic global culture that could sustain world citizenship, and wherein multiple particular cultures could interact harmoniously, or at least without mutual destruction. The global aspirations of twenty-first century Confucianism involves aspiring to exemplary world citizenship through communicating with cultural others in a civilized manner at the local level.

### Civilized Local Communicator:
### Confucianism's Pragmatic Role in Intercultural Communication

In Confucianism, the exemplary person is one who is authoritatively human; such a person would conduct herself according to *li* 禮 in every respect (*Analects* 12.1; Tu, 1968). *Li*, translated as 'rites', 'rituals', or 'ritual propriety', is the constitutive cultural means to humanity. If Tu's Confucian humanism transforms the human ideal into an exemplary world citizen, Robert Neville's interpretation of *li* through pragmatist semiotics shows how one begins and continues the quest for that ideal by being a civilized local communicator. Neville's 'Boston Confucianism', which he calls a 'portable tradition in the late modern world', offers us insights into how to attempt a Confucianization of liberal democratic system through a communication approach to Tu's ideal of a global community of exemplary world citizens. In cultural terms, this must be realized from below, at the most basic level of day-to-day interpersonal encounters. A culture of citizenship is constituted by the interpretive resources available for interactions among citizens, and between citizens and the environment. According to the *Analects* (16.13), we would not know where to stand in society, vis-à-vis our fellow human beings, without *li*. The Confucian notion of *li* comprises symbolic resources that facilitate the practice of citizenship by enabling a person to find a place in a community that orientates her interaction with other members of the community and, where the community is smaller than the entire world, with other communities.

Though particular in its meanings, Confucianism is also 'universal' as a 'portable tradition' that could be practiced anywhere in the world. Neville uses the Confucian notion of *li* to critique Boston society and suggest ways of civilizing its day-to-day interactions (Neville, 2000, pp.15-23). To Neville, Confucian *li* 'can be generalized to include the entire pyramid of signs or of organic and social habits' (*ibid.*, p.14). Confucian *li* creates culture in a continuous, spontaneous, and aesthetic process. It is conventional but normative, constituting a kind of harmony.[18] Neville argues that Confucian notion of *li* could help Boston society develop certain meaningful significatory forms to shape social habits to improve its family, working, social, and civic life. Among these ritual forms are those of family, friendship, and civility – the last having to do with how individuals relate to and play official and semi-official roles in their community. The theme of civility has received some attention in recent civil society discourse, which could be linked to the search for global citizenship (Rouner, 2000, pp.187-221; Tan, 2003). Richard Falk and others have argued that instead of imposing a new world order through top-down globalization, we should aim for global civil society, or focus on transnational communities and social movements that involve individuals on an everyday basis (Falk, 1993; Delanty, 2000, pp.58-64). We act as global citizens by participating in activities that affect each of us individually, but also have global impact.

Neville interprets Confucianism from a pragmatist perspective. Communication is central to the pragmatist understanding of democracy (Dewey, 1927). If the political is more than resolving and preventing conflicts, abstract reasoning about common humanity alone will not create a global community of world citizens. A legal order on a global scale may prevent conflicts from being too destructive, but it is often a process of separation rather than connection – like a fence preventing two parties from trespassing on each other's properties. This is crucial in acute crises when those in conflict are already going for each other's throats, but more is needed for long term peace and harmony. While good regulatory institutions also contribute to a suitable environment for peaceful rather than acrimonious social relations, untiring efforts to communicate in ways that could generate trust and good will at the local level are even more important, be it between neighbours in a residential locale, between a resident and a visitor to a locale or country, between a voter and her political representative, or between representatives negotiating for groups or countries. Such civilized communication is especially difficult between individuals of different cultures, and even more so if anyone's cultural identity is at stake.

To accommodate cultural diversity in the political resolution of conflicts, some theorists turn to discourse theory and communicative ethics for a framework to understand how cultures are reproduced and modified, and provide more control over the processes of cultural reproduction.[19] Kantian influence inclines these theorists towards too rationalistic an account of cultural reproduction. A pragmatist Confucian approach such as Neville's recognizes that communication is more than rational discourse; it includes much that is affective, non-verbal, even non-verbalizable. Human conflicts and the fundamental political and moral problems they raise cannot be resolved by the exercise of reason alone, they require what

Martha Nussbaum (1994), explicating Greek ethics, calls the 'therapy of desire'. Nussbaum herself emphasizes reason in this therapy, but her cognitive approach also stresses the importance of 'narrative'.[20] Narratives are cultural forms which provide the context for our understanding and evaluation of any situation, including those of political conflicts; culture therefore plays a part in both the genesis as well as the possible resolution of conflicts.

Confucians share the belief that dealing with passions well play an important role in moral life, but they go further than Nussbaum in recognizing that *non-cognitive* cultural forms also have significant impact on our passions and desires. Xunzi was especially emphatic that emotions (*qing* 情), if given license, will result in conflict and chaos, given inevitable competition for scarce resources and differences among individuals and groups who have to live together (Knoblock, 1994, pp.55-7). For Confucians, *li*, comprising non-cognitive as well as cognitive cultural forms, channels passions and desires appropriately and thereby makes social harmony possible. Such harmony does not eliminate differences (*Analects* 13.23). Disagreement and contention will always exist, but in an ideal Confucian polity, parties to any conflict act in an exemplary manner by following *li* – they employ appropriate cultural forms of expressing disagreement and competition that ensure the continued possibility of mutual respect, good will and trust.

Confucians today should aspire to become world citizens by learning to be civilized local communicators. Confucianism in the new millennium needs a global orientation, even as it remains rooted in its tradition. This transformation will enable those who claim a Confucian legacy to participate from their particular cultural contexts in the intercultural dialogues that will hopefully shape the future world. Besides participation, does Confucianism have anything unique to offer its dialogue partners? I offer only a tentative suggestion. Advances in technologies of communication are central to globalization; but we have not achieved as much in creating cultural forms in communication to bring about global order and world peace. We stand in desperate need of cultural renewal. Confucianism could contribute to the efforts to nurture a global citizenship culture by supplementing intercultural discourse with *li* that facilitate mutual understanding and respect.

## Notes

1    When asked where he came from, Diogenes the cynic was reported to have replied, 'I am a citizen of the world' (Hicks, 1970, p.63); Kant, 1798; see also Nussbaum, 1997.
2    Kant (1798), p.106; there are however several racist remarks in Kant's works on anthropology. On the complicity of other Enlightenment thinkers in European imperialism and ethnocide in various colonized territories, see Coleman and Higgings, 2000. Stoic cosmopolitans were straightforward in their support for colonialism (Nussbaum 1997, p.14).
3    In contrast, Bryan Turner (2000, p.29) argues that 'cosmopolitan coolness and indifference towards the claims of traditional patterns of solidarity' could be functional in a globalized postmodern world.

4     For efforts to construct global ethics, see Kung, 1991; for Huntington's thesis and the controversies it generated, see Huntington, 1993; responses to Huntington in *Foreign Affairs*, vol.75, no.4; Rasheed, 1997.

5     Gerard Delanty (2000, pp.68-75) argues that 'human rights are now overriding the rights of citizenship and reshaping democratic politics'. Yasemin Soysal (1994) suggests that, after two centuries of divergence, the present situation is one of a blurring of human rights and citizenship rights.

6     Richard Rorty (1993) highlights the 'ethnocentrism' of human rights as a core value of liberalism, but is unapologetic about promoting human rights from an ethnocentric position.

7     Wm. Theodore de Bary (1998, p.54) argues that greater political participation and freedom of expression in China depend in part on 'agreement that human rights should not be understood or defined solely in Western terms; rather, they are a growing, expandable concept that will be enhanced through shared multicultural learning and experience'.

8     Traditional politics of discrimination also 'assumes an essentialist meaning of difference; it defines groups as having essential different natures'. Young (1990, p.157) contrasts this with an egalitarian politics of difference, which 'defines difference more fluidly and relationally as the product of social processes'.

9     On the complexity of cultural identity, unity and fragmentation of culture in late modernity, see Hall, 1996; Featherstone, 1995.

10    Bauböck, 1994, p.7. Beginning with T.H. Marshall's 1950 classic *Citizenship and Social Class* almost every work on citizenship has affirmed that close association between citizenship and rights, even if an increasing number argues for active or deep citizenship that goes beyond rights regimes.

11    In Engin Isin's and Patricia Wood's (1999, p.152) multilayered conception of citizenship, for example, 'cultural citizenship' is more than rights to produce and consume cultural goods and services or redistributive justice concerning cultural capital; it 'is about becoming active producers of meaning and representation and knowledgeable consumers under advanced capitalism'.

12    The ambivalence and contradictions in the cultural identity of Chinese outside the People's Republic of China is especially acute in the case of Taiwan, where the search for cultural identity in the last few decades is inseparable from its politics, and 'is often predicated on a critique of Sino-centrism' (Tu, 1998, p.75).

13    Keightley, 1983, part II; Chang, 1986; Fei *et al.*, 1989; Tu, 1991. Participation in globalization is creating a unique hybrid culture among highly mobile Chinese international managers and professionals who have 'the material and symbolic resources to manipulate global schemes of cultural difference, racial hierarchy, and citizenship to their own advantage' (Ong, 1998, p.135); see also Chan, 2003.

14    Fung Yu-lan's response at the Columbia University Convocation in his honor on 10 September 1982, in *Proceedings of the Heyman Center*. This was also taken for granted by Qian Mu, Tang Junyi, Xu Fu Guan and Mou Zongsan (Chang Hao, 1976).

15    For Ching, this means that the Chinese are left with the unprecedented freedom of 'making one's own culture'.

16    Han Yu of Tang dynasty condemned Buddhism as 'a cult of the barbarian people'. That the Buddha 'did not speak the language of China and wore clothes of a different fashion' bothered him as much as the fact that Buddhist teachings 'did not concern the ways of (Chinese) ancient kings' (de Bary and Bloom, 1999, pp.583-4). Even the *Analects* (3.5) and the *Mencius* (3A4) have passages disparaging other cultures.

17 *Analects* 6.30, 12.2, 15.24. Wing-tsit Chan (1963, pp.14-18) translates *ren* as 'humanity' and considers it the general virtue that is the source of all specific Confucian virtues (Chan, 1975).
18 As a descriptive category, *li* may not be conducive to harmony and solidarity. On political rituals as a crucial element in the 'mobilization of bias' instead of promoting value integration, see Lukes, 1975.
19 An example is Chambers, 1996, chapter 15; though critical of Habermas's commitment to universalist normative reason, Young's (1990, p.34) position also endorses and follows this general framework.
20 Nussbaum's emphasis on reason is more pronounced in 'Kant and Stoic Cosmopolitanism', despite her expressed preference for Aristotle's approach to passions rather than the Stoic approach of eliminating them (1997, p.22).

## References

*Analects*, in Roger T. Ames and Henry Rosemont (trans.) (1998), *The Analects of Confucius*, Ballantine, New York.
Barber, Benjamin (1995), *Jihad vs. McWorld*, Random House, New York.
Bauböck, Rainer (1994), *Transnational Citizenship*, Edward Elgar, Aldershot and Brookfield.
Bauer, Joanne R. and Daniel A. Bell (eds.) (1999), *The East Asian Challenge for Human Rights*, Cambridge University Press, Cambridge.
Bauman, Zygmunt (1999), *Culture as Praxis*, 2nd edition, Sage, Thousand Oaks.
Bridges, Thomas (1994), *The Culture of Citizenship*, State University of New York Press, Albany.
Calhoun, Craig (2003), 'The Class Consciousness of Frequent Travelers: Towards a Critique of Actually Existing Cosmopolitanism', in Vertovec and Cohen, 2003, pp.86-109.
Chambers, Simone (1996), *Reasonable Democracy*, Cornell University Press, Ithaca and London.
Chan, Kwok-Bun (2003), 'Both Sides, Now: Culture Contact, Hybridization, and Cosmopolitanism', in Vertovec and Cohen, 2003, pp.191-208.
Chan, Wing-tsit (1975), 'Chinese and Western Interpretations of *Jen* (Humanity)', *Journal of Chinese Philosophy*, vol. 2, pp.107-29.
Chan, Wing-tsit (trans. and comp.) (1963), *A Source Book in Chinese Philosophy*, Princeton University Press, Princeton.
Chang, Hao (1976), 'New Confucianism and the Intellectual Crisis of Contemporary China', in Charlotte Furth (ed.), *The Limits of Change: Essays on Conservative Alternatives in Republican China*, Harvard University Press, Cambridge.
Chang, Kwang-chih (1986), *The Archeology of Ancient China*, Yale University Press, New Haven.
Ching, Julia (2000), 'Chinese Culture is Dead', interview with Kao Chen, *Straits Times*, 14 May, Singapore.
Coleman, Ann and Winton Higgings (2000), 'Racial and Cultural Diversity in Contemporary Citizenship', in Vandenberg, 2000, pp.51-76.
de Bary, Wm. Theodore (1998), 'Confucianism and Human Rights in China', in Larry Diamond and Marc F. Plattner (eds.), *Democracy in East Asia*, John Hopkins University Press, Baltimore, pp.42-54.
de Bary, Wm. Theodore and Irene Bloom (eds.) (1999), *Sources of Chinese Tradition*, Columbia University Press, New York, vol.2.

de Bary, Wm. Theodore and Tu Wei-ming (eds.) (1998), *Confucianism and Human Rights*, Columbia University Press, New York.

Delanty, Gerard (2000), *Citizenship in a Global Age*, Open University Press, Buckingham and Philadelphia.

Dewey, John (1927), *The Public and Its Problems*, 1954 edition, Ohio University Press, Athens.

Falk, Richard (1993), 'The Making of Global Citizenship', in Jeremy Brecher *et al.* (eds.), *Global Visions: Beyond the New World Order*, South End Press, Boston, pp.39-50.

Fareed Zakaria (1994), 'Culture is Destiny – A Conversation with Lee Kuan Yew', *Foreign Affairs*, vol.73, pp.109-26.

Featherstone, Mike (1995), *Undoing Culture: Globalization, Postmodernism and Identity*, Thousand Oaks, Sage.

Fei Xiaotong *et al.* (1989), *'Unity in Multiplicity' of Chinese People*, Central People's College Press, Beijing.

Hall, Stuart (ed.) (1996), *Questioning Cultural Identity*, Sage, Thousand Oaks.

Hicks, R.D. (trans.) (1970), *Life of the Philosophers*, Harvard University Press, Cambridge.

Huntington, Samuel (1993), 'The Clash of Civilizations?' *Foreign Affairs*, vol.72, pp.22-49.

Isin, Engin and Patricia Wood (1999), *Citizenship and Identity*, Sage, Thousand Oaks.

Kant, Immanuel (1798), 'Perpetual Peace: A Philosophical Sketch', in Hans Reiss (ed.), *Kant: Political Writings*, Cambridge University Press, Cambridge, pp.93-130.

Keightley, David (ed.) (1983), *Origins of Chinese Civilization*, University of California Press, Berkeley.

Knoblock, John (trans.) (1994), *Xunzi: A Translation and Study of the Complete Works*, Stanford University Press, Stanford, vol. 3.

Kung, Hans (1991), *Global Responsibility: In Search of New World Ethic*, John Bowden (trans.), Crossroad, New York.

Kuo, Eddie C.Y. (1992), *Confucianism as Political Discourse in Singapore: The Case of an Incomplete Revitalization Movement*, Department of Sociology Working Paper Series, National University of Singapore, Singapore.

Kymlicka, Will (1995), *Multicultural Citizenship*, Oxford University Press, Oxford.

Lukes, Steven (1975), 'Political Ritual and Social Integration', *Sociology*, vol.9, pp.289-308.

Marshall, T.H. (1950), *Citizenship and Social Class and Other Essays*, Cambridge Univeristy Press, Cambridge.

*Mencius*, in D.C. Lau (trans.) (1970), *The Mencius*, Penguin, Harmondsworth.

Mouffe, Chantal (1997), 'Democratic Identity and Pluralistic Politics', in Ron Bontekoe and Marietta Stephaniants (eds.), *Justice and Democracy*, University of Hawai'i Press, Honolulu, pp.381-94.

Neville, Robert Cummings (1994), 'Confucianism As A World Philosophy: Presidential Address for the 8th International Conference on Chinese Philosophy, Beijing, 1993', *Journal of Chinese Philosophy*, vol.21, pp.5-25.

Neville, Robert Cummings (2000), *Boston Confucianism: Portable Tradition in the Late Modern World*, State University of New York Press, Albany.

Nussbaum, Martha (1994), *The Therapy of Desire*, Princeton University Press, Princeton.

Nussbaum, Martha (1997), 'Kant and Stoic Cosmopolitanism', *The Journal of Political Philosophy*, vol.5, pp.1-25.

Ong, Aihwa (1998), 'Flexible Citizenship among Chinese Cosmopolitans', in Bruce Robbins and Pheng Cheah (eds.), *Cosmopolitics: Thinking and Feeling Beyond the Nation*, University of Minnesota Press, Minneapolis, pp.134-62.

Onuma, Yasuaki (1999), 'Toward an Intercivilizational Approach to Human Rights', in Bauer and Bell, 1999, pp.103-23.

Parekh, Bhikku (2000), *Rethinking Multiculturalism*, London, Macmillan.

Rasheed Salin (1997), *Clash of Civilizations? Asian Responses*, Oxford University Press, Karachi.

Rorty, Richard (1993), 'Human Rights, Rationality and Sentimentality', in Stephen Shue and Susan Hurley (eds.), *On Human Rights*, Basic Books, New York, pp.111-34.

Rouner, Leroy S. (ed.) (2000), *Civility*, University of Notre Dame Press, Notre Dame.

Soysal, Yasemin (1994), *Limits of Citizenship: Migrants and Postnational Citizenship in Europe*, University of Chicago Press, Chicago.

Tan, Sor-hoon (2003), 'Can there be a Confucian Civil Society', in Kim-Chong Chong, Sor-hoon Tan and C.L. Ten (eds.), *The Moral Circle: Chinese and Western Approaches*, Open Court, La Salle, pp.193-218.

Tan, Sor-hoon (2005), 'Three Corners for One: Creativity and Tradition in the *Analects*', in David Jones (ed.), *Contemporary Encounters with Confucianism*, Open Court, La Salle.

Tang Yijie (1988), *Confucianism, Daoism and Buddhism in Traditional Chinese Culture*, Peace Press, Beijing.

Taylor, Charles (1995), 'The Politics of Recognition', in *Philosophical Arguments*, Harvard University Press, Cambridge, pp.225-56.

Tu Wei-ming (1968), 'The Creative Tension between *Jen* and *Li*', *Philosophy East and West*, vol.18, pp.29-39.

Tu Wei-ming (1986), 'Toward a Third Epoch of Confucian Humanism: A Background Understanding', in Irene Eber (ed.), *Confucianism: the Dynamics of Tradition*, MacMillian, New York.

Tu Wei-ming (1989), *Confucianism in a Historical Perspective*, Institute of East Asian Philosophies, Singapore.

Tu Wei-ming (1991), 'Cultural China: The Periphery as Center', *Daedalus*, vol.120, pp.1-32.

Tu Wei-ming (1992), 'Core Values and the Possibility of a Fiduciary Global Community,' in Katharine and Majid Tehranian (eds.), *Restructuring for World Peace*, Hampton Press, Cresskill, pp.333-45.

Tu Wei-ming (1993), 'The Structure and Function of Confucian Intellectual in Ancient China', in *Way, Learning and Politics: Essays on the Confucian Intellectual*, State University of New York Press, Albany, pp.13-28.

Tu Wei-ming (1995) Unpublished text of the 1995 Inaugural Wu Teh Yao Memorial Lecture in Singapore, p.5; most of it has been published in 'Epilogue: Human Rights as a Confucian Moral Discourse', in de Bary and Tu, 1998, pp.297-307.

Tu Wei-ming (1998), *Humanity and Self-Cultivation*, first published in 1978, Cheng and Tsui, Boston.

Turner, Bryan (2000), 'Liberal Citizenship and Cosmopolitan Virtue', in Vandenberg, 2000, pp.18-32.

Vandenberg, Andrew (ed.), *Citizenship and Democracy in a Global Era*, Macmillan, London.

Vertovec, Steven and Robin Cohen (eds.) (2003), *Conceiving Cosmopolitanism*, Oxford University Press, Oxford.

Waldron, Jeremy (2000), 'Cultural Identity and Civic Responsibility', in Will Kymlicka and Wayne Norman (eds.), *Citizenship in Diverse Societies*, Oxford University Press, Oxford, pp.155-74.

Young, Iris Marion (1990), *Justice and the Politics of Difference*, Princeton University Press, Princeton.

# Chapter 14

# Conclusion: Meeting Challenges

Sor-hoon Tan

The contributors to this volume have reached no consensus on a singular conception of citizenship that would meet all the challenges of this global age. They do not even agree completely on the problems that need solving if the concept is to continue to be meaningful. Nevertheless, the diverse discussions have hopefully cast light on the complexity of being a citizen in a time of increasing cultural diversity within nation-states and greater fluidity of boundaries.

Some perennial issues continue to demand our attention. Citizenship as passive legal status seems inadequate. The rights of citizenship are at risk unless citizens play more active roles in governance. For some, the desire for active citizen participation in public life must be qualified by respect for the individual's moral integrity in deciding on the justifiability and limits of participation. If we are sceptical of the wisdom of relying on wise individuals to rule on our behalf, then we should also avoid assuming that the results of public discourse or social inquiry necessarily achieve the best outcome for individuals or groups. These are issues relevant both within and beyond the boundaries of the nation-state.

The opportunities and resources made available through globalization have empowered some individuals and groups, sometimes in their struggles with the state they reside in. The possibilities of this new era also throw into high relief the inequities that exist around the globe. We have overcome many physical limits to the movement of goods, people, and information; we have made less progress in solving the distribution problems that divide the world into haves and have-nots, the powerful and the powerless. Some believe there is a need to extend the rights of citizenship to long term residents who enter a nation-state either as refugees or migrant workers who are unlikely to return to their countries of origin. However, there is no one-size-fits-all solution. In some cases, migrant workers fear that agitation for citizenship rights may jeopardize their chances of working abroad to make a better life for their family back home. The problems of global inequalities need imaginative and bold rethinking, perhaps even fundamental change to the current structure of nation-states and other political organizations.

At some level, we need to consider our transnational responsibilities and how to balance them with our responsibilities to those closer to home. The difficulties of active citizenship are even more glaring at the global level. The average individual has even less influence on global events than on national events; or does she? If we continue to think only in terms of international relations and global capital, then it appears that a few powerful individuals, by virtue of the resources they command or the organizations they control, will decide the future of the world, and it is questionable how far their decisions take into consideration the welfare of all. This approach overlooks the potential of technology in facilitating grass-roots organization and popular participation in politics at both national and international level. Ordinary citizens could and should communicate better among themselves and organize better by tapping new resources to improve their influence on what is happening around them, and around the world.

Improvement of communication and organization for active citizenship is difficult because unfortunately human reason, even if it is universal, does not produce instantaneous understanding and unanimity of views. How do we achieve better communication and create something in common across diverse cultures? Cultural encounters are meetings of persons, of peoples. Conflicts arise because those with very different worldviews and ways of life have to share a living space; people living in different corners of the earth find their interests clashing. Might not the universal rights and obligations designed to limit and resolve earlier struggles serve our purpose? Many do not think so, for these are the products if not of a single culture, at least of a fairly coherent tradition of thought shared to a large extent by many Western societies. If citizenship is to serve us in a multiethnic and multicultural world, it needs to be modified to take cultural differences more seriously. Furthermore, the modifications that serve one society may not serve others with very different concerns in different conditions.

It is difficult, if not impossible to be an active citizen on one's own. Active participation requires a community. Rights and duties may define the minimum for peaceful coexistence, but may be insufficient for sustaining community. We need to find ways of bringing "outsiders" and "strangers" into our existing communities, ways to reach across cultural boundaries, ways to listen and respond to others sympathetically and constructively, ways to create common ground where none exists before.

Membership in a nation-state today has many transnational and local rivals that fight for primacy in an individual's sense of identity and her loyalty. To be an effective citizen requires us to look beyond the nation-state, to recognize global demands, especially demands of justice, on us as individuals and as members of groups less extensive than the whole world. To overcome the many existing inequalities and divisions that obstruct meeting such global commitments, we need to reform or build new institutions at various levels; we also need to re-evaluate and improve on processes of human interaction at all levels by making better use of technology and creating new knowledge of such processes.

Global commitments are not incompatible with local attachments. Some go further to argue that global memberships can be effective only if they are grounded locally. Personal motivations and justifications must be sought in the cultural or other local affinities of individuals. Global citizenship has to be more than membership with legal rights and duties; it needs cultural depth and must be reconciled with local identities. Cultural differences present both opportunities and risks in this global age. The problems of globalization require us to understand cultures and their interaction in new ways so that, rather than create more problems themselves, they could provide the resources for solving problems.

# Index

Aristotle 2, 64, 65, 67, 76, 148
assimilation 2, 16, 107, 112, 127, 128
authority 64-5, 67, 69, 76, 78, 173-4, 175
autonomy 17, 21, 77, 91, 95, 99, 104,
        107, 117, 118, 119, 120
Barry, Brian 19, 151, 152, 158, 160, 164,
        166
capitalism 87, 176, 183
choice 5, 20, 21, 48, 49, 51, 52, 53, 55,
        57, 76, 95, 96, 98, 99, 101-4, 154,
        165, 175, 186
citizen of the world 21, 24, 25, 33, 183
civil society 16, 25, 26, 42, 45, 64, 65, 69,
        80, 83-5, 162, 189, 191
common humanity 21, 34, 35, 36, 39,
        156, 191
communication 39, 92, 93, 105, 121, 157,
        161, 190-2
communitarianism 120, 121, 162, 177
community 4, 6, 16, 18, 27, 51, 64, 65,
        66, 70, 79, 95, 98-9, 102, 106, 107,
        112, 121, 130, 137, 152, 154, 162,
        162, 170, 172, 176-81, 186-91
conflicts 17, 20, 38, 45, 47, 90, 110, 117,
        139, 151, 165, 183-4, 185, 191
Confucianism 59, 76, 121, 157, 158,
        169-81, 186-92
contract 32, 49, 51
    contract theory 66, 67, 91-2
cosmopolitanism 18-9, 20, 21, 23, 26-7,
        72, 165, 184, 189
culture 5, 17-22, 24, 27, 37, 50, 54, 56-9,
        80, 83, 107, 112, 120, 151-2, 153,
        162-6, 183-92
deliberations 80-82, 90-91, 93-5
democracy 5, 6, 16, 20, 36, 42, 46-7, 55,
        70-71, 75-6, 81-3, 89-96, 114, 165,
        170, 172-4, 176, 183, 184, 187
Dewey, John 75, 78-81, 192
diversity 2, 17, 20, 22, 38, 108, 111-4,
        116, 122, 124, 154-5, 184, 191
economic development 22, 54, 55, 127,
        130
education 18, 34, 44, 56, 69, 77, 91, 103,
        108, 130, 164

elitism 72, 80, 90, 170, 172, 173
emotions 179, 192
engagement 16, 22, 38-9, 43, 45, 159,
        185
Enlightenment 21, 24, 72, 183-4
equality 2, 19, 37-8, 42, 46, 49-50, 69,
        76, 82, 92, 93, 98, 114, 116, 152,
        153-65, 170, 172, 175, 186
ethnocentrism 2, 187, 189
family 50, 52, 57-9, 66, 76, 77, 101-2,
        104, 108, 113, 148, 189, 191
federalism 111, 114-21, 124
freedom 22, 24, 26, 38, 47, 60, 71, 75, 77,
        91, 93, 95, 98, 102, 106, 115, 143,
        164
French Revolution 1, 16, 24, 175
global citizenship 15, 21, 23, 26, 34, 155,
        163, 165, 181, 191
globalization 4, 24-6, 27, 34, 42, 56, 63,
        68, 70, 78, 122, 155, 181, 189, 191,
        192
governance 64, 70, 71, 82, 83
government 19, 23, 25, 35, 39, 42-9, 51-
        6, 64, 65, 67, 69, 70, 76, 78, 80, 82,
        90, 186
    self-government 111, 116, 117, 118,
        119, 120, 121, 126-7
Habermas, Jürgen 24, 89, 91-3, 165
harmony 180-1, 186, 191-2
hybridity 5, 165, 184, 186
identity 5, 22, 23, 34, 36, 37, 39, 71, 95,
        99-103, 105, 106, 107-8, 112, 122,
        162, 175, 180, 187
    cultural identity 5, 23, 36, 38, 145,
        155, 177, 185, 191
    national identity 5, 15, 111, 114, 153
identity politics 17, 99, 183, 184, 185
immigrants 33, 37-9, 43, 49, 112, 116,
        121
    illegal immigrants 23-4, 53, 54, 113
imperialism 2, 5, 68, 70, 72, 163, 184
indigenous people 18, 111-2, 116, 125-8
individualism 93, 98, 104-5, 162, 171
individuality 89, 93, 171

interest 43-8, 50, 54, 56, 58, 77, 80, 81,
    82, 83, 90, 91, 143, 175, 177
    common interest 34, 38, 64, 65, 76,
        79, 82
    personal interest 78, 179
    public interest 91, 143
    self-interest 35, 50, 17
Islam 16, 20, 38, 157-8, 163, 165
justice 25-7, 33, 35-6, 39, 48, 51, 53, 56,
    90, 92, 94, 119, 130, 146, 154
Kant, Immanuel 17, 26-7, 106
language 16-18, 24, 39, 50, 104, 105,
    111, 112, 115, 118, 153, 157, 161,
    170, 178
law 21, 38, 44-6, 53-4, 67, 69, 80, 121,
    146, 156
    international law 19, 23, 24, 25, 67,
        126, 184
legitimacy 92, 93, 130
liberalism 5, 15, 17-21, 25-7, 37, 63, 70,
    91, 92, 98, 101-2, 105-6, 114, 153,
    157-9, 175-6, 188
    neo-liberalism 25-6, 69, 176
market 50, 64, 65, 69, 77, 82, 83, 85, 176
Marshall, T.H. 7, 67, 68, 69, 71
Mill, John Stuart 17, 20, 91, 175
minorities 1, 20, 39, 98, 102, 105, 107-8,
    117, 118, 120, 122, 124, 126, 130,
    146, 153, 162, 165, 180
multiculturalism 17, 18-21, 23, 45, 107,
    110, 111, 113, 116, 120, 145-9,
    154, 188
nationalism 6, 16, 21, 24-5, 111, 115,
    116-8, 121, 122, 124, 157, 161
nation-state 5, 6, 15-16, 18, 21, 24-7, 80,
    81, 85, 114, 115, 175, 176, 183,
    185
Nussbaum, Martha 27, 33-4, 36
Parekh, Bhiku 18-19, 23, 154, 159, 185
participation 2, 16, 27, 35, 36, 69, 71, 76,
    77, 80, 83, 89, 94-6, 119, 188
pluralism 2, 17, 19, 20, 188
poverty 21, 23, 26-7, 42, 56, 57, 69, 153,
    159, 179-80
private 16, 18, 78, 79, 83-5, 143, 147,
    178
public 16, 24, 36, 46, 47, 76-80, 83-5,
    89-91, 93-6, 138, 142, 143, 184
public and private 16, 77, 165, 175, 178,
    179
public sphere 27, 59, 163

racism 17, 22, 36,
Rawls, John 17, 35-6, 90, 93-5, 154, 156,
    164
reason 138, 139, 140-3, 190, 191
refugee 26, 31-3, 66, 113
relativism 138-9, 144, 152
religion 37, 38, 95, 112, 122
republicanism 16, 24-5, 75, 77-8, 80, 83,
    91, 188
respect 17, 19, 20, 22, 26, 27, 28, 39, 58,
    59, 98-9, 102, 103, 107, 108, 148,
    152, 154-5, 156, 157, 161, 163,
    164, 174, 185, 186, 192
rights 15-17, 20, 22, 24, 33, 43, 45, 49-
    50, 69, 71, 90, 92, 96, 101-3, 111,
    112, 114, 126-7, 130, 153-4, 159,
    165, 170, 172, 174, 178-9, 186
    civil and/or political rights 2, 47, 68-
        9, 120, 129, 154, 177
    cultural rights 15, 20, 23, 162
    group rights 16, 17, 145, 189
    human rights 19, 21, 23, 26, 66, 70,
        121, 124, 157, 163, 184-5, 187
    individual rights 17, 20, 21, 25, 26,
        98, 115, 121, 177, 186, 189
    minority rights 110, 111, 121, 124,
        126, 154, 162, 176
rights and duties 2, 6, 16, 26, 33
rites/rituals (*li*) 180, 190-1
Rousseau, Jean Jacques 82, 90, 94
secession 116, 117, 124
security 114, 118, 122-4, 127, 129-30,
    175
sovereignty 27, 66, 67, 82, 89, 91, 94
state 31, 34, 36, 65-71, 78, 80, 95, 165,
    175
terrorism 27, 34, 114, 157-8, 165
tolerance 21, 33, 108, 124, 164-5
toleration 38, 98
tradition 101-3, 106, 108, 137, 138, 139,
    141, 142, 144, 145, 146, 148, 187
trust 44, 51, 59, 130, 191, 192
universal and particular 21, 22, 36, 39,
    99-100, 137-9, 141, 143, 145, 153,
    154, 159, 160, 163, 184, 189, 191
universalism 17, 19-21, 27, 72, 139, 141,
    143-5, 152, 153, 189, 191
values 17, 19, 21, 34, 38, 101, 102, 104,
    124, 154, 160, 185, 187
welfare 22, 26, 33, 43-5, 66, 67, 72, 94